MAY GOD REMEMBER

Memory and Memorializing in Judaism

Yizkor

Other Jewish Lights Books by
Rabbi Lawrence A. Hoffman, PhD

My People's Prayer Book:
Traditional Prayers, Modern Commentaries, Vols. 1–10

My People's Passover Haggadah:
Traditional Texts, Modern Commentaries, Vols. 1 & 2
(Coedited with David Arnow, PhD)

The Art of Public Prayer, 2nd Ed.:
Not for Clergy Only
(A book from SkyLight Paths,
Jewish Lights' sister imprint)

Rethinking Synagogues:
A New Vocabulary for Congregational Life

Israel—A Spiritual Travel Guide:
A Companion for the Modern Jewish Pilgrim

The Way Into Jewish Prayer

What You Will See Inside a Synagogue
(coauthored with Dr. Ron Wolfson)

Also in the Prayers of Awe Series

Who by Fire, Who by Water—Un'taneh Tokef

All These Vows—Kol Nidre

We Have Sinned: Sin and Confession in Judaism—Ashamnu *and* Al Chet

MAY GOD REMEMBER

Memory and Memorializing
in Judaism

Yizkor

Edited by
Rabbi Lawrence A. Hoffman, PhD

JEWISH LIGHTS Publishing
Nashville, Tennessee

May God Remember: Memory and Memorializing in Judaism—Yizkor

Requests to the Publisher for permission should be addressed to Turner Publishing Company, 4507 Charlotte Avenue, Suite 100, Nashville, Tennessee, (615) 255-2665, fax (615) 255-5081, E-mail: submissions@turnerpublishing.com.

Library of Congress Cataloging-in-Publication Data
May God remember = Yizkor : memory and memorializing in Judaism / edited by Rabbi Lawrence A. Hoffman, PhD.
   pages ; cm — (Prayers of awe)
   Includes bibliographical references.
ISBN 978-1-58023-689-8 (hc)
ISBN 978-1-68336-188-6 (pbk)
   1. Hazkarat neshamot. 2. Kaddish. 3. Judaism—Liturgy. 4. Jewish mourning customs. I. Hoffman, Lawrence A., 1942- editor. II. Title: Yizkor. III. Title: Memory and memorializing in Judaism.
  BM670.H39M39 2013
  296.4'545—dc23
                                        2013022920

10 9 8 7 6 5 4 3 2
Manufactured in the United States of America
Front Cover Design: Jeff Miller
Cover Mechanical Design: Grace Cavalier

Published by Jewish Lights Publishing
A Division of LongHill Partners, Inc.
An Imprint of Turner Publishing Company
4507 Charlotte Avenue, Suite 100
Nashville, TN 37209
Tel: (615) 255-2665
www.jewishlights.com

For Hanka Kornfeld-Marder,
who remembers

Contents

Acknowledgments

As a good deal of the book makes clear, the *Yizkor* liturgy is inextricably tied up with the communal memory of Jewish martyrdom: first, the Crusades; and second, the Chmielnicki massacres of the seventeenth century. I am, therefore, particularly grateful to Dr. Carole Balin for drawing my attention to recent scholarship on the subject. In addition, my thanks are due to Yoram Bitton, who supplemented his discussion of *Hashkavah* by identifying geographic place names in the complex document memorializing the Chmielnicki pogroms (Appendix B). He also drew my attention to the musical heritage of *El Malei Rachamim* and made available the fascinating manuscript of 1888 (Appendix C). I am grateful to the Klau Library of Hebrew Union College for use of this valuable resource. Appreciation goes also to Dr. Mark Kligman, who offered help in issues of musicology.

I would be remiss in not giving special mention to two scholars of enormous importance who are no longer with us: Rabbi Solomon B. Freehof, PhD (*z"l*) and Rabbi Jakob J. Petuchowski, PhD (*z"l*). Freehof's classic article first appeared in the *Hebrew Union College Annual* (1965); Petuchowski's contribution comes from *Prayerbook Reform in Europe* (1968), a publication of the World Union for Progressive Judaism. I am grateful to these two institutions for allowing me to reproduce the two articles in question.

The goal of this series is, in part, to make available English translations of the liturgy and some of its attendant source material that is otherwise unavailable to most readers. In that regard, I thank two scholars for their help. First and foremost, Dr. Joel M. Hoffman, who regularly translates the liturgy of this series, went beyond the call of duty, as usual—this time, in the enormous task of translating and annotating the memorial from the Chmielnicki period (Appendix B), a literary masterpiece whose every line contains implicit allusions to other instances of biblical and Rabbinic literature. In addition, Dr. Annette M. Boeckler was kind enough to help translate the German of the 1888 manuscript from Königsberg. My thanks are due to both of these contributors who never fail to involve themselves in the project as a whole and who make valuable suggestions throughout it.

As with previous volumes in this series, I wish to express enormous gratitude to the many colleagues, artists, composers, poets, philosophers, theologians, and critics whose contributions make this series the rich resource that it is. I continue to be blessed also with support from my extraordinary publisher, Stuart M. Matlins, founder of Jewish Lights, and from Emily Wichland, vice president of Editorial and Production there. It was Stuart who first approached me with the idea for the Prayers of Awe series, as suggested to him by Dan Adler in response to a High Holy Day program developed by Rob Eshman, editor in chief of the *Jewish Journal of Greater Los Angeles*, and David Suissa. Their program sprang from an idea first conceived by Rabbi Elazar Muskin of Young Israel of Century City. Emily continues to amaze me in all she does: her abundant wisdom, skill, patience, and perseverance are precisely what an author most desires. For her copyediting, my thanks go again to Debra Corman. I happily include as well all the others at Jewish Lights, especially Tim Holtz, director of Production, who designed the cover for this book and typeset the English text.

ᏬᏊᏍᎧᎧ

Introduction

Yizkor *and Memorial in Jewish Tradition*

Rabbi Lawrence A. Hoffman, PhD

Memory is dear to Jews. As Isaac Bashevis Singer is said to have commented (I wish I could remember where), "We Jews have many faults; but amnesia is not among them." In insisting on memory, we are apparently in good company, however, because God too (we say) can be importuned to remember. That, at least, is the claim of *Yizkor*, known in English as the memorial service, originally a relatively modest liturgical staple attached in Ashkenazi tradition to the *Shacharit* ("morning")

Rabbi Lawrence A. Hoffman, PhD, has served for more than three decades as professor of liturgy at Hebrew Union College–Jewish Institute of Religion in New York. He is a world-renowned liturgist and holder of the Stephen and Barbara Friedman Chair in Liturgy, Worship and Ritual. He has written and edited many books, including *My People's Prayer Book: Traditional Prayers, Modern Commentaries* series, winner of the National Jewish Book Award; and *Who by Fire, Who by Water*—Un'taneh Tokef, *All These Vows*— Kol Nidre, and *We Have Sinned: Sin and Confession in Judaism*—Ashamnu *and* Al Chet, the first three volumes in the Prayers of Awe series; and he is coeditor of *My People's Passover Haggadah: Traditional Texts, Modern Commentaries*, a finalist for the National Jewish Book Award. He is a developer of Synagogue 3000, a transdenominational project designed to envision and implement the ideal synagogue of the spirit for the twenty-first century.

service for Yom Kippur. As we shall see in greater detail later, the custom arose in Germany, following the devastation of Rhineland Jewry during the Crusades, a trauma that was exacerbated in the fourteenth century when Jews were attacked for "causing" the Black Death. The practice of *Yizkor* then spread eastward, where Polish Jews added a prayer commemorating the Jewish victims massacred in the 1648 Cossack uprisings under Ukrainian leader Bogdan Chmielnicki. They also extended this slightly elaborated *Yizkor* for inclusion on the last day of the three festivals (Passover, Shavuot, and Sukkot). All of this is primarily true of Ashkenazi Jews only. Most Sephardi congregations follow their own custom of memorializing the dead: an even more modest unit of prayer called *Hashkavah*, literally, "Laying Down," as in the sense of "laying down the dead for final repose" (see Bitton, pp. 19–21).

This entire development must be seen against the backdrop of the flexibility that characterized Jewish prayer until the advent of printing.

Yizkor as Liturgical Innovation

Contrary to popular opinion, the liturgy throughout most of history has been relatively fluid. For centuries after its Rabbinic origins around the turn of the Common Era, worship was altogether an oral discipline, in which prayer leaders freely composed new versions of even those segments of the service that nowadays seem absolutely fixed. To be sure, as Rabbinic Judaism spread, the kind of wide-ranging creativity that had marked the early years was dampened by prayer leaders who were unable to match the earlier masters in improvisational skills. Balancing that development, a new form of creativity developed: complex poems called *piyyutim* that were inserted into prayers that were becoming too encrusted with habit.

The process of fixity continued, and a set of precise wording found its way into our first known prayer book, *Seder Rav Amram* (c. 860), but as long as scribes were necessary for the spread of books, a written siddur was rare enough that only the local prayer leader had one—a situation that left him free to add, subtract, or otherwise alter the norm to some extent; and alternative scribal traditions permitted widespread variance in any case, to the point where fourteenth-century Spanish savant David Abudarham said he knew of no two Spanish synagogues where the *Amidah* was recited precisely the same way. Throughout the Middle Ages, imaginative authors created new compositions that easily found their way into the service: an unknown medieval poet gave us *Adon Olam,* for example, and in the fifteenth century, Daniel ben Judah of Rome staked out his claim to being a Maimonidean by putting the latter's Thirteen Principles of Faith into the poetic form that we now sing as *Yigdal Elohim Chai.* Perhaps the greatest testimonial to this ongoing liturgical ingenuity is *Kabbalat Shabbat,* the service for welcoming the Sabbath, which kabbalists in sixteenth-century Safed created entirely *de novo.*

By then, however, the printing press was already spreading throughout Europe, and it was printing that threatened to bring this enormous creativity to an end. Here and there, conditions conspired to keep creativity alive to some extent—individual Hasidic masters, for example, enshrined their own personal customs as mandates among their followers. But the technological capacity of the printing press to set a single authoritative text in stone very largely ended the opportunity to make widespread changes in at least the basics of the prayer service, which cantors now chanted word for word as it appeared in their text, while worshipers followed along in their own prayer-book copies to make sure nothing was omitted, altered, or otherwise "improved upon."

The technology of printing was not the sole reason behind this move toward conservation of the past, however. It was aided and abetted by the impact of kabbalistic theology, which rapidly spread throughout Europe precisely because kabbalistic authors predominated in the very years when printing arose. For the first time in history, books could be produced in bulk and sold everywhere.

To a remarkable degree, the kabbalists resisted any significant alteration of precedent. To be sure, they gave us *Kabbalat Shabbat,* and they also introduced *kavvanot,* meditations that introduced each prayer by providing a mystical understanding of its esoteric significance. But *Kabbalat Shabbat* preceded the dominance of the new print technology, and the *kavvanot* (most of which were oral anyway) were meditations on liturgy, more than they were the liturgy itself. Especially as time wore on and printing developed the capacity to codify wording, these same kabbalists were quick to argue that not a single word should be changed, because each and every word of each and every prayer had profoundly magical merit. This conclusion followed from the kabbalistic notion of *tikkun olam* ("repair of the world"), a term that went far beyond the idea of social justice, as our modern-day liberalism imagines it to be.

Kabbalists were convinced that the universe was inherently flawed from the very moment of creation, when *k'lipot*, "shards of evil," as it were, had crept into the divine light that was intended to saturate the world. The practice of *mitzvot*, especially prayer, could remedy the situation, but only if performed properly. The process was thoroughly mechanical, as if the world were a gigantic machine dependent on a multitude of cogs that could be edged forward bit by bit, one impacting the other. With each properly performed *mitzvah*, the world would creak slowly forward from its initially imperfect state toward a better day of universal harmony and perfection. The whole exercise of worship was to be undertaken just for this esoteric end.

Every word, therefore, had its own theurgic power; nothing could be changed. In 1613, a kabbalist named Sabbetai Sofer of Poland tried his hand at establishing a single authorized version of the liturgy, going so far as to compose a warning to cantors not to make even a single mistake, lest altering even one word might defeat the underlying mystical purpose. Kabbalistic thought thus combined with printing to standardize prayer texts, not just through technological possibility but by theological necessity.

We have seen that the traditional form of *Yizkor* developed following the Crusades—prior to printing and kabbalistic conservatism. The lateness of its entrance into the liturgy made it somewhat exempt from halakhic scruple (see Landes, pp. 30–38), but given the technology of printing and the dominance of Kabbalah, it took a major trauma in Jewish life for anything to be added to it. The trauma was the Chmielnicki massacres. But thereafter, the service remained tiny, a printed set of three prayers only, appended to the end of the morning service. Had the pre-modern mentality of medieval Kabbalah remained regnant, the elaborately designed memorial service we now have would never have come about. But at least in the West, Kabbalah lost its dominance, under the colossal impact of modernity.

Modernity arrived for Jews only in the nineteenth century, in the wake of the Napoleonic reforms. For some time, these impacted Western Europe only, because Napoleon was defeated before he was able to conquer territories in the east. Upon his defeat, old-guard interests managed to roll back much of what Napoleon had put in place, but once Jews had left the ghetto, it proved difficult to put them back in, and as they went to university, they reacted against the dampening of creativity that had hitherto prevailed. The will to change was especially prominent among rabbis whom we nowadays call "reformers," not yet with the technical sense of representing a Reform Movement, however. Rather, they represented a broad swath of modernist Jewish thought, including what we now would call Conservative Judaism and even, to some extent, modern Orthodoxy. Still, the rabbis who pioneered what became the Reform Movement were especially vocal about performing radical surgery on what had been received as utterly sacrosanct wording beyond the possibility of change.

We saw how creativity had been dampened under the twin impacts of printing and Kabbalah. The reformers' later demand that creativity be reinstated was similarly hastened by technology and ideology. Technologically speaking, printing became inexpensive enough for rabbis to undertake their own independent prayer books; the invention of the steam press in 1814 sped up the printing process, and by the 1860s, the substitution of wood pulp for rags made paper abundantly available. They were able, therefore, to create well over a hundred prayer books throughout Europe and North America. As for ideology, these university-educated Jews were learning the evolution of the liturgy and then using that knowledge to refashion prayer for their time. Armed with historical knowledge of earlier times and demanding a liturgy that was honest in its theology and universal in its ethics, they shortened the accumulated mass of prayers that the liturgy had become, translated much of it into the vernacular, and composed new prayers to match the spiritual yearnings of their era. Among the prayers they inherited was the tiny *Yizkor* service of their ancestors, which they then expanded mightily with psalms of the Jewish past and newly created prayers in the vernacular to express the Jewish present. They moved the whole thing out of *Shacharit* and made it into a service of its own.[1] *Yizkor*, newly refashioned as an entirely novel service, represents a reassertion of the mandate that had dominated Jewish thought prior to printing and Kabbalah—the commitment to reformulate the liturgy in each new era.

The reformers varied in their degree to which they were willing to innovate but were unified in their commitment to the historical evolution of Jewish tradition, which, they were convinced, gave them not just permission but even the obligation to alter the liturgy at least to some extent. They were attacked by traditionalists who took a different approach to the Jewish past. These traditionalists too varied significantly, of course: no less than the reformers can they be said to have occupied a unified stance on each and every issue that modernity had imposed on Jewish consciousness, and those with a modern education knew the historical facts as well as the reformers did. Both sides, moreover, were talmudically well trained, graduates, at times, of the same yeshivot. But while reformers gave priority to evolution, traditionalists felt obliged to abide by the codes of Jewish law and their multiplicity of commentaries. They largely agreed, therefore, that prayer had changed through time but found that fact irrelevant to the need to remain true to the way worship had been defined by the legal literature.

Politics played a further role—the way it always does among people with deep commitments to different perspectives that have significance for communal policy. Germany was not yet a free environment where groups of Jews could build separate synagogues and pray differently. Not everywhere, but in many places, the local government saw Jews as a single community that was to be allotted only a single synagogue where all Jews should pray. Quarrels between reformers and traditionalists were, therefore, matters of deep consequence, because the winners would determine the shape of Jewish prayer throughout the entire community. Personal status was at stake as well, because spokesmen for both parties staked their reputation and rabbinic calling on the results. Finally, leaders on both sides believed that what was at stake was nothing short of the shape of the Jewish future, which would live or die, and follow the dictates of the one true God or veer shamelessly away from it.

As we have seen, however, the memorial service was an anomaly, in that its prayers were matters of custom more than they were of law. To be sure, custom has its own elevated standing in Jewish tradition, but the prayers of *Yizkor* were not of such antiquated vintage as to have attracted the reams of halakhic precedent that characterized staples like the *Sh'ma* and the *Amidah*. Traditionalists too, therefore, found it possible, in this case, to sometimes borrow from experiments undertaken by reformers (although, politically speaking, they rarely were able to admit the source from which they borrowed). Memorial services as we know them are, therefore, creative expansions by German reformers, which then migrated to become commonplace in traditional services as well.

Yizkor in Greater Detail

People nowadays express enormous curiosity about these memorial services, not just because they are so popular but because of the beliefs on which they inevitably impinge. People who rarely attend any other service at all come for *Yizkor*, where they usually expect not just a liturgy but a sermon as well. Even people who rarely give much thought to the hundreds of other *mitzvot* to which Jews are obligated intuit a deep sense of personal responsibility when it comes to remembering their deceased relatives—and doing so, moreover, publicly, as part of a prayer service that they may otherwise consider irrelevant. And once they are there, they join the many worshipers who come to that service—including the worshiping "regulars"—in confronting theological issues of the greatest magnitude: What happens to us after we die? Is there really an afterlife? Do we agree with the Rabbis of antiquity who considered bodily resurrection a defining dogma that all Jews must hold? Do we believe (either alternatively or in addition) in a soul that is pure and eternal, a soul that returns to God even though the body decays? Does our fate after death depend on the goodness with which we have pursued our earthly life—that is, is eternal life for body or soul a reward for goodness? And if so, do we believe that the afterlife contains the opposite, not just reward for goodness but also punishment for evil? If so, what exactly is this "reward and punishment"? And is our sentence fixed upon death, or can it be altered by the acts of those who say *Kaddish* and remember us after we die?

Communally too, sentiments run deep on what *Yizkor* is all about. It began with martyrdom in the Crusades, then expanded with martyrdom in Poland, and now encompasses reflections on our own more recent martyrs, those of the Shoah first and foremost, but also the many who have died defending Israel in its wars against those who fought its foundation or oppose its continuity.

For all these reasons, curiosity about *Yizkor* is widespread and profound. It is that curiosity that this volume seeks to address by collecting not just contemporary reflections on liturgical memorial in Judaism but also essays that explore the history of the memorial service as we have it.

Like the other volumes in the Prayers of Awe series, this book elucidates a variety of approaches to a prayer that is both well known and problematic in some way. It also provides scholarly understanding on how that prayer came to be what it is. Where it differs is the decision to expand the scholarly contributions relative to what we have in prior volumes. The expansion follows from two considerations: first, the intense interest in the history of memorializing the dead; and second, the fact that there is no other single sourcebook where a relatively full treatment of that history can be found. In part 2, "Historical Insights," we have included two classic essays, now out of print: the account of the origins of *Yizkor* as provided by the late expert on Jewish law and its developments Rabbi Solomon B. Freehof, PhD, "*Hazkarat N'shamot* ('Memorial of Souls'): How It All Began";[2] and a survey of German memorial services among reformers, from the work of the late liturgist, theologian, and Rabbinics scholar Rabbi Jakob J. Petuchowski, PhD, "*Kaddish* and Memorial Services."[3] The most significant work on the subject, however, has been done by master liturgist Dr. Eric L. Friedland,[4] who has graciously provided a signal summary of his larger research for this volume, "*Yizkor*: A Microcosm of Liturgical Interconnectivity"; and that overview has been augmented by yet another one, "'Service for the Souls': The Origin of Modern Memorial Services, 1819 to 1938," the work of Dr. Annette M. Boeckler, who (among other things) locates *Yizkor* as a reflection of national German culture following the Napoleonic Wars.

All four historical essays expound on overlapping, but different, aspects of the memorial service as we have it today. They look at *Yizkor* from its medieval origins to its modern expansions, all of which builds on understandings that we call Rabbinic, the system of Judaism that began in the centuries surrounding the Common Era and culminated in the two Talmuds, traditionally dated to 400 CE (from the Land of Israel) and 550 CE (from Babylonia). But what about before that? To answer that question, Dr. Marc Zvi Brettler ("Would Jeremiah Have Recited *Yizkor*? *Yizkor* and the Bible") gives us the biblical basis for this Rabbinic system, a time with a very different conception of death and the afterlife than what we are used to hearing. It was well before we had synagogues, prayer-book liturgies, and certainly *Yizkor*.

Yizkor is of such current concern, that we have prefaced these historical reflections (part 2) with a section on "Theology and Practice" (part 1). Because *Yizkor* is so thoroughly Ashkenazi, Yoram Bitton ("*Hashkavah*: Memorializing the Dead in Sephardi Practice") opens the section by describing the foundational Sephardi memorial practice of *Hashkavah*. What follows is my own essay, "Remembering the Dead: By Us and by God," a theological understanding of memory and memorial in Jewish tradition. As he does elsewhere in the series, Rabbi Daniel Landes then summarizes a halakhic perspective on *Yizkor*. Turning to the present, Rabbi Dalia Marx, PhD ("Memorializing the Shoah"), surveys the ways in which we have (or have not) successfully included the victims of the Holocaust in today's memorial services; and Dr. Wendy Zierler

("Sites and Subjects: Memory in Israeli Culture") looks at the complex network of memory in Israeli culture.

With this backdrop—from Bible to the Rabbis; the *Yizkor* of the Middle Ages to the independent memorial services of nineteenth-century Germany; the evolving Ashkenazi ceremony on one hand and the Sephardi *Hashkavah* on the other; the halakhah of memorial and the theology of memory; and the issues raised specifically by the Holocaust and the continual deaths through defensive wars in Israel—we are ready for part 3, the traditional *Yizkor* liturgy newly translated and annotated by Dr. Joel M. Hoffman, the translator of our entire series. In part 4, that liturgy receives its full complement of modern commentaries discussing the way contemporary observers, primarily rabbis, understand this age-old Jewish practice of memorializing the dead. As appendix A, we include the Hebrew and English translation of the *Hashkavah* from the prayer book of Congregation Shearith Israel, New York's Spanish and Portuguese Synagogue. In appendix B, Dr. Joel M. Hoffman translates an exceptionally moving seventeenth-century account of the attacks that resulted in the third and final prayer in the *Yizkor* service, *El Malei Rachamim*. The account is composed in florid literary style with an abundance of biblical and Rabbinic allusions that Hoffman elucidates in his running commentary. Finally, in appendix C, we turn to the music of this stirring prayer.

Because *El Malei Rachamim* is chanted at funerals, not just at memorial services, a great many Jews get used to hearing it sung while they prepare to follow the casket out of the funeral home or synagogue on the way to its final resting place in the cemetery; it is likely also to be sung a second time, at the graveside, as an urgent testimonial to the age-old Jewish faith in the soul's ultimate repose beyond the vagaries of the material reality that constrains our bodies on the one hand and our imagination on the other. Those in attendance at a funeral have no prayer books in hand; all they know is the haunting chant of a song that then turns up again at memorial services, a reminder through the sense of sound, rather than of sight, that we are remembered beyond the grave.

This is not the first time we have encountered the centrality of music—how could it be, in a series devoted to public prayer? Can we imagine a world of liturgy without song? I worked for four years as a rabbi to the deaf, and they too established a choir to "sing" the prayers with their hands, like a dance troupe engaging the text with bodies in fluid signing motion to acknowledge the need for liturgy to speak to the sense of rhythmic unison that song provides. We wished we had been able to provide musical accompaniment to round out the reader's experience of all these volumes—certainly for the volumes on *Un'taneh Tokef* and *Kol Nidre*; and the same is true of the prior series on the liturgy generally, the ten volumes of *My People's Prayer Book*, where every other page, it seemed, demanded music to more fully represent the experience of the prayers that were otherwise discussed in such evident detail, but without the emotionality that prayer, by its very nature, demands.

We rarely know just when even our most familiar tunes came into being. The oldest Ashkenazi melodies, at least, are said to be *misinai*—very old, that is, as if to say "from Sinai." These were once dated somewhere between the twelfth and the fifteenth centuries. We now think they are more recent still—it is hard to say, without record of sound the way we have record of speech (musical notation is a relatively recent development, after all). But music is an aural thing, in any event; it changes more rapidly—like a game of broken telephone where a sound is received but very unlikely to end up being the same after it has been passed along the chain of liturgical usage for a while. From the very moment a prayer is composed, it attracts a plethora of ways for it to be musically delivered.

In *El Malei Rachamim*, we have a prayer that goes back "only" to the seventeenth century—not to antiquity or even the Middle Ages, for that matter—and it was chanted from the very beginning (see pp. 251–256). We have no way to reconstruct that original chant, but we do have some nineteenth-century versions. The earliest known manuscript, says musicologist Mark Kligman, dates from 1825, where it was used in the Aarhus synagogue in Denmark. The one we include here was made available by Yoram Bitton, the librarian at Hebrew Union College in New York. It is of particular interest because of the occasion that prompted it.

As we have already seen, Dr. Annette M. Boeckler links our expanded memorial services to German civil religion, the memorials of the German war dead from the Napoleonic Wars. The connection of specifically denominational liturgy to national religious sentiment is not all that unusual—think of Thanksgiving services in American churches and synagogues, for example; or the singing of "God Bless America" in some synagogues following 9/11. Mordecai Kaplan's original Reconstructionist prayer book contained readings for nearly all American holidays, some of which (Arbor Day, Flag Day) we barely recognize today. The connection of Jewish mourning and German national consciousness did not, therefore, go away as the nineteenth century progressed. On the contrary: as Jews felt more and more at home in the evolving German amalgam that would eventually (1871) become a united Germany, they also, more and more, wanted to show their loyalty and gratitude to the political entity that was including them so fully as citizens. In 1888, Kaiser Wilhelm I, the man under whom the unified Germany had finally come into being, died; and for that occasion, a remarkable cantor and musicologist, Eduard Birnbaum, composed a version of *El Malei Rachamim*. We are happy to include that composition here, as appendix C.

As always, we are proud of the international collaboration that these essays represent. Taken as a whole, our volume juxtaposes authors not just from the United States, but also from Canada, France, Germany, Israel, and the United Kingdom. They identify as Sephardi and Ashkenazi; denominationally, they span the spectrum of movements that characterize North America, Europe, and Israel. They are men and women, old and young. It is an honor to edit a volume that represents them all.

What remains here is a summary statement on the historical conclusions that are detailed in part 2.

Historical Summary: How *Yizkor* Came to Be

The broad outline of *Yizkor*'s evolution is provided above, and the abundant detail on which such an outline is based is given in part 2. Here, I supply something in between: a summary statement of the overall evolution of the prayers in question. There are basically three: *Yizkor Elohim* ("May God remember"), *Av Harachamim* ("Father of mercy"), and *El Malei Rachamim* ("God, full of compassion").

As we saw, the first two were composed in the wake of the devastation wrought by Crusading masses who set out from France in 1096 and bivouacked in the Rhineland before moving on to fight their intended victim: the Muslim armies engaged in ongoing war with Byzantine Christians centered in Constantinople. Jews had settled the Rhineland in the tenth century by moving overland across the Alps from Italy. By the eleventh century, they had established an exceptional set of yeshivot with rabbinic authorities of international renown. The devastation left its mark in a variety of ways, not the least being each community's practice of assembling a memory book (*Memorbuch*) in which were kept the names of the dead, introduced with the prayerful wish "May God remember [*Yizkor Elohim*]." That pious preamble was later detached from the names and used as the central prayer in *Yizkor*. Another prayer from the same era was "Father of mercy" (*Av Harachamim*). It reflected the powerlessness of a Jewish community that had no options but to ask God to wreak vengeance on the enemy who had so brutally brought destruction upon them.

Both *Yizkor* and *Av Harachamim* dealt originally with communal memorials, opportunities for an entire community to recall its martyrs. *Yizkor* was eventually uncoupled from the acts of martyrdom that occasioned it, and from the specific names of those recorded in the memory books, so as to become a prayer for personal memories of one's own family, regardless of how they had perished. *Av Harachamim* retained its connection to martyrs, to the point where it became common to recite *Av Harachamim* on two "martyr Sabbaths": the Sabbath before Shavuot and the one preceding Tisha B'av (the ninth of Av). These two dates were associated with especially traumatic attacks on Jews during the First Crusade and then from the era of the Black Death.

The period of Shavuot is simple enough. It had been associated with deaths in the Rhineland and never lost its association with them. Tisha B'av is more complicated. It was a time of mourning anyway, and the Middle Ages, when this all occurred, was an era that preceded the demand for historical accuracy, so that rather than establish times of mourning that corresponded to actual historical events, it was usual to designate an already existent memorial day as a time for martyrs generally. Even though slayings from the Black Death were spread over a year or so, it seemed logical to lump them together on Tisha B'av, when martyrs were already being memorialized anyway. As these more contemporary martyrs were added to the folk recollection of those lost in the razing of the two Temples, the Sabbath before it was labeled the "Black Shabbat."

But memorializing had become more common even prior to the Black Death. By the end of the thirteenth century, we have a record of particularly significant martyrs in one community (Nuremberg) being remembered on every Shabbat, not just on a specially designated "martyr Sabbath." Eventually too—although we have no firm date at which it began—ordinary people asked to have their own dead recalled with some regularity, whether or not they had been martyrs. Toward this end, *Yizkor* as we know it evolved, not as a communal memorial for martyrs but as a family memorial that was set on the holiest day of the year, Yom

Kippur. In its earliest form, it would have made use of the two martyrs' prayers from the Crusades: *Yizkor* and *El Malei Rachamim*.

The final addition to the service is "God, full of compassion" (*El Malei Rachamim*), first mentioned in *Yeven M'tzulah* ("Abyss of Despair"), a book by Nathan of Hanover, the seventeenth-century chronicler of the Chmielnicki revolts. By Shavuot of 1648, a combined force of Ukrainian Cossacks and their Tatar allies from the south had fallen on the Jewish population in cities west of the Dnieper River—a natural geographic landmark that runs through the heart of Ukraine and empties into the Black Sea. After describing the horrible deaths that these Jews had suffered, Nathan turns to the situation of Jews on the other side of the river. Having heard of the massacre, they decided to surrender to the local Tatar population before the marauding forces crossed the river to reach them, in the hope that these Tatars would allow them to be ransomed by Jews living in Tatar areas of settlement in Turkey to the south. Among the Jewish population, Nathan says, "was a certain cantor, named Reb Hirsch of Zywotow. As the Tatars arrived, he began mournfully to chant *El Malei Rachamim* over the slaughtered kin of the house of Israel [at which time] everyone broke out in loud cries, which must have been heard on high because their captors were moved to show them compassion."[5] Nathan's wording need not imply that the prayer was composed specifically for the occasion, so a version of it may have preceded the events being described. Nonetheless, a poetic description of the Polish Jews who perished is indelibly associated with the prayer, so that we now understand it as a memorial that arose for them specifically (see part 4, which provides the description in question).

Jews of the nineteenth century inherited all three prayers as an appendix to the morning service. The personal version of *Yizkor* (by then no longer associated with the Crusades) was recited first, so that people might recall their own dead; then came *El Malei Rachamim*, a petition for the soul to live on under the protective custody of God's healing presence. It too was by then separated from its historical origins, so that it stood for all the dead, including particularly (it must have seemed) those recollected personally in the previous prayer, *Yizkor*. Finally, worshipers recited *Av Harachamim*, with its cry for vengeance upon Israel's enemies.

Traditionally speaking, the time taken to recite the prayers in question was not great—not more than fifteen minutes, if no sermon was attached. But the emotional ambience of that quarter of an hour was enormous, especially because of the superstition attached to the occasion. Believing firmly that our prayers of memory have an impact on the soul of our beloved dead, people recited the liturgy with more than a little fervor; and adding to the drama was the commonplace practice of sending anyone whose parents were still alive out of the sanctuary while *Yizkor* was recited, a custom rooted in superstitious fears that the presence of those whose parents are still alive might bring harm to them or to others. It was felt that they might prematurely become orphans so as to have to recite the prayer in earnest the next year; also, nineteenth-century adults felt that children should not have to see their parents demonstrating emotion (see Boeckler, pp. 113–126).

The theurgic power of prayer to heal even the dead from punishment in the afterlife comes through most clearly in the practice of pledging *tz'dakah* (charity) on their behalf. The giving of charity on fast days generally is attested to in the Talmud, which says, simply, "There is no fast day without charity." Yom Kippur is such a fast day, so giving charity on it need not have been associated with the dead originally. But giving charity to help the dead on their course through the afterlife was commonplace in and of itself, unconnected with *Yizkor*—the practice is regularly referred to throughout the twelfth and thirteenth centuries. The two practices—giving charity on Yom Kippur and memorializing the dead through charity—were easily connected in popular imagination, so that, already a century earlier, the chief liturgical work of French Jewry, *Machzor Vitry*, says, "As for our allotting charity for the dead, it is because it is a day of atonement, pardon, and absolution for them." The selection of Yom Kippur for the family memorial is probably connected to the fact that charity for the dead was being allotted then anyway.

As we saw, Eastern Europe extended *Yizkor* also to the final day of the three Pilgrimage Festivals, despite the obvious difficulty of scheduling a memorial moment at an occasion intended as joyous! The practice is associated with the day's Torah portion, which notes (Deuteronomy 16:17) the need to give charity ("each according to the gift of his hand [*k'matnat yad*]"). This act of charity was likened to the one associated with remembering the dead, who were, therefore, it seemed, appropriately memorialized on those occasions as well.

The next step in the evolution of *Yizkor* was the nineteenth-century transformation of a simple memorial ritual of just three prayers into its own memorial service. But following the tortuous path by which this transformation occurred is no easy matter, because the Jews of Central Europe who were responsible for it lived in no hierarchically organized manner, so there is no single linear line of development for us to follow. The three contributions in this book (Petuchowski, Friedland, and Boeckler) that deal with the phenomenon provide complementary but overlapping views on the process.

What they all emphasize, among other things, is the key role played by the Reform synagogue that was established in Hamburg in 1818. As an independent port city, Hamburg had attracted a variety of Jewish mercantile interests for centuries—first, Spanish and Portuguese traders, financiers, and shipbuilders who came as conversos in the fifteenth century, and then Ashkenazim, who were slowly admitted to the region as the seventeenth century got under way. While other areas in Germany were not free to establish rival synagogues, Hamburg was, and the Reform Temple of 1818 quickly designed its own liturgy, the influential *Hamburg Temple Prayer Book* of 1819. As the first major liturgical reform, it attracted enormous attention from detractors and supporters alike, each of whom collaborated to publish a set of responsa arguing the case for and against reform, and setting the stage for an entire century of reform that would follow. Hamburg would establish such staples as the following:

- A reconsideration of the role of the *Kaddish*
- The use of Sephardi as well as Ashkenazi tradition
- Prayer in the vernacular
- New compositions to frame the emerging memorial service
- Emphasis on the immortality of the soul, rather than on bodily resurrection
- Moving the service to its own independent liturgical position later in the day of Yom Kippur

Even as all three authors describe the Hamburg prototype, each one looks at different aspects of the memorial service's unfolding story as well. Dr. Annette M. Boeckler makes the remarkable case for its being part and parcel of German civil society, an outgrowth of *Totensonntag* ("Sunday of the Dead"), the holiday established throughout Prussia as a remembrance of those who had died in the Napoleonic Wars. Dr. Eric L. Friedland looks also at other models of Reform: the 1855 *Order of Prayer* for Temple

Emanu-El in New York, for instance; and he brings the tale up to date by surveying the situation in Great Britain and North America, emphasizing the contemporary move toward therapeutic personalism. Where German Jews were concerned with defining ideas, even dogmas, for which Judaism stands, our age seems more content with evocative appeals to the psychological and emotional quest that marks current spirituality.

My goal here is hardly to summarize the entirety of the tale that emerges from a close reading of these singular studies in liturgical development. The process was far too rich to allow for such a simple summary—hence the decision to include the three narratives in the first place and to urge readers to read them through for all their richness of detail.

I do, however, wish to treat, in some detail, a theological understanding of memory as it pertains to *Yizkor* in my essay in part 1, "Remembering the Dead: By Us and by God." We more or less know what it means for human beings to remember, in general, and to remember the dead, in particular; it is not as clear exactly *why* we choose to remember them. Further, we should wonder what it means for God to remember. God, after all, has no body, no brain; and doesn't a plea for God to remember imply that God can sometimes forget? To be sure, all talk of God is metaphoric in some way, an extrapolation from human experience to the divine. But a close look at this particular metaphor of "memory" reveals enormous profundity that should not go unrecognized.

⚮

PART I
Theology and Practice

Hashkavah

MEMORIALIZING THE DEAD IN SEPHARDI PRACTICE

Yoram Bitton

When I go to my parent's Moroccan synagogue on Shabbat, I am often honored with an *aliyah* to the Torah. Following the *aliyah*, without even asking me, the *chazzan* recites a *Hashkavah* on my behalf. Because he knows my family from Morocco, he populates the *Hashkavah* with the names of my deceased relatives whom I have never met and barely heard of. Although the recitation of the *Hashkavah* after each *aliyah* lengthens the Torah reading, it maintains a record of the family trees of the synagogue members.

In most Ashkenazi communities, *Yizkor* is recited four times a year and is marked as an important time on the Jewish calendar. It is laden with emotional significance to the point where it is often preceded by a related sermon from the rabbi. By contrast, the *Hashkavah* of the *edot hamizrach* (the Sephardi communities in the Mediterranean and the Middle East) is a regular occurrence, barely noticed by the congregants.

A person normally buys the privilege of being called to the Torah, and with that purchase comes an automatic *Hashkavah* for the person's family. As I said, the *chazzan* usually knows the family of the person and doesn't even need to ask the names of the deceased. That is not true of guests attending services, of course, so they will usually be asked if they would like a *Hashkavah* to be recited and then given the opportunity to provide the names they wish mentioned to the *chazzan*. Often, also, those who are not called to the Torah provide the names of their own deceased

---

Yoram Bitton is the director of the Klau Library at Hebrew Union College–Jewish Institute of Religion in New York.

to the *chazzan*, while he is reciting the prayer for the person who has the *aliyah*.

The actual *Hashkavah* is somewhat lengthy (see the full text in appendix A), so it is common for the *chazzan* to recite just an abridged version after each *aliyah*, as follows:

הַמְרַחֵם עַל כָּל בְּרִיּוֹתָיו הוּא יָחוֹס וְיַחְמוֹל וִירַחֵם
עַל נֶפֶשׁ, רוּחַ וּנְשָׁמָה שֶׁל (פלוני). רוּחַ יְהֹוָה תְּנִיחֶנּוּ
(לאשה -תְּנִיחֶנָּה) בְּגַן עֵדֶן.

May He who is merciful to all his creatures have pity, compassion, and mercy upon the lower soul, spirit, and higher soul of (name of the deceased). May the spirit of God place him (for a woman: her) in the Garden of Eden.

Reference to the "lower soul, spirit, and higher soul" refer to the three Hebrew words for "soul" that kabbalistic tradition associated with different aspects of "soulness," arranged in a hierarchy. This version was preferred by the famed kabbalist Isaac Luria (the Ari, Safed, 1534–1572) and his followers, as it did not automatically praise the deceased, an action that might not be appropriate in all circumstances.

However, if the person called to the Torah is marking a family member's *yahrzeit* (a term also used among Morrocan Jews), is marking the conclusion of the *sh'loshim* period, or is sitting shivah (*Shabbat p'kudato*, "the week that he was summoned," referring to the deceased being summoned by God), the original, and longer, version of the *Hashkavah* is recited (appendix A). The full version is recited also for the person called for the seventh *aliyah*, which is considered the most prestigious (and expensive), as whoever buys it also gets the right to recite the *Kaddish* following the reading of the Torah.

The full version of the *Hashkavah* is usually recited twice, once for men and once for women. There are significant differences between the language of the men's version and the women's version. The men's version is mostly in Hebrew, while the women's version is primarily in Aramaic.

The full version for a man usually begins *tov shem mishemen tov*, "Better is a good name than precious ointment." However, if the deceased was considered a *chacham*, a distinguished rabbi or righteous person, the *chazzan* recites additional verses at the beginning of the prayer, which begin, "Where shall wisdom be found.... "

Hashkavah is also recited following the evening service (*Arvit*) when one of the congregants is marking the *yahrzeit* of a close family member. The mourner says the *Kaddish*, and then the *chazzan* recites the full version of the *Hashkavah*.

In contrast to *Yizkor* and other prayers in the Ashkenazi tradition that use the father's name, the *Hashkavah* uses the first and last names of the deceased for both men and women, although sometimes women are referred to as "wife of" their husband's first and last name.

Although my experience with *Hashkavah* is from Moroccan synagogues, *Hashkavah* is also said in the Spanish-Portuguese tradition. In the Spanish-Portuguese synagogue Shearith Yisrael in New York, the text of the prayer is the same as it is in Moroccan synagogues. However, the short version that I mentioned above is limited to a *nachalah* (*yahrzeit*). The prayer is recited at the *Arvit* (evening) service on the evening of the *nachalah* and also on the Shabbat before the *nachalah* when the mourner is called to the Torah, usually for the seventh *aliyah*. The name of the deceased is recited using his or her name, the father's name, and the surname.

Spanish-Portuguese custom also precedes *Hashkavah* for a *chacham* with the verses mentioned above, but it may add verses to the beginning of the prayer if the deceased was a man of eminence, like a community supporter or leader. These verses begin, "How great is your goodness."

Hashkavah is recited primarily on Shabbat, as that is the day when, traditionally, the deceased are said to have rest from judgment in the beyond. Therefore, it is an appropriate day to pray for their rest and well-being, which are major themes in the *Hashkavah*.

☙

Remembering the Dead
By Us and by God
Rabbi Lawrence A. Hoffman, PhD

Why We Remember

We know what memory is. Indeed, a good number of the contributions in this volume rely on recent findings from neuroscience that describe the physiological infrastructure of the brain where memories are mapped, stored, and accessed.[1] We also know some of the reasons for memory. At its most elemental level, remembering has evolutionary value: it allows us to recognize threats to survival (that we can avoid) and pathways to food, sex, and safety (which we can pursue). Insofar as human beings are part of the animal kingdom as a whole, those basic functions of memory remain relevant. But human beings have advanced to an evolutionary stage where memory does much more. It is essential to the passing on of culture, which is, perhaps, the most consequential achievement of the human race.

It is no wonder, then, that the commandment to remember shows up so universally in the way our cultures shape us. The first- to second-century Greek Stoic philosopher Epictetus advised, "Remember never to say that you are alone, for you are not alone; but God is within." Americans "remember the Alamo." Jews "remember Amalek." Christians remember that at his last supper, Jesus said, "Do this in memory of me." But why, exactly, do we do all this? And why, by extension, do we remember our teachers, parents, mentors, or friends who have died and are no longer with us?

Medieval tradition was convinced that remembering the dead hastens them on their way to a better afterlife. It was more or less firmly believed that when we die, we receive reward or punishment on account of our deeds and that we can more hastily find our way to reward by the acts of those who remember to pray for us and, perhaps, who even donate money on our behalf.

That traditionalist answer, however, was subsidiary to the religious claim, "Because you should!"—a rationale that encompassed all the *mitzvot*, this one included. That normative approach to remembering is common to more than Jews. People generally memorialize because they feel that they *should*. Stopping all activity for a moment of silence on Israel's Day of Remembrance (Yom Hazikaron), buying poppies on the Remembrance Day that grew out of World War I, offering intercessory prayers for the deceased during a Sunday morning Mass, and observing *Yizkor*—these are all of a piece, all occasions where tradition bids its followers to remember just because it is the right thing to do. It is, in secular terms, an obligation; in Jewish terms, a commandment, a *mitzvah*. Our ancestors who passed on the obligation to remember our dead rarely spoke at all about the benefit it might have for worshipers who do it. The point was not the worshiper, but God, who had commanded the act in the first place, whether or not personal benefit (to the worshiper or the deceased) flowed from it.

Religion as obligation has fallen into hard times nowadays. The late anthropologist Victor Turner described contemporary religion as playful, a realm of human activity that is in competition with everything from opera to sports, as a way to fill one's discretionary time. Similar insight comes from sociologist Robert N. Bellah who, as early as 1985, drew our attention to "expressive individualism": Unlike America's early days, where the individualism of leaders like Franklin, Jefferson, and Adams was focused on constructing lives of service, our era emphasizes individuality as self-expression, service of the self to the self, in whatever ways the self feels proper. Bellah's dichotomy leads naturally to philosopher Charles Taylor's exploration of the revolutionary new way we think of authenticity: once it corresponded to the obligation one felt to be true to a higher order of reality outside the self; now it means the right to self-expression. The spirituality of personal fulfillment is everywhere, then—among Jews as well, to no one's surprise, as we see from Steven M. Cohen and Arnold M. Eisen's discovery of what they called a "sovereign" Jewish self: the modern search to define a Jewish life not because of an overwhelming sense of obligation but because one just naturally has the right to select a lifestyle that is therapeutically useful, not necessarily divinely commanded.

It is striking, therefore, to find that the obligation to remember one's parents and to extend that obligation to the martyrs of our past has not yet fallen prey to the expectation that such memory must be good for the person doing the remembering. People still attend memorial services because they think they should. For whatever reason, the obligation to remember runs deep inside our psyche. As we prepare each year for *Yizkor*, it is worth remembering that Jewish practice is based on obligation to those who came before us, a peculiar notion of *k'vod hamet*, "honor due the dead," not on pleasuring the self.

How God Remembers

Whatever problem we may have in locating the reason for our own remembering, we are at least not troubled by the idea that human beings can and do remember. Of course we remember; we can also forget; we need reminding. But what about God? What possible sense can it make to say that God remembers? Can God, then, also forget? Is that why we remind God to remember us? Put another way, isn't memory a temporal function, and thus beyond God who is eternal? What exactly is time, anyway?

The question was put famously by the philosopher and church father Augustine of Hippo some sixteen hundred years ago. "For what is time?" he asked and then answered:

> Certainly we understand when we speak of it; we understand also when we hear it spoken of by another. What, then, is time? ... If nothing passed away, there would not be past time; and if nothing were coming, there would not be future time; and if nothing were, there would not be present time. Those two times, therefore, past and future, how are they, when even the past now is not; and the future is not as yet?[2]

Augustine realized that we naturally picture time as what we today call a video strip, passing slowly frame by frame through the window of our consciousness. Unless we are historians, detectives, or reactionaries intent on salvaging nostalgia, we naturally keep our eyes on the screen, perhaps to anticipate what will come into view next, but surely wasting no time on the part of the film that has already been played. In this model, memory is what is left of yesterday's movie show.

But time is only one metaphor to which memory might apply. Space is another, as physicists know when they link space and time along a single continuum. Space and time differ in metaphorical use. Time "passes"; space does not. Because time passes us by, bit by bit, we tell people to pay attention to what's happening; for a time "comes" and then it inevitably "goes." Space, on the other hand, is a huge undifferentiated terrain in which we must locate ourselves and through which we may pass back and forth if we like, endlessly visiting and revisiting sites that exist simultaneously on a map.

My point is that the Rabbis treated God's memory other than we do; it was, for them, a spatial, not a temporal thing.[3] We can see this clearly by looking in detail at the use of the Hebrew verb for "remember," *yizkor*, from the root letters *z.k*[or *kh*].*r*. The same root gives us two nouns for "memory" or "memorial" and sometimes even "reminder": *zekher* and *zikaron*.

Seder Rav Amram (our very first prayer book and a reliable source, therefore, for what the words meant liturgically in the crucially formative era when our liturgy was taking final shape) uses the terms interchangeably. Shabbat, for instance, is both *zekher l'ma'asei v'reshit* ("a reminder, memorial, or memory of the act of creation")[4] and *zikaron l'ma'asei v'reshit*[5] (the same thing). Temporally speaking, that means that on Shabbat, we think back to the past. It is as if we were to say, while dozing off for a Shabbat nap perhaps, "This must have been what it was like when God rested that first Shabbat afternoon." All of that is well and good for us, who do, in fact, live in the reality of time, pressed as we are between the urgent bookends of a biography that may turn out to have fewer chapters than we plan on. We can do worse than plot our lives according to different forces of the word "remember" (in the temporal sense). We can variously live in the present, the future, or the past, as our mental health requires. It makes sense for humans to think in terms of time.

But what about God, who, we say, is *melekh ha'olam*, "ruler of the world"? If an earthly monarch, "a king of flesh and blood" (*melekh basar vadam*), as the Rabbis put it, were to rule the whole earth, would he also be *melekh ha'olam*, do you suppose? The answer is no, because such a ruler would hold sway only over the *space* of the earth, but not its existence in *time*. God, by contrast, is *melekh ha'olam*, but also, *mei'atah v'ad olam*, "from now until eternity"—when applied to God, *olam* has the sense of space *and* time, for God lives in time the way humans live in space. That is the Rabbis' best philosophical insight—the insistence that time is to God what space is to us.

God, then, does not "remember" the way we do. To remind God of something is not just to dredge up some old memory that was once alive but now is only a faded outline of what it was when it was "real." Reminding God about an instance in time is more akin to pointing out to humans a distant place on the map of space, which thereby moves into focus, if you like, even though it never actually stopped being there. The closest *we humans* can come is the science fiction of time travel, when we imagine that time is space and that, like the *Star Trek* team, we can awaken one morning to find ourselves not just with memories but with the reality of Al Capone's Chicago or Julius Caesar's Rome. Travelers in time or space need pointers to show the way. And that is where *zekher/ zikaron* comes into play for God. *Zekher/zikaron* is not a memorial; it is a pointer.

Space and time are only two maps of the human spirit. There are others. Maps are charts of distances, but the distances they encode may belong to any medium. Take human reason, for instance. In the ethereal realm of logic, you get synapses of reason that need to be charted on maps of mental acuity. Apply logic to life, and you get a map called halakhah. The very best way to image halakhah is precisely as a map of the mind but applied to human reality rather than as pure mathematics or symbolic logic. Join two distant points in the map of halakhah and you have a logical demonstration of various sorts, an exercise in Talmudic logic for which the Talmud actually has terms—*kal vachomer*, for example, "arguing from a minor or lenient assumption to a major or more stringent conclusion." Some terms of halakhic logic are actually cartographical, drawn, that is, from the world of mapmakers. *M'na lan* ("Whence do we know this?") and *M'na hanei milei* ("Whence do we get this opinion?"), for example, are calls for tracing what we have on hand to a distant place whence it came. It is as if the Rabbis knew they were in receipt of indubitable places in the map of halakhah but had to join them logically, the way Marco Polo knew there was a place called Cathay but had to join it to Europe.

Like the dots in a connect-the-dots game, the things we experience in the world make sense only when they are joined together. The kind of line we use to join the dots depends on the nature of the map. The map of time uses lines of memory; space features highways, shipping routes, and air corridors; logic uses Aristotelian propositions, algebraic equations, and halakhic hermeneutics.

And in the map of halakhah, we find this: *im ein r'ayah ladavar, yesh zekher ladavar*, "Although there is no proof for the matter under discussion, there is a *zekher* for it." Yes: *zekher*—not "memory," "remembrance," "reminder," or "memorial," however, but "pointer." That is to say: "Though there is no proof for the thing, there is a *zekher*, a pointer, to it." Physics speaks of a strong and a weak force, and philosophy differentiates a strong sense of an argument from a weaker one. So too in halakhic proof-texting. One would prefer a strong text that proves one's case absolutely; when that cannot be found, however, the Rabbis sometimes cite a verse that is short of real proof in their minds but is at least a *zekher*, an "indication," let us say, that at least points the way to the thing under discussion. When a verse is cited as evidential demonstration short of absolute proof, that verse is called a *zekher*.[6]

Now we know what it is for God to remember us or, for that matter, to remember all the other things that our liturgy evokes as reminder. Our prayers ask God not just to remember our beloved dead, but also to "remember for us the covenant of our fathers" or "remember ... Abraham, Isaac, and Jacob.... Remember the thirteen [divine attributes of Exodus 34:6–7]."[7] If you doubt that the Rabbis treated these things as transhistorical—part of God's space, not God's time—consider the obvious fact that the thirteen divine attributes do not belong to history. They are eternal, as God is.

Or what about this petition: "Remember your mercy, O Adonai, and your compassion, for they are eternal."[8] For God, remembering "your mercy"[9] is like remembering the covenant of thirteen attributes. Neither is evanescent. The word "memory" thus cannot fully capture the sense of *zekher/zikaron* when applied to the divine.

Even the things that *seem* historical from our perspective are not, when we point them out to God. When we say of God, *Zokher chasdei avot*, "God remembers the righteousness of the ancestors," it is not that God flips through an old picture album to remember the good old days of Abraham, Isaac, and Jacob. Imagine God instead surveying space like time: God looks at our ancestors and then at us and links the two with the connective tissue of divine grace. It may be, therefore, that *ein banu ma'asim*, "we have no good deeds" with which to plead our merit, but trust God to *choneinu va'aneinu*, "graciously answer us" anyway, on account of the *avot* and *imahot*, the "forefathers and foremothers," who are not dead and gone, but still alive and well somewhere else on the map that God alone comprehends.

Many consequences flow from our revisiting Rabbinic theology with a map of space, not time, as primary. Our haftarah for Rosh Hashanah insists that God "visits" Sarah, for instance—another geographical, not temporal, term. But elsewhere, the liturgy uses "visit" and "remember" in interchangeable apposition: "Remember us on it for good and visit us on it for blessing."[10] "Visiting" is the same as "remembering," but geographical as to space, rather than temporal as to time. That is why the Talmud rules that liturgical references to God's remembering may include instances of divine visits as well.[11] God visits across time as we visit across space.

In sum, pointers are necessary in any act of thought. They get us across gaps that are otherwise unbridgeable. In a gap of Talmudic logic, a biblical verse may point the way. In the domain of time, memory does so. In space, our landmarks announce, "Jerusalem, this way." So *zekher* means memory only when time is at stake, and only accidentally, not essentially. More precisely, *zekher* is the function of pointing.

We can now see what prayers for God to remember do. They provide pointers that, as it were, attract God's attention on the divine map of space-time. With regard to our deceased, it is as if we understand that they are dead only from the perspective of human beings, for whom space is unending but time is not. In God's mind's eye, however, time too is all-present, so that even those who die are as alive as ever. We point them out to God.

On the High Holy Days, we are asked to stretch our mind to the point of imagining that we see things as God does. Rosh Hashanah and Yom Kippur provide this sweeping vision of a universe of space and time that is visible, in its entirety and all at once—but only to the eternal perspective of God. The map, however, is neither homogeneous nor static; it has shifting highlights, and the highlighted areas are open to our design. We can weigh the relative significance of different points on the map, "reminding" God to attend to this quadrant rather than that. One of the grandest things we aspire to do is point God's way to our beloved who have passed from that quadrant of time that houses us but who still remain alive in the eternity of time that God alone inhabits.

This foray into liturgical theology says something also about the character of human beings. In this religious anthropology, we are not mere victims of the grains of sand that descend inexorably in the hourglass of being and bury us under a virtual tel of time, as if we had never existed; nor, in our own lives, need we feel inundated by the detritus of civilization gone awry, the screaming headlines and mega-events that relegate us to mere statistics in a universe that is presumed to be too impersonal and too large to keep us in mind.

The grand message of God's memory is that human beings are never out of mind. They may always be kept in mind, because our liturgy evokes their existence in the mind of God. Liturgy is the means by which they are pointed out, visited, remembered, even saved. There can be no nobler hallmark of the human spirit than this: the chutzpah to believe that even the lowliest human being is worthy of God's attention and that human culture at its best calls us together, even across generations, to be remembered by God, pointed out on the divine map of eternity!

 srwo

Remembering the Dead as Halakhic Peril

Rabbi Daniel Landes

Hazkarat n'shamot ("remembering the souls") or *hazkarat hametim* ("remembering the dead") is a set of prayers and charitable actions inspired by the memory of deceased family members—especially parents. *Hazkarat n'shamot* has come to occupy a major place in Jewish religious consciousness, but it in no way derives from an original halakhic prescription. Rather, it is a popular practice that halakhah subsequently chose to regulate and to establish as normative.

As this book makes clear, there are three prayers that are classically associated with *hazkarat n'shamot*:

- *El Malei Rachamim* ("God, full of compassion")
- *Av Harachamim* ("Father of mercy")
- *Yizkor Elohim* ("May God remember")

More than just prayers, each of these is its own form or type of remembrance; each was attached to its own specific set of halakhic regulations and underlying considerations.

Rabbi Daniel Landes is the director and *rosh hayeshivah* of the Pardes Institute of Jewish Studies in Jerusalem. Pardes brings together men and women of all backgrounds to study classical Jewish texts and contemporary Jewish issues in a rigorous, challenging, and open-minded environment. Rabbi Landes is also a contributor to the *My People's Prayer Book: Traditional Prayers, Modern Commentaries* series, winner of the National Jewish Book Award; *My People's Passover Haggadah: Traditional Texts, Modern Commentaries*, a finalist for the National Jewish Book Award; and *Who by Fire, Who by Water*—Un'taneh Tokef; *All These Vows*—Kol Nidre, and *We Have Sinned: Sin and Confession in Judaism*—Ashamnu *and* Al Chet (all Jewish Lights).

The first, *El Malei Rachamim* ("God, full of compassion"), which parallels the Sephardi practice of *Hashkavah* ("Laying down to eternal rest"), is recited on the closest Torah reading to the *yahrzeit* (annual memorial day of the deceased's death date). It is recited between *aliyot* or at the end of the Torah reading, prompted by a relative of the deceased who rises for an *aliyah* with the deceased in mind. *El Malei Rachamim* is associated with the Chmielnicki pogroms of 1648 (in present-day Ukraine) but is by now recited for anyone who has died and for martyrs generally, as well. It is a liturgical centerpiece, therefore, not just an accompaniment to an *aliyah* that commemorates a person's date of death. It is recited at the funeral itself and at any memorial that has a *minyan* (prayer quorum)—a memorial service following *sh'loshim* (the "thirty" days of mourning following a death), or a service for Yom Hashoah (Holocaust Memorial Day), for example.

The second, *Av Harachamin* ("Father of mercy"), is recited weekly as part of the Shabbat morning liturgy. As a memorial prayer, however, it is linked conceptually to the dirgeful set of prayers we call *Tachanun* ("Supplications"), a daily rubric that reflects on the sinfulness of the human condition (see *My People's Prayer Book*, vol. 6, *Tachanun and Concluding Prayers*). *Tachanun* is omitted on Shabbat (whose character makes such cheerless liturgy inappropriate) and on a variety of similar weekday occasions—Chanukah, for instance. So too, then, *Av Harachamim* is not said on those Sabbaths that if they were weekdays, *Tachanun* would not be recited. Like *El Malei Rachamim*, *Av Harachamin* too began in the wake of a disaster, the slaughtering of Jewish martyrs at the time of the First Crusade. But unlike *El Malei Rachamim*, it has remained primarily associated with martyrs—not just the original Ukrainian victims, but all of our martyrs throughout the generations. *El Malei Rachamim* does not actually mention the martyrs, whereas *Av Harachamim* does, so that the wording alone guarantees that this original nexus will not be lost.

Av Harachamim is recited at the end of the haftarah reading on Shabbat, before *Ashrei* and the return of the *Sefer Torah*, a moment of maximal synagogue attendance and ritual drama according to the *Bi'ur Hagra* (a classic commentary on the *Orach Chayim* section of the *Shulchan Arukh*, by the Vilna Gaon, Rabbi Elijah ben Shlomo Zalman Kremer of Vilnius [1720–97]; see 284:7). But more importantly, as pointed out by the *Shibolei Haleket* 81 (Rabbi Zedekiah ben Abraham Anav, thirteenth century, Rome), it is located directly after the blessing for the community, its members, leaders, and supporters: "After we [first] bless the living, because their respect comes first."

The third form of *hazkarat n'shamot* is *Yizkor Elohim*, the prayer that gives the entire *Yizkor* "service" its name and that is sometimes referred to itself, simply, as *Yizkor*. It is recited primarily on Yom Kippur, more properly known as Yom Hakippurim. Indeed the *Darkhei Moshe* (Rabbi Moses Isserles, 1520–72, Poland; on the *Tur*, 21) points to the reason given for *kippurim* (literally, "atonements") being in the plural is that this day is for both the living and the dead. In most Ashkenazi traditions, *hazkarat n'shamot* is also recited during the last of the three Pilgrimage Festivals (Passover, Sukkot, and Shavuot).

These three forms of *hazkarat n'shamot* reflect three modes of connecting one's prayers to the dead. *Yizkor* is said individually, privately, and quietly, by the relative (or student) for the beloved one (or teacher) within the community. *El Malei Rachamim* is said publicly, out loud, and communally, by a representative of the community that has gathered for prayer that day—the prayer leader (*sh'liach tzibbur*). Both are recited with a pledge to give *tz'dakah* ("charity") in memory of the deceased. *Av Harachamim* is recited regularly by all worshipers within the Shabbat service, without a pledge of *tz'dakah*.

The original reference to *hazkarat n'shamot* within the traditional corpus of Rabbinic literature is actually aggadic, not halakhic—the influential post-Talmudic (eighth century) *Midrash Tanchuma*, as part of a discussion on the human journey through life based on the astrological signs (*Ha'azinu* 1):

> Once judged on the scales [Libra] ... even if a person has sinned, he is rendered to be like a virgin [Virgo]. But if he continues to sin [thereafter] he is sent down to the bottom of Sheol and *Gehinnom* [biblical names for places associated as a sort of hell for sinners] as a crab [Cancer]. If he repents, however, he is thrown out like an arrow shot from a bow [Sagittarius]. Therefore we mention the dead on Shabbat so that they, the dead [who are assumed to have been spared the torments of hell on Shabbat], shall not return to *Gehinnom* [once Shabbat is over]. Similarly, we are accustomed to remember the dead on Yom Kippur and to pledge in their memory a specific amount of *tz'dakah* [charitable] funds.

For we have learned in *Torat Kohanim* [the halakhic midrash of the Talmudic period known as *Sifra*] [this citation cannot be found in our editions]: "'Atone for your People Israel' (Deut. 21:8)—these are the living; 'whom you have redeemed'—those are the dead. From here we learn that the living redeem the dead."

[The text now turns to a further discussion of itself, namely, the lesson that] "therefore we are accustomed to remember the dead on Yom Kippur and to pledge in their memory a specific amount of *tz'dakah*." [*Torat Kohanim* itself wonders out loud]: "Could it be that once they have died, *tz'dakah* will not help them? [No, because] the verse instructs us [explicitly] 'whom you have redeemed,' from which we learn that when a specific amount of money is pledged in their memory, they are taken out [of *Gehinnom*] and raised up as an arrow shot from a bow."

Immediately, such a person is rendered as tender and clean as a kid [Capricorn], and he is purified as the hour he was born, and pure water from a ladle [Aquarius] is poured over him, and he grows up with great pleasure as a fish [Pisces] who enjoys the water.

We need to see what is present and what is absent in this rationale for *hazkarat n'shamot*. Absent is any form of prayer directed to or through the dead. A memorial could have taken two such forms: (a) a prayer to the dead asking them to be intercessors to God on our behalf, or (b) a prayer through the dead, a prayer, that is, that claims God's mercy on the basis of our relationship to the dead, who are presumed to be righteous enough to help us. Neither option has a place in *hazkarat n'shamot*. Our prayers are delivered to God directly (not to the dead), and they are on behalf of the dead (not on our own behalf). We ask—we actually come close to demanding—mercy for them, that their rest be perfect. We offer both prayer and *tz'dakah*, attempting to convince God of the justness of our request.

We can see in the *Tanchuma* source a great wish to justify a ritual practice that had already achieved widespread social acceptance by the time of its composition. It provides a Pentateuchal verse with Rabbinic exposition to anchor the practice in Torah. The verse with its accompanying explication is used to exemplify a great Torah/Rabbinic concept—that of *pidyon* ("redemption"), a concept that should now occupy our full attention.

Pidyon is utilized as a description of God's qualities, best understood, in Maimonidean terms, as a quality of divine action. God is the one who redeemed us from Egypt: "for I brought you out of the land of Egypt and *redeemed* you from the house of slavery" (Micah 6:4). The term is applied halakhically in three contexts. The first is *pidyon* of agricultural products, which are held to be holy, by their very nature, and requiring redemption from God's domain in order to be available for creaturely consumption. Ideally, one is to take a tenth of any particular agricultural harvest (a *ma'aser sheni*, or "second tithe") and eat it in the sacred confines of Jerusalem. If the owner finds this burdensome, he is allowed to redeem that crop for its monetary worth plus 20 percent. The redeemed crop is rendered free of its original sanctity and may be used for any purpose, while the newly sacralized money is used in Jerusalem for a pleasant holiday.

The second context is *pidyon haben*, "the redemption of the first-born male child." The first-born is considered to belong to God and is therefore born into a state of holiness. Like the harvest, he must be redeemed in a ceremony whereby the parent or guardian "pays" a *kohen* ("priest") five silver coins to get him back. This payment frees him from being "owned" by God's representative, the priest (and destined for Temple service). So redeemed, the child is then free to live a normal life under parental guidance and responsibility.

Finally, we have *pidyon sh'vuyim* ("redemption of captives"), which became so highly valued as a *mitzvah* that it was known as a *mitzvah rabbah* ("great mitzvah") according to the Talmud (Bava Batra 8b). This mitzvah arose because of the commonplace capture of Jewish notables by authorities (or by pirates), who then ransomed them back to the Jewish community for a price. The *mitzvah* of *pidyon sh'vuyim* is overridden only (1) when it is felt that paying the redemption money as ransom will incite further kidnapping, or (2) if the captured person's own reckless behavior has repeatedly put him in the situation of having to be ransomed by the community. But in general, we follow Maimonides's affirmation that "the ransom of captives takes precedence over the feeding and clothing of the poor. There is no greater *mitzvah*" (*Mishneh Torah*, Laws of Gifts to the Poor 8:10–11).

In all three cases, redemption alters the status of the person or thing being redeemed. In our case too—the redemption assumed to occur in *hazkarat n'shamot*—altered status must occur. We should ask, therefore, what new status is granted the deceased when we "remember" them.

The imagery of the *Midrash Tanchuma* suggests a double transformation: first, "geographically" the dead are freed from the prison of *Gehinnom*, as if shot upward to the bliss of paradise or, at least, to some sort of waiting station short of heaven but still better than hell! The second transformation is more interesting to us, because it has to do with the essential quality of the deceased. The dead are described as being rendered "tender and clean as a kid [Capricorn] ... purified as the hour he was born." They are reborn as new children: innocent, pure, and readied by *hazkarat n'shamot* for a second chance at whatever Judaism holds out as the promise for life after death.

But the *Tanchuma* is clear that prayer and remembering are not enough by themselves. On their own, they are only words or thoughts. So a pledge for a specified amount of money to *tz'dakah* is also required, on the understanding that "charity saves from death" (*tz'dakah tatzil mimavet*, Proverbs 11:4). That phrase is generally used Rabbinically as cautionary advice for a person to embrace charity while still alive—before death arrives, with its final judgment. Here it is used as a life saver that we, the living, can toss to the helpless dead as at least a temporary reprieve from their condition in *Gehinnom*.

An important discussion of these issues is found in the responsa of the medieval Jewish legalist *par excellence*, Rabbi Shlomo ben Aderet (the Rashba, 1235–1310, Barcelona), who examines the issue of what a son—and, by extension, daughters and others as well—can do to improve the moral standing of the dead (Rashba, reponsum 539). The hypothetical case in question is a man who dies with "a standing debt or obligation" that has come about because of some unethical act of which he is guilty. It may be a case of outright theft, ill-gotten gain acquired through oppressive misuse of power, or just the false denial of owning something that this man actually has in his possession at the time. According to the Rashba, this man who has died has two problems:

> One is the amount of the money owed to the aggrieved party; the second is the punishment that is owed to heaven for his transgression of the commandments (e.g., not to steal). Regarding his financial obligation incurred on account of theft or oppression, his children, brothers, relatives, and friends can pay that up, leaving nothing owed.... As regards the punishment that he owes to God for transgressing a *mitzvah*, it is no different from other

transgressions: there is no one who can for certain lessen that reality.

The living can easily make up the debt that their deceased owe to people they have cheated or robbed. But how might they mitigate the punishment incurred before God? That is the Rashba's question.

The Rashba begins by expressing some faint hope that a pious man's prayerful remembrance of the dead *might* be effective in erasing this moral debt before God, but he seems doubtful. He includes reference to the *Tanchuma* and *Midrash Kohanim* (cited above), as well as other, later, sources, but is lackluster about the efficacy of the "custom in some places to remember the dead." He does make the effort to defend the practice, as he often defends community customs, but he is silent regarding recommending it.

His evidently real feelings are summed up in a prior paragraph where he definitively says:

> One's elevation to greatness and the pleasure that arises from being in the divine presence is only according to one's deeds. Even if all the righteous of the world were to request money for him [to repay his debts after he has died] and even if all conceivable *tz'dakah* were given for his merit, none of this would help.

The Rashba's understanding of these issues is persuasive. It is true that one's monetary debt or fine can be made up by a surviving son or daughter (or anyone else, for that matter). This debt is a finite "external" amount—specific, discrete, and tangible. To be sure, paying off such debt is conducive to creating a responsible sense of order and balance within society and needs to be encouraged. But paying off the debt is not the same as paying off the sin. Attempting to use our own prayers or charity to expunge a sin of others smacks of bribery, for the sin "belongs" inalienably to the human being who did it—just as his merit for good deeds does. The Rishonim (early Rabbinic authorities, prior to the *Shulchan Arukh*, sixteenth century) frequently put it this way: "One eats only what one has prepared [by oneself] for the Sabbath." In short, the halakhah is opposed to the notion of a free lunch. Insofar as *hazkarat n'shamot* involves the tending of prayer and charity for the dead's credit, it is perilous to the halakhic notion of individual moral responsibility.

Considering all this, one might be persuaded to call the whole thing off. I myself have toyed with that option. But *hazkarat n'shamot* has taken root so pervasively and persistently that it would be better to investigate its alternative potential for ennoblement and transcendence.

There are three arguments for the efficacy of the *tz'dakah* that is attached to *hazkarat n'shamot* in freeing the dead from the punishments of *Gehinnom*. The first is presented by the Rashba in a different responsum (5:49), where he argues that a son can alter his deceased father's morally difficult situation because the son (and by the same logic, a daughter) is a natural product of the parent, having been formed by that parent's nature and nurture. Thus the child's good deeds can be understood as emerging as an extension of the parent who is now imprisoned in the hell of his or her own making. Having been born to and raised by this parent, the child's actions (including *tz'dakah* and prayer) are in a real way an extension of the parent him- or herself.

The second argument is that of Rabbi Joseph Caro (1488–1575, Safed) in his monumental commentary *Beit Yosef* on the *Tur* (1269–1343, Germany). He writes (*Orach Chayim* 621:6):

> How does it help that the living gives *tz'dakah* on behalf of the dead? God examines the hearts of the living and the dead to determine that if the deceased in question were alive they would have given *tz'dakah* [themselves]. Even if they were poor but their hearts were good and they would have given [the money] if they had it, then this [the living who give *tz'dakah* on their behalf] is [at least] somewhat efficacious, for the living can ask to lessen the [negative] judgment on the dead.

We thus find two arguments for *tz'dakah* on behalf of the deceased: first, the child's good deeds are the extension of the parent; second, the *tz'dakah* is given as the content of a presumed intention on the part of the deceased. Regarding this second argument, however, Caro notes that this would certainly not work for an actual *rasha* ("a truly evil person")!

There is a third argument too, however; one that follows from the concept with which we began: *pidyon* ("redemption"). The idea seems to be that *pidyon* is so deeply rooted in Judaism, it is inconceivable that there might be a place in our lives—death!—where it cannot be employed. *Pidyon* was experienced in the flesh by those present at the Exodus from

Egypt and will again be experienced the same way by those alive at the time when history as we know it gives way to a better time to come. We need to extend as well the possibility of experiencing redemption to those who have passed away and are seemingly beyond being present for it bodily when it comes again. It must, therefore, be available also to the deceased. We thus allow and even celebrate *hazkarat n'shamot* when accompanied by the genuine effort of transformation such as giving *tz'dakah*. And as *tz'dakah* works its miracles for its beneficiaries—the recipients and the actual givers—it also delivers the deceased in whose names it is given, from their status as prisoners of sin and death.

☙❧

Memorializing the Shoah

Rabbi Dalia Marx, PhD

A story is told of Napoleon Bonaparte, who heard wailing coming from a Parisian synagogue on the ninth of Av. Upon learning that people were mourning the destruction of the Temple, he is said to have asked, "What Temple? Why wasn't I informed? When did this happen?" "A thousand and seven hundred years ago," was the reply. Astonished, Napoleon responded, "Surely a people who have mourned the loss of their Temple for so long will survive to see it rebuilt!"

However legendary, this story reflects the remarkable nature of the Jewish collective memory. Through the symbolism of liturgy, Jews have regularly reenacted their past so as to understand their present and shape their future.[1] My interest here is the Holocaust and the ways in which it has been memorialized in the realm of the synagogue and through prayer and ritual. I begin with liturgical responses to tragedies in the past, in order to develop a benchmark for the manner and extent to which Jewish memorials have become the norm. Other forms of memorializing, such as

Rabbi Dalia Marx, PhD, is a professor of liturgy and midrash at the Jerusalem campus of Hebrew Union College–Jewish Institute of Religion and teaches in various academic institutions in Israel and Europe. Rabbi Marx earned her doctorate at the Hebrew University in Jerusalem and her rabbinic ordination at HUC–JIR in Jerusalem and Cincinnati. She is involved in various research groups and is active in promoting progressive Judaism in Israel. Rabbi Marx contributed to *Who by Fire, Who by Water—Un'taneh Tokef; All These Vows—Kol Nidre;* and *We Have Sinned: Sin and Confession in Judaism—Ashamnu and Al Chet* (all Jewish Lights). She writes for academic journals and the Israeli press, and is engaged in creating new liturgies and midrashim.

non-religious ceremonies, poetry, visual arts, or trips to Poland, will not be discussed here. They merit a separate discussion.

We can focus on two prior eras of persecution, both of them in Ashkenazi Europe: first, the Crusader slaughter of Jews in the Rhineland in the spring of 1096; and second, the execution of the Jews of Blois in 1171.[2]

The Crusades "provoked the first major attempt to exterminate an entire Jewry in Europe."[3] Its Jewish martyrs "left a scar in Jewish collective memory in the German Empire."[4] Poignant *piyyutim* (liturgical poems) marking the disaster were composed, as was the prayer *Av Harachamim* ("Father of mercy"), a requiem for the martyrs that calls on God to avenge the "spilled blood of his servants" who perished in sanctification of the divine name (*al kiddush hashem*). *Av Harachamim* is also recited after the Torah reading on Shabbat.[5] It can reliably be traced back to the end of the twelfth century, but may have been composed soon after the First Crusade of 1096. *Kaddish* was already part of the fixed liturgy, but it became a prayer of mourners, particularly orphans, only in the generation after the First Crusade.[6]

Some of these innovations remained within the Ashkenazi world, while others spread to become practices of the entire Jewish People. The recitation of *Av Harachamin* and the practice of *Hazkarat N'shamot* (literally, "commemoration of souls," the memorial service, which takes place at the end of the festivals and Yom Kippur, called simply *Yizkor* here) are strictly Ashkenazi, as are the many liturgical hymns written by eye witnesses of the atrocities. The recitation of the *Kaddish* as the mourners' prayer, however, along with related ritual innovations resulting from that era, such as the *yahrzeit* (a commemoration of the anniversary of the death)[7] and lighting candles for the deceased, have become general Jewish practice.

Some commemoration rituals remained local. For example, a fast day was decreed by Rabbenu Tam, Rashi's grandson, to be observed in the communities of France, England, and the Rhineland each twentieth day of Sivan, because on May 26, the Hebrew date of the twentieth of Sivan, 1171, some three dozen Jews of the small Jewish community of Blois (part of central France) were burned at the stake following a blood libel. Special *kinot* (lamentations) were composed to commemorate the event.[8] Some scholars argue that the custom of reciting *Alenu* daily stems from the fact that the Blois martyrs sang it when they were executed—and then became a general practice. Commemorations of later tragedies, such as Chmielnicki's pogroms (1648–49 in present-day Ukraine), were folded into the same day. Memorializing on the twentieth day of Sivan was widely retained until the Holocaust,[9] and it is still a custom to not get married on this day.

The Memory of the Holocaust in the Standard Liturgy

The Holocaust presents a different category of tragedy. Never before has the Jewish People (and arguably any other people) experienced such a coordinated and planned attempt at total annihilation. The Nazis openly declared their intention to eradicate Jews from the face of the earth and pursued their deadly aims with determination and persistence, even when it was clear that Germany was losing the war.

Yet compared to the outpouring of ritual following the Crusades, the Holocaust has made little impact upon the fixed liturgy of the synagogue—a marked contrast to its significant imprint on contemporary literature, art, and discourse. Why is that?

To be sure, commemorating the Holocaust is not altogether absent from the synagogue service. We should begin by seeing what, in fact, we do have.

El Malei Rachamim for Victims of the Holocaust

Special versions of the Ashkenazi memorial prayer *El Malei Rachamim* are the most commonly accepted prayers that memorialize Holocaust victims. They are widely recited in synagogues of most, if not all, denominations, both in Israel and in the diaspora.

El Malei Rachamim can be traced to the Chmielnicki pogroms. The prayer (multiple versions of which exist) became the standard Ashkenazi memorial prayer. As a flexible text, modified over time, it lent itself easily to the task of commemorating victims of the Shoah.

Several different versions of *El Malei Rachamim* for the Holocaust are presently in use. They differ in style, emotionality, and religious tenor. The following example refrains from focusing on the perpetrators; instead, it stresses the communal obligation to memorialize the victims:

O God, full of mercy, who dwells
on high,
grant a perfect rest
under the wings of the *Shekhinah*,
among of the holy and the pure,
whose brightness shines like the
firmament,
the souls of our brothers and sisters,
the children of Israel
the holy and pure
who fell at the hands of the murderers
and whose blood was spilled
in Auschwitz, Majdanek, Treblinka
and in the other death camps in
Europe
those who were murdered, burnt,
slaughtered, and buried alive
in all manner of cruel and unnatural
deaths
for the sanctification of the name,
for the charity that we,
their sons and daughters, brothers and
sisters
vow to give charity for the remembering of their names—
in the Garden of Eden may they find
rest.
Therefore, the master of mercy will
protect them forever, and bundle
their souls in the bundle of life.
Adonai is their heritage,
And may they find peace in their last
resting place.
And let us say: Amen.[10]

אֵל מָלֵא רַחֲמִים שׁוֹכֵן
בַּמְּרוֹמִים הַמְצֵא מְנוּחָה
נְכוֹנָה תַּחַת כַּנְפֵי הַשְּׁכִינָה
בְּמַעֲלוֹת קְדוֹשִׁים וּטְהוֹרִים
כְּזֹהַר הָרָקִיעַ מְאִירִים
וּמַזְהִירִים לְנִשְׁמוֹת אַחֵינוּ בְּנֵי
יִשְׂרָאֵל הַקְּדוֹשִׁים וְהַטְּהוֹרִים
שֶׁנָּפְלוּ בִּידֵי הָרוֹצְחִים
וְנִשְׁפַּךְ דָּמָם בְּאוֹשְׁוִיץ מַיְדָנֶק
טְרֶבְּלִינְקָה וּבִשְׁאָר מַחֲנוֹת
הַשְׁמָד בְּאֵירוֹפָּה שֶׁנֶּהֶרְגוּ
וְנִשְׂרְפוּ וְנִשְׁחֲטוּ וְנִקְבְּרוּ חַיִּים
בְּכָל מִיתוֹת מְשֻׁנּוֹת
וְאַכְזָרִיּוֹת עַל קְדֻשַּׁת הַשֵּׁם
בַּעֲבוּר שֶׁאֲנַחְנוּ בְּנֵיהֶם
וּבְנוֹתֵיהֶם אֲחֵיהֶם וְאַחְיוֹתֵיהֶם
נוֹדְרִים צְדָקָה בְּעַד הַזְכָּרַת
נִשְׁמוֹתֵיהֶם בְּגַן עֵדֶן תְּהֵא
מְנוּחָתָם לָכֵן בַּעַל הָרַחֲמִים
יַסְתִּירֵם בְּסֵתֶר כְּנָפָיו
לְעוֹלָמִים וְיִצְרֹר בִּצְרוֹר
הַחַיִּים אֶת נִשְׁמָתָם ה׳ הוּא
נַחֲלָתָם וְיָנוּחוּ בְשָׁלוֹם עַל
מִשְׁכָּבָם וְנֹאמַר אָמֵן.

Holocaust versions of *El Malei Rachamim* are commonly included in the memorial service for Yom Kippur and the last day of the Pilgrimage Festivals (Sukkot, Pesach, and Shavuot). In many prayer books, particularly those used in Israel, it is recited alongside another version memorializing soldiers lost in the defense of Israel.

The reason for the popularity of *El Malei Rachamim*, is clear—its paradigmatic text is well known and predates the Holocaust. However, it hardly exemplifies liturgical innovation composed exclusively for the occasion.

Liturgical Poetry (*Piyyutim*)

By contrast, a few liturgical poems (*piyyutim*) have been composed specifically with the Holocaust in mind and are widely included, especially in traditional synagogues, on Tisha B'av, the day we mourn the destruction of the Temple and other tragedies suffered by the Jewish People. Some were composed by survivors themselves. One example, *Eli, Eli, Nafshi B'khi* ("Lament, lament, my soul"), for example, was composed by Yehudah Leib Bialer in 1945, when he returned home to Warsaw at the end of the war. Here are a few of its stanzas:

Lament, lament, my soul;	אֱלִי אֱלִי נַפְשִׁי בְּכִי
Cry out and mourn, O Daughter of Israel,	וְזַעֲקִי בַּת יִשְׂרָאֵל
In eulogy, in howls of grief,	מִסְפֵּד שְׂאִי וְהִתְיַפְּחִי
For the flames have consumed Israel.	אָכְלָה הָאֵשׁ בְּיִשְׂרָאֵל
For the genocide, so carefully planned;	עַל טֶבַח עַם אֲשֶׁר הוּכַן
O pangs of grief for the cascades of blood—	יִסּוּרֵי שְׁכוֹל אֲשָׁדוֹת דָּמִים
None were spared, not old, not young;	זָקֵן גַּם טַף לֹא רֻחַם
All were sacrificed—holy and pure.	עַל עֲקֵדָה קָרְבָּן תָּמִים
. . . .	. . . .
For the generations that were cut down,	עֲלֵי דוֹרוֹת אֲשֶׁר נִגְדְּעוּ
Blood of the fathers with blood of the sons.	דְּמֵי אָבוֹת עַל דְּמֵי בָּנִים

In the valley of Auschwitz they were
    expunged,
In the furnaces of the crematoria.

For the imprisoned, clothed only in rags,
Expiring in droves, in multitudes;
In Treblinka and Majdanek,
Their bones were scattered, left to rot.

For the cattle cars, crammed with
    human cargo
That were cushioned with nothing but
    tar and chalk.
Bleached by thirst, their souls parched
    and dry,
They called for water; no hand reached
    out.

For those frozen in fields of snow,
Young children in their mothers' arms.
For the martyrs whose wailing could be
    heard,
Buried alive in the communal graves.

For the decimation of a nation we
    raise a lamentation,
Bound up in sorrow, cloaked in
    destruction.
Will hatred's shadow forever reign?
Will the struggle never end?

בְּגֵיא אוֹשְׁבִיץ תַּמּוּ גָוְעוּ
עֲלֵי מוֹקְדוֹת הַכִּבְשָׁנִים

עֲלֵי כְּלוּאִים חֲגוּרֵי שַׂק
הַנְּמַקִּים בְּרִבְבוֹתֵיהֶם
בְּטְרֶבְּלִינְקִי וּמַיְדָנֶק
וְאֵין מְלַקֵּט עַצְמוֹתֵיהֶם

עֲלֵי קְרוֹנוֹת צְפוּפֵי אָדָם
אֲשֶׁר רוּפְּדוּ גָפְרִית וָסִיד
צַחֵי צָמָא כִּכְלוֹת נַפְשָׁם
צָעֲקוּ מַיִם וְאֵין מוֹשִׁיט

עֲלֵי קְפוּאִים בִּשְׂדוֹת שְׁלָגִים
יְלָדִים רַכִּים בְּחֵיק אִמָּהוֹת
וְעַל קְדוֹשִׁים הַשׁוֹאֲגִים
קְבוּרֵי חַיִּים מִתּוֹךְ בּוֹרוֹת

עַל שֶׁבֶר עַם נִשָּׂא קִינָה
כְּבוּלֵי יָגוֹן עֲטוּיֵי שׁוֹאָה
הֲלָנֶצַח תַּאֲפִיל שִׂנְאָה
וְלֹא תִּפָּרֵשׂ הַנִּגְהָה

See, O God, how my skin has shriveled;
My heart is broken as my enemies rise up.
Hear my pleas, provide a haven;
Save my soul from the murderous mob.[11]

רְאֵה אֱלֹהִים עוֹרִי צָפַד
נָפַל לִבִּי שׂוֹנְאַי קָמִים
הַקְשִׁיבָה שַׁוְעִי חִישָׁה מִפְּלָט
הַצִּילָה נַפְשִׁי מֵאַנְשֵׁי דָמִים

The style of this hymn echoes *Eli, Zion* ("Mourn, Zion!"), the lamentation that is recited in many synagogues at the conclusion of the Tisha B'av service.

A second example is the poem *Eikh Al Acha'i* ("How my brothers"[12]) composed by Rabbi Haim Sabato, an author who, uniquely, had no personal or familial contact with the Holocaust at all. Sabato was born in 1954 to Syrian-Jewish parents in Egypt. The family moved to Jerusalem when Haim was a child, where he learned about the Holocaust from his neighbors and wrote the poem. Yehudah Kadari composed touching music for the *piyyut*. To the best of my knowledge, this is the only known Holocaust-related poem composed by a Sephardi Jew. This is the final part of the poem:

They were crammed, rushed, into the animal wagons,
With their suffering children. And the sound of their crying
didn't rend the heavens, just their hearts.
No one had compassion on them as they left.
Can the land atone for their blood?
No one had compassion on them as they left.
Can the land atone for their blood?

They were gathered like fish and herded like sheep.

נִדְחֲפוּ נִבְהֲלוּ תּוֹךְ קְרוֹנוֹת בְּהֶמְתָּם
עִם יַלְדֵיהֶם נְפוּחִים וְקוֹל בְּכִיָּתָם
לֹא קָרַע רְקִיעִים רַק קָרַע לִבּוֹתָם
לֹא חָמַל עֲלֵיהֶם אִישׁ בְּצֵאתָם
הֲעַל דָּמָם תְּכַפֵּר אַדְמָתָם

נֶאֶסְפוּ כִּדְגֵי יָם וְהוּבְלוּ כְשֶׂה תָם

Where is the heavenly place where their fate was sealed?	אֵי מָדוֹר בַּשָּׁמַיִם נֶחְתְּמָה גְּזֵרָתָם
What is the secret of their binding and their trial?	וּמַה סוֹד עֲקֵדָתָם וְדָתָם
Where is their covenantal sign, where is the scent of their worship?	אֵי אוֹתוֹתָם וְנִיחוֹחַ עֲבוֹדָתָם
Can the land atone for their blood?	הֲעַל דָּמָם תְּכַפֵּר אַדְמָתָם
Can the land atone for their blood?[13]	הֲעַל דָּמָם תְּכַפֵּר אַדְמָתָם

In addition to his poignant expression of Jewish suffering, Sabato adds a novel theological concern when he lodges a grievance against heaven—a theme that cannot be found to this extent in earlier, more traditional, lamentations. Even the cries of the children did not split the heavens, he laments; they split only their parents' hearts. The refrain "Can the land atone for their blood?" refers to the last part of the biblical verse: "O nations, acclaim his people! For He'll avenge the blood of His servants, wreak vengeance on His foes, and cleanse the land of His people" (Deut. 32:43). But while the verse celebrates God's revenge of His people's enemies, the poem questions it.

The poet and partisan leader Abba Kovner composed a moving memorial text titled *Nizkor* ("Let Us Remember"). The text is framed in the form of traditional liturgy, in the sense that it calls for remembrance. Kovner uses the traditional liturgical formulation *Yizkor Elohim* … ("May God remember …"), but here it is not God that has to remember but the survivors or the entire people of Israel. Secularizing the text serves as a theological charge. Here is the first part of the poem:

Let us remember our brothers and sisters	נזכור את אחינו ואחיותינו
The homes in towns and villages	את בתי העיר ואת בתי הכפר,
The small town streets, gushing like rivers	את רחובות העיירה שסאנו כנהרות
The mother in her kerchief	

The young girl in her braids	את האם בסודרה
The children	את הנערה בצמותיה
The thousands of Jewish communities	את הטף
Together with the families of man	את אלפי קהילות ישראל
The entire Jewish people	על משפחות האדם
That was assigned to slaughter in Europe	את כל עדת היהודים
At that hands of the Nazi reaper. [...]	אשר הכרעה לטבח על
	אדמת אירופה
	מידי הכורת הנאצי [...]

Some poems were not originally composed for the Holocaust but became associated with it. The best example may be *Ani Ma'amin* ("I believe"), a song that is based on Maimonides's twelfth principle of faith: belief in the coming of the messiah. Its popularity is associated with a particularly mellow tune attributed to Reb Azriel David Fastag, a Modziser Hasid, who allegedly composed it while on a transport to Treblinka. According to a Hasidic tradition, Fastag promised half of his share in the world to come to anyone who would bring the song to the Modziser Rebbe. Two young men volunteered. One jumped from the train but perished, while the other succeeded in reaching the Rebbe, who was already in New York. The Rebbe supposedly responded in tears, saying, "With this *niggun* [melody] the Jews went to the gas chambers and with this *niggun* they will greet the messiah."[14]

Some *kinot* (lamentations) read on Tisha B'av, originally composed to commemorate earlier tragedies, were read for the Holocaust as well. As we will see below, religious authorities often found them sufficient and either saw no need for or actually prohibited new ones. But overall, inclusion of *kinot* for Holocaust victims are not uncommon in many traditional synagogues.[15]

The Passover Haggadah

The synagogue service already contains lengthy liturgies for Tisha B'av with (as we have seen) *piyyutim* that might serve as models for similar poetry to mark the Holocaust. The same cannot be said for the home ritual of the Passover seder, where such *piyyutim* are relatively sparse. The seder does, however, celebrate deliverance from bondage and has traditionally been seen as a time to anticipate future redemption as well.[16] Its treatment of Jewish suffering in Egypt has also recommended it as an occasion to consider more contemporary Jewish tragedies. As a home ceremony, moreover, the seder was especially amenable to local adjustments, and as the most well-attended Jewish family event of the year, it was the obvious place to make a statement of importance to one's family.

Understanding all of this, the American Jewish Congress's Seder Ritual Committee, headed by Rufus Learsi (Israel Goldberg), introduced a ritual component to the Haggadah in 1953—a prayer to be recited after the festive meal and before the door is opened for Elijah. The title of the one-page text is "Seder Ritual of Remembrance—For the Six Million Jews Who Perished at the Hands of the Nazis and for the Heroes of the Ghetto Uprisings."[17]

Despite significant efforts by the committee to publicize and distribute the prayer, however, it never became a standard part of the American seder. The campaign began successfully enough. According to researcher Abe Katz, a 1958 internal committee memo reports that 266 synagogues and organizations had ordered and paid for 44,235 copies of the text, and by 1962 it had distributed several hundred thousand copies, a significant number for the days before photocopy machines. But few, if any, printed Haggadot ever included the prayer. Dr. Philip Birnbaum, the influential editor of daily, Shabbat, and festivals prayer books, considered adding it to his edition of the Haggadah. However, as a prerequisite for his including the prayer, Birnbaum asked that changes be made to both the Hebrew and the English texts. After a short exchange of letters, Birnbaum decided not to include the prayer, and after the death of Learsi in 1968, the committee's work came to a halt.[18]

Concerning Orthodox Haggadot, Katz writes, "A review of tens of Haggadahs that have been published since 1953 yielded only one Haggadah which included any reference to the Holocaust"[19]—any reference at all, that is (not, specifically, the Learsi text). The same cannot be said for non-Orthodox Haggadot. In the 1975 American Haggadah published by the Reform Movement (edited by Rabbi Herbert Bronstein), an entire section is dedicated to the memory of the Holocaust. The memorial prayer appears after the statement "For more than one enemy has risen against us to destroy us. In every age, they rise up to plot our annihilation. But a Divine power sustains and delivers us."[20] The unit contains a citation from Anne Frank's diary, the Hebrew poem *Neder* ("Vow" to remember the Shoah) by Abraham Shlonsky, a poem in Yiddish by Samuel Halkin, and a prose text by Anthony Hecht.[21]

Rabbi Irving Greenberg composed a special section commemorating the Holocaust titled "The Fifth Son."[22] It is an addition to the traditional story of the Four Children, each of whom addresses the deliverance from Egypt from a different point of view. The fifth child is the one that did not survive and cannot question at all:

> On this night we remember a fifth child.
> This is a child of the Shoah (Holocaust), who did not survive to ask.
> Therefore we have to ask for that child—Why?
> We are like the simple child. We have no answer
>
> . . . .
>
> We answer that child's question with silence.
> In silence, we remember that dark time.
> In silence, we remember that Jews preserved their image of God in the struggle for life.
> In silence we remember the Seder night spent in the forests, ghettos and camps. We remember that Seder night when the Warsaw Ghetto rose in revolt.
>
> (*lift the cup of Elijah*)
>
> In silence, let us pass the cup of Elijah, the cup of the final redemption yet-to-be. We remember our people's return to the land of Israel, the beginning of that redemption. Let us fill Elijah's cup with some of our wine, expressing the hope that through our efforts, we will help bring closer that redemption.
>
> . . . .

We rise now and open our door to invite Elijah, the forerunner of the future which will bring an end to the nights of our people. We sing as they did:

Ani maamin b'emunah shleimah, beviat Hamashiah ...
For I firmly believe in the coming of the Messiah,
and even though the Messiah may tarry, in spite of this,
I still believe.

Some families also sing *Zog Nit Keinmal,* known as "The Jewish Partisans' Song."[23] And it is not uncommon for Holocaust survivors who may otherwise hesitate to share their personal experiences to do so during the ritual ambience of the seder.

In Israel too the seder service has been viewed as an appropriate time to memorialize the tragedy of the Shoah. Contrary to popular opinion, a seder has been rather widely practiced in Israel even in secular and atheist kibbutzim. Despite its being the vanguard of the socialist, secular, young State of Israel, the Kibbutz Movement has demonstrated impressive ritual innovation, creating editions of the Haggadah in which references to the Holocaust are many.

References to the tragedy of European Jewry began to appear in kibbutz Haggadot during the years of the Holocaust and even in anticipation of it. Kibbutz Sdot Yam's Haggadah from 1939, for example, expresses fear for the well-being of Jews in Europe in the wake of the "wicked kingdoms which plot our annihilation."[24] These texts reflect a wide range of reaction to the tragedy—shock, grief, anger, and defiance. Nevertheless, they share the common conviction that building a Jewish national homeland is the proper response to persecution.

As might be expected, these kibbutz texts contain harsh accusations directed toward the Divine—in whom its members did not believe. For example, the Haggadah of the Kibbutz Ha'artzi (the most left wing of the kibbutzim), from 1943,[25] declares:

Suddenly a fearless mighty generation would shake off:	פֶּתַע יִתְנָעֵר דּוֹר עַזּוּז וְגִבּוֹר:
"A last generation of servitude and the first one of redemption Us"!	״דּוֹר אַחֲרוֹן לְשִׁעְבּוּד וְרִאשׁוֹן לִגְאוּלָה אֲנַחְנוּ!״

Our hand alone
our mighty hand
has removed the burden from our
    strong neck
And even now if the avenging God
    has confined us in His desert,
in spite of the heavens and their wrath
Here we are
We shall come forth!

יָדֵנוּ לְבַדָּה

יָדֵנוּ הַחֲזָקָה

אֶת כֹּבֶד הָעוֹל מֵעַל גְּאוֹן

צַוָּארֵנוּ פָּרְקָה

גַּם עַתָּה, אִם סָגַר עָלֵינוּ

מִדְבָּרוֹ אֵל נָקָם

אַל אַף הַשָּׁמַיִם וַחֲמָתָם —

הִנְנוּ וְעָלִינוּ!

"Even now," the text reads, "if the avenging God has confined us in his desert, in spite of the heavens and their wrath"—a vow to continue with the pioneer endeavor, even against the will of God who appears here as the enemy. God only hinders the pioneers, who, however, are confident of ultimate victory.

    Editors of more traditional Haggadot who have refrained from adding Holocaust-related texts have nonetheless represented the Holocaust visually, through illustrations. The traditional text's description of Israelite suffering in Egypt is accompanied by pictorial representations of Jews tormented by the Nazis.

The Shoah Scrolls

A few attempts were made to create a liturgical reader to commemorate the Holocaust in the form of a scroll. Avigdor Shinan, professor of Hebrew literature at the Hebrew University in Jerusalem, created a special text to be read on Holocaust Memorial Day. Moved by Alex Eisen, a Canadian Jew, who expressed regret about the failure of the Jewish community to compose appropriate liturgical responses to the Holocaust, Shinan approached the Israeli Chief Rabbinate with this initiative but was rebuffed. He then turned to Bar-Ilan University, an Orthodox institution, and it too showed no interest. Eventually the Israeli Masorti (Conservative) Movement took up the project, with Shinan being recruited to devise the actual composition.[26]

The Holocaust memorial that Shinan created took the form of a religious scroll to be read on the eve of Holocaust Memorial Day. It contains six chapters to memorialize the six million Jews who perished:

1. "In the Beginning" (the historical background of the Holocaust)
2. "The Earth Filled with Chaos and Confusion" (a testimony of a Christian witness who infiltrated the Ghetto)
3. "The Darkness Spread over All" (a letter written by a Jewish woman in a concentration camp)
4. "Confronting the Abyss" (a testimony of a young Jew who was ordered to discard the victims' bodies, his brother among them)
5. "A Heavenly Voice, Hovering, Cries Out" (a lamentation for those who died)
6. "Let There Be Light Again" (the survivors and the establishment of the State of Israel)

The text was published in 2004 in Hebrew, English, French, German, Spanish, and Russian. Shinan intended it to be viewed as an additional scroll to the five biblical ones that are read on the Jewish festivals and holidays. The instructions to the fifth chapter of the scroll direct that it be chanted with the mournful tropes by which the scroll of Lamentations is read each Tisha B'av night. Here are a few of the lines of this chapter:

A heavenly voice cries out: For these do I weep.[27] For Gertrude's parents, who were torn away from each other[28] *Congregation:* For these do I weep For Gertrude and Anushka, Gittel, Helen, and Gratzia, whose vitality came to an end in the labor camps *Congregation:* For these do I weep. For members of the *Judenrat* and for the Jewish Kapo, who were asked to fulfill a task that no human being could fulfill *Congregation:* For these do I weep.	בת קול משמים מרחפת ואומרת: על אלה אני בוכייה על הוריה של גרטרוד, שנקרעו זה מזה בפראות קהל: על אלה אני בוכייה על גרטרוד ואנושקה וגיטל והלנה וגראציה, שכלה כוחן במחנות העבודה קהל: על אלה אני בוכייה על אנשי היודנראט ועל

For Yaakov-David ben Yoel-Tzvi
Halevi who died twice and was born
    four times
Congregation: For these do I weep.

[...] For these do I weep, for infants
who never learned to say "Mommy,"
for boys and girls whose youth was
stolen from them, who withered
before coming to blossom; for young
men and women who never were
blessed beneath the wedding canopy,
for the elderly denied the privilege of
a gracious old age; for the orchestras
and for the music, and for all the
world's beauty whose color was lost,
replaced by only brown and gray and
black. For these do I weep.

הקאפו היהודייה, שנדרשו
למלא תפקיד שאין אדם
יכול למלאו
קהל: על אלה אני בוכייה
על יעקב־דוד בן יואל־צבי
הלוי, שמת פעמיים ונולד
ארבע
קהל: על אלה אני בוכייה
[...] על אלה אני בוכייה,
על עוללים שלא למדו
להגות "אמא", על ילדים
וילדות שנעוריהם נגזלו
מהם והם קמלו טרם פריחה:
על עלמים ועלמות שלא
נתברכו מתחת לחופה, על
זקנים שלא זכו לשיבה של
חסד: על התזמורות ועל
המוסיקה ועל כל יפי העולם
שאבדה לו צבעוניותו וכולו
רק חום ואפור ושחור. על
כל אלה אני בוכייה:

The scroll ends with these words:

Do not mourn too much, but do
not sink into the forgetfulness of
apathy. Do not allow the days of

אל תתאבלו יותר מדי,
אך אל תשקעו בשיכחה של

darkness to return; weep, but
also wipe the tears away.
Do not absolve and do not
   exonerate,
Do not attempt to understand.
Learn to live without an answer.
Through our blood, live!

אֲדִישׁוּת אַל תַּנִיחוּ לִימֵי הַחוֹשֶׁךְ
שֶׁיָשׁוּבוּ, בְּכוּ וְגַם מְחוּ אֶת
הַדִּמְעָה;
אַל תִּמְחֲלוּ וְאַל תִּסְלְחוּ,
אַל תְּנַסּוּ לְהָבִין;
לִמְדוּ לִחְיוֹת לְלֹא מַעֲנֶה.
בְּדָמֵינוּ חָיוּ!

The practice of reading the scroll was accepted in several communities. Some organizations still recite parts of it. Nevertheless, the initial hopes of those who envisioned the text as a "sixth scroll (*megillah*)" were not met, and *The Shoah Scroll* did not take its place within wider circles as the means by which the Holocaust is commemorated.

In America too, totally independent of Shinan's Israeli experiment, attempts were made to introduce a Holocaust scroll. Irving Greenberg surbeys some early examples of *Megillah* commemoration texts.[29] Rabbi Lawrence A. Hoffman recalls making that suggestion to the Liturgy Committee of the CCAR, the Reform rabbinic organization of North America. It was to be one of two such special scrolls, the other being a ritualized history of the founding of the State of Israel from its earliest Zionist settlements to the Day of Independence. The two scrolls would be bound with the five traditional scrolls under the subtitle *Megillot Shel Yameinu* ("Scrolls for Our Days"), and read on Yom Hashoah and Yom Ha'atzma'ut, respectively.

As chair of the committee at the time, Hoffman wrote letters to various people to initiate the writing. The Holocaust scroll was to be composed by Albert Friedlander, then rabbi of Westminster Synagogue in London, and a child of Holocaust refugees who fled in 1939. Friedlander actually completed a draft of the scroll, but before it could see the light of day, the project was rejected by the CCAR board on the grounds that contemporary Jews have no right to compose scrolls that might be treated with the same liturgical authority as the *chamesh m'gillot,* the five traditional biblical scrolls that were to have been part of the same volume. Hoffman's term of office as committee member (and chair) expired the year after, and the project was forgotten.

Services Included in Prayer Books

A number of prayer books, particularly ones with a liberal bent, include a special service for *Yom Hashoah V'hag'vurah* (Holocaust and Heroism Remembrance Day), commemorated on the twenty-seventh of Nisan. Some liturgical pieces have become standard—*El Malei Rachamim* and the Mourner's *Kaddish* (of course), but also the prophecy of the dry bones (Ezekiel 37), "The Partisans' Song," and Abraham Shlonsky's *Neder* ("Vow").

One of the interesting liturgical pieces is what some refer to as the Camps' *Kaddish*, a form of *Kaddish* that juxtaposes the traditional Aramaic text with the names of the concentration camps and ghettos where massacres occurred. The following is Elie Wiesel's version, which appears in the North American Conservative and Reform prayer books:[30]

יִתְגַּדַּל Auschwitz

וְיִתְקַדַּשׁ Lodz

שְׁמֵהּ רַבָּא. Ponar

בְּעָלְמָא דִּי בְרָא כִרְעוּתֵהּ, Babi Yar

וְיַמְלִיךְ מַלְכוּתֵהּ Maidanek

בְּחַיֵּיכוֹן וּבְיוֹמֵיכוֹן Birkenau

וּבְחַיֵּי דְּכָל בֵּית יִשְׂרָאֵל Kovno

בַּעֲגָלָא וּבִזְמַן קָרִיב, Janowska

וְאִמְרוּ: אָמֵן

יְהֵא שְׁמֵהּ רַבָּא מְבָרַךְ לְעָלַם
וּלְעָלְמֵי עָלְמַיָּא

יִתְבָּרַךְ וְיִשְׁתַּבַּח Theresienstadt

וְיִתְפָּאַר וְיִתְרוֹמַם Buchenwald

וְיִתְנַשֵּׂא וְיִתְהַדָּר Treblinka

וְיִתְעַלֶּה וְיִתְהַלָּל Vilna

שְׁמֵהּ דְּקֻדְשָׁא, בְּרִיךְ הוּא, Bergen-Belsen

לְעֵלָּא Mauthausen

מִן כָּל בִּרְכָתָא וְשִׁירָתָא, Dachau

תֻּשְׁבְּחָתָא וְנֶחֱמָתָא Minsk

דַּאֲמִירָן בְּעָלְמָא, Warsaw

וְאִמְרוּ: אָמֵן

יְהֵא שְׁלָמָא רַבָּא מִן שְׁמַיָּא וְחַיִּים עָלֵינוּ
וְעַל כָּל יִשְׂרָאֵל, וְאִמְרוּ: אָמֵן.
עֹשֶׂה שָׁלוֹם בִּמְרוֹמָיו, הוּא יַעֲשֶׂה שָׁלוֹם עָלֵינוּ
וְעַל כָּל יִשְׂרָאֵל, וְאִמְרוּ: אָמֵן. [31]

Despite the fact that a number of prayer books provide such Holocaust memorial services or at least a set of readings for such a service, not all congregations and organizations actually hold such services, a sign, perhaps, of the synagogue's declining vitality—an issue to which we will return.

Another powerful ritual is *L'khol ish yesh shem* ("every person has a name"), which is comprised of an ongoing recitation of the names of victims. Since 1989, the Knesset, the Israeli parliament, the Yad Vashem organization, as well as synagogues and other institutions hold public recitations of victims' names. The names are read by Knesset members, victims' relatives, and by members of the public. This ritual traces back to traditional memorial services in medieval Ashkenaz where communities recited the names of the deceased during *Yizkor* services. These were recorded in a form of *memorbikher* (memorial books). The ritual in its contemporary form is observed mostly outside of the synagogue.

The Virtual Absence of Standard Liturgy Commemorating the Holocaust

With all of this creativity and its prominence in Jewish consciousness, it becomes hard to explain the virtual absence of a standard liturgy commemorating the Holocaust. Given the enormity of the trauma in our time, one would have expected a commonly accepted collection of prayers, a standard ritual for synagogue use, or at least some form of widespread Holocaust memorializing that would be taken for granted by now. But none exists! Why is that?

We have to settle for partial answers. I divided them into historical, theological, halakhic-cultural, and social dimensions.

Historical Dimensions

A review of the liturgical responses to past tragedies reveals a paradox: the greater the magnitude of the tragedy, the fewer the liturgical responses. Tragedies of lesser severity often receive a greater liturgical response. The blood libel that struck Blois, for example (see above), involved the death of some dozens of Jews by fire, yet it became the basis for holding a fast day each twentieth of Sivan for many centuries. Several *piyyutim* were composed to mark the event, and the practice of reciting *Alenu* was initiated to commemorate the testimonies that the martyrs of Blois recited the prayer as they were led to their deaths. By contrast, tragedies that encompassed broader numbers of Jewish communities have tended to receive less liturgical attention, in some cases because few were left to remember the deceased.

The Holocaust is such a horrific event, but it is more—it is of such magnitude that it may just be impossible to capture its horror in words. Not only was it directed against the entire Jewish people, but throughout Europe, it was largely successful. Its very enormity may have militated against its receiving a proper religious response.

In addition, the wound of the Holocaust is still fresh. Many survivors are still alive. The passage of time may be needed before a proper religious response can be formulated. In his book on medieval European lamentations, published only a few months after the end of World War II, the medieval literature scholar Abraham Meir Haberman spoke to this point, urging patience and caution in the light of such a recent ordeal:

And especially in our days we need to return and read these ancient words [the liturgical poems about the suffering of the Jews of Ashkenazi]. We did not expect that the [pains inflicted upon us in] the Middle Ages would recur. We thought that what happened in the past could not happen in our days. And, lo, we are bitterly disillusioned. The Middle Ages have returned even more fiercely.

... There is yet no expression of what has happened in our generation; apparently, it is too early to do so. One whose dead lay unburied before him and whose heart is in pain is not up to eulogizing, even if he wants to, even if he needs to.

For the time being, let us concentrate on the ancient pages, in which we occasionally may hear an echo of what has happened to our generation. May we also draw from them the strength to bear the pain and consolation to continue and build: our enemies wanted to annihilate us, and we continued living, as then, so also now.[31]

Theological Dimensions

In premodern times, tragedies were readily assimilated into the traditionalist theology of punishment, atonement, pardon, and renewal once again.[32] By the time of the Holocaust, that paradigm had been almost universally abandoned, so that theologians were challenged to come up with some other way to explain why God would permit the destruction of the six million.[33] Not surprisingly, no widely accepted explanation has been found. Liturgical editors have had trouble arriving at proper responses. With nothing to say, religious silence may have seemed like the most appropriate religious response.

In any event, the nature of the liturgical response to the Holocaust was dependent on the day chosen for its commemoration, a calendar issue that prompted much debate. The Knesset (Israeli parliament) chose the twenty-seventh of Nisan, marking the Warsaw Ghetto Uprising. The Israeli Chief Rabbinate declared the tenth of Tevet, a day associated with the onset of the siege on Jerusalem, at the time of the First Temple, as *Yom Hakaddish Haklali* ("the general *Kaddish* day") for those whose date of death was unknown. A third option proposed by some, among them Menachem Begin, former prime minister of Israel, was to hold the commemoration on the ninth of Av itself, the ultimate day for national Jewish mourning. Other proposals included the Reich's Pogrom Night (known as *Kristallnacht*), November 9. More recently, a suggestion was floated to target January 27, the international commemoration day of the Holocaust, corresponding to the liberation day of Auschwitz.[34]

Liturgy and calendar intersect of course, but it is hard to differentiate cause from effect. To some extent, failure to determine calendar caused the parallel failure to develop liturgy. But equally, perhaps, the failure to agree on a suitable date reflected the prior uncertainty as to the proper way to commemorate the Holocaust in the first place. Had the classical theology still been tenable, the calendar issue would have been less troublesome. The Holocaust would have been folded into the universal Jewish calendar with standard liturgical responses no less than the Chmielnicki massacres were.

Halakhic-Cultural Dimensions

To some extent, the failure to adopt and encourage liturgical innovation stems from an unwillingness on the part of contemporary halakhic authorities to accept anything other than permutations on the old theological theme. Take the statement by Rabbi Joseph B. Soloveitchik, for example:

> Of course the six million Jews deserve to be eulogized on Tisha B'av. But we do so within the frame of reference of the *Kinot* [lamentations] we already recite on that day. Instead of Vilna, we mention Worms or Mayence. It does not make much difference, because the scenes described and the words of despair, mourning and grief are the same.[35]

Unlike Haberman, for whom the Holocaust is too recent to address adequately, Soloveitchik sees no need for liturgical innovation whatsoever.

The reluctance of Orthodox authorities to create liturgies concerning the Holocaust reflects their reluctance to create any new liturgies at all today. But what about liberal denominations that have no such restriction? Here, we must differentiate two cases. First, there is the loose amalgam of institutions associated with the Jewish Renewal Movement, which regularly create new liturgies. But in large part, the capacity for this ongoing creativity is its own enemy, because it militates against the expectation that anything new should become *keva* (permanent); rather, the goal is to maintain spontaneity by constantly creating new liturgies to replace old ones.

A more likely source of ongoing liturgical consolidation would be the prayer books used by Conservative, Reconstructionist, and Reform Jews. These do include special memorial services for the Holocaust, but it seems that many of these services are not widely attended, at least not as part of the synagogue services—the issue we raised above.

Social Dimensions

Unlike prior tragedies that took place within established borders—the First Crusade in the Rhineland, for example—the Holocaust was associated with no specific Jewish community. To some extent, commemorating it became a cause with no particular advocate. The entire Jewish world does not make decisions easily—least of all concerning a matter of such symbolic consequence as remembering its six million.

In addition, the Holocaust was experienced primarily (though not exclusively) by European Jews and is still perceived by many Sephardim as an Ashkenazi-"owned" phenomenon.[36] Perhaps one of the reasons for this is the lack of acknowledgment of Sephardi suffering in the Holocaust (in Greece and North Africa).[37]

Memorializing the Holocaust has to take on the responsibility of the entire Jewish People, but it is not quite clear who has the authority (or legitimacy and willingness) to exercise that responsibility.

Hesitance over taking responsibility may be tied up with the haunting, and not often openly discussed, questions surrounding the tragedy. Many have felt guilty for not having done more to save the victims; others express embarrassment that their fellow Jews went "like sheep to the slaughter."

Finally, for the most part, the synagogue as an institution and prayer as an activity are not "on the radar screen" of many contemporary Jews. I alluded to this underlying concern above; I now conclude with it.

The Eclipse of the Synagogue?

Any discussion of liturgical memorialization must come to terms with the fact that the synagogue where liturgies are enacted no longer enjoys the widespread loyalty of Jews. Secular Jews assign only little importance to it, and even many of those who define themselves as religious do not always expect it to provide meaning to their lives or solutions to the quandaries of life. The liturgy (at least, in its classic definition) has simply ceased to be the main language through which Jews deal with their realities, anxieties, and fears.

The relative scarcity of liturgical responses for synagogue commemoration does not mean that the memory of the Holocaust is being neglected. On the contrary, the last decades have seen a wide variety of national, local, and organizational ceremonies, rituals, and commemorations. We have witnessed tremendous creativity related to the Holocaust in such media as literature, film, theater, and visual arts, some of them having clear ritualistic aspects. The Holocaust receives enormous scholarly attention, and many institutions of higher learning feature "Holocaust Studies" as an academic discipline. Holocaust museums and monuments proliferate throughout Europe, Israel, and the Americas. Ritualized trips to Poland, like the March of the Living, are attended annually by tens of thousands of youths and adults.

For the first time in two millennia of Jewish history, commemorations of a Jewish tragedy are taking place mainly outside the walls of the synagogue. In understanding Holocaust memorialization, we encounter a long-term trend that may be nothing less than a paradigm change in Jewish consciousness.

We should therefore expand our definition of the field of liturgy and ritual to include institutions other than the synagogue, and we should ascribe religiosity to broader phenomena than we have in the past. The journeys to Poland, for example, though somewhat controversial, can be considered genuine pilgrimages; the central ceremony of the Holocaust Memorial Day at Yad Vashem in Jerusalem has a clear religious tone, not only because the *Kaddish* and *El Malei Rachamim* are recited in it, but because it is constructed as such. Similar religious undertones should be seen in a multitude of ceremonies taking place in schools, universities, social centers, and organizations—even if the people within them claim secular rather than religious motives. These events are manifestations of the Jewish People's civil religion, in process.[38]

The larger question before us is whether the synagogues have the capacity still to represent the Jewish People in its gravest fears and highest expectations, whether it is still able to serve as the central meeting place for Jews, or whether it will settle for marginalization. This survey of Holocaust memorial demonstrates not so much a failure to remember the Shoah, but to do so in the usual synagogue and liturgical setting. The issue, then, is not just that the Holocaust is well remembered, but also the synagogue.

This is not to say that the synagogue may not yet respond with vigor and reclaim its former role as the meeting place of history past and destiny yet to come. Perhaps the visionary leaders of Jewish life should see it as a call to reconsider its mission, its message, and its means of achieving its goals in order to make this ancient institution relevant again.[39]

❧

Sites and Subjects

MEMORY IN ISRAELI CULTURE

Dr. Wendy Zierler

In his well-known essay "Between Memory and History: *Les Lieux de Mémoire*," French (and Jewish) historian Pierre Nora laments the loss of collective memory in modern life: "There are *lieux de mémoire*, sites of memory," observes Nora, "because there are no longer *milieux de mémoire*, real environments of memory."[1] What Nora means to say is that once upon a time, we had a traditional mode of memory that linked us organically to our past.[2] By contrast, memory for moderns is consigned to historical reconstructions in impersonal sites and objects like museums, archives, videotapes, and storehouses of documents that can never possibly be incorporated in the living, breathing lives of communities.

Interestingly enough, around the same time that Nora composed these thoughts, Israeli poet Yehuda Amichai (1924–2000) published a poem in which he expressed longing for the very thing Nora seemed to bewail. A veteran of several Israeli wars and of the yearly commemorations

---

Dr. Wendy Zierler is professor of modern Jewish literature and feminist studies at Hebrew Union College–Jewish Institute of Religion, New York. She is translator and coeditor with Rabbi Carole Balin of *To Tread on New Ground: The Selected Writings of Hava Shapiro* (forthcoming) and *Behikansi atah* (Shapiro's collected writings, in the original/Hebrew). She is also author of *And Rachel Stole the Idols* and the feminist Haggadah commentary featured in *My People's Passover Haggadah: Traditional Texts, Modern Commentaries* (Jewish Lights), a finalist for the National Jewish Book Award. She contributed to *Who by Fire, Who by Water*—Un'taneh Tokef, *All These Vows*—Kol Nidre, and *We Have Sinned: Sin and Confession in Judaism*—Ashamnu *and* Al Chet (all Jewish Lights).

of fallen soldiers—and living, therefore, in a culture so rife with firsthand experiences of bereavement—Amichai begged for the opportunity to offload his surfeit of memories onto external sites: "Let the memorial hill remember instead of me, that's its job."[3] Amichai went on to enumerate a host of sites, buildings, objects, and creatures that might do the remembering in his stead: the memorial park; a street named after a departed historical figure; a famous building; a synagogue bearing God's name; the Torah scroll; the physical shrouds of the dead and the metaphorical shrouds of history, the flags; the dust (to which the bodies of the dead returned); the dung at the gate; the beasts of the field and the birds of the heaven—if only any of all of these would remember, so that the speaker of the poem could rest and rid himself of this constant burden!

Unlike Nora's essay, Amichai's poem betrays no nostalgia for collective memory, that is, for the mode of *Yizkor*—precisely what Amichai wishes to escape! His poem, however, contains no fewer than twelve separate repetitions of the verb *zakhar*—*yizkor, tizkor, yizk'ru*—a sign of how hard it is for Israelis to do the escaping. Even if the poet were actually able to outsource all of this memory, it would saturate each and every object and site of his environment. Walking around with visual memory cues constantly in his trail, how would he ever manage to forget?

Smack in the middle of the list of possible material sites of memory, Amichai mentions the *Yizkor* prayer itself. *Shehayizkor yizkor,* he says: "Let the *'He will remember'* remember." Would that he could siphon off the stinging pain of remembering onto the prayer itself, as if prayer could be a vessel for overflowing feeling, or (better yet) a person, the subject of a future-tense verb. This personification of a prayer only adds to its commanding presence, however—how does one dare shirk memory in the presence of the walking, talking *Yizkor?* Any of us who regularly attend synagogue services and see how many otherwise non-synagogue-goers show up to services on the days when *Yizkor* is being recited can attest to the power this prayer has for us.

In the context of Israel's fallen soldiers, however, who is the subject of *Yizkor*—who actually is supposed to be doing the remembering? In the traditional *Yizkor* text, dating back, in all probability, to the post-Crusade era of the twelfth century, it is God who is adjured to remember the dead. Secular Zionist *Yizkor* services change the subject of the verb, putting the onus of memory on ourselves—hence the burden felt by Amichai, who wishes he could avoid it! The first such *Yizkor* text for fallen soldiers in the Land of Israel was composed in 1920 by pioneering labor Zionist Berl Katznelson (1887–1944), for a ceremony honoring those who died defending Tel Hai on 11 Adar, 1920. Katznelson borrowed something of the structure from the traditional *Yizkor* service but secularized the language and made the people of Israel the principal agents of memory:

> May the People of Israel remember the pure souls of its loyal and brave sons and daughters, people of Labor and Peace who walked after the plough and risked their lives for the honor of Israel and the land of Israel. Israel shall not rest and not be comforted until it returns and redeems its surviving land.[4]

This version of *Yizkor* for fallen soldiers appeared in the first Israeli *Yizkor* book published by the Israeli Ministry of Defense in 1955. Rabbi Shlomo Goren, the chief rabbi of the Israeli Defense Forces at that time, reported having ripped this page out of his copy of the book in protest against the removal of God as the agent of remembering.[5] Religious groups have continued to advocate for an official version of *Yizkor* that replaces "May the People of Israel remember" with "May God remember." They have composed and instituted for their communities alternative texts that employ language reminiscent of traditional sources, including quotations from David's lengthy lament for Jonathan from 2 Samuel 1:19–27, references to soldiers dying *al kiddush hashem* ("for the sanctification of God's name"), and requests that the memory of the fallen be "bound in the bundle of life," as per the traditional *El Malei Rachamim* (pp. 236–250). In 2011, with the appointment of army chief of staff Benny Ganz, this controversy erupted anew, with Ganz appointing a committee to arrive at an official version. In the end, the committee and Ganz decided to retain the secular original: "May the People of Israel remember."

Other modern Israeli versions of *Yizkor* have gone even further in taking up the personal mantle of memory. S. Yizhar (pen name of Yizhar Smilansky, 1916–2006), an Israeli writer and former member of the Kenesset, composed *Yizkor Lalochamim*, "A *Yizkor* for the Fighters," which changes the opening verb to first-person plural ("*We* shall remember") and transforms it into a kind of oath of everlasting comradeship:

> We shall remember our brothers and friends
> Who went out together with us

In the fighters' brigades.
We returned but they will never again return.
Wave upon wave they rose, they flooded and returned
and were left here
on the banks of No-Return.
Young and powerful they went out,
lovely and upright like plants of the field,
until the lead caught up with them,
and the slivers of death killed them.
Man after man were felled and did fall in the fields
each a son to his mother, each a father to his children,
each a lover to his loved ones—filling the entire land.
Brigades and divisions of youngsters, powerful and
upright like plants of the field—
for life and not destruction, for love, labor,
for the obligation—to bestow a blessing of peace upon
the land.
That is how we shall remember the fallen,
who are no longer with us here today.[6]

Unlike other versions of *Yizkor*, including that of Katznelson, which fold the experience of the fallen soldiers into a secularized commemoration of such abstract, even religious qualities as bravery and martyrdom, the ultimate values expressed in Yizhar's *Yizkor* are human, earthly, and interpersonal: the fallen should be remembered primarily for the beauty and nobility of their young selves, for their relationships with others, and for their intention to bestow a blessing of peace on the land.

The authors of these neo-*Yizkor* texts wrestle with the role of human memory—who remembers and how. Other authors return to Amichai's idealized alternative: not "human memory," but "sites of memory" that might fill in for the remembering that people do. One of the most famous songs about fallen soldiers—by now a canonical part of Yom Hazikaron (Israeli Memorial Day) and, in effect, a kind of *Yizkor* prayer in its own right—is *Bab el Wad*, the lyrics of which were composed by the 1948-era poet Haim Gouri (b. 1923). The name *Bab el Wad* (or *Sha'ar Hagay* in Hebrew) refers to a site on the Tel Aviv–Jerusalem highway, twenty-three kilometers from Jerusalem, where the road rises into a ravine between cliffs. During the 1948 War of Independence, this stretch of road was captured by the Arabs, and many Israeli soldiers were killed. To this day, the road is lined with rusted armored cars from that battle, an ongoing monument to the fallen. In Gouri's lyrics, a first-person speaker passes by and calls upon the site to remember "our names," the names, that is, of the fighters and their fallen comrades:

> Bab el Wad
> Forever remember our names,
> Convoys burst on the route to the City!
> On the side of the road our dead have been laid
> The iron skeleton is silent like my comrade.
> Bab el Wad,
> Forever remember our names
> Bab el Wad, on route to the City.[7]

Amichai's poem does more than call for sites of memory; it reflects a decided weariness with respect to the lives of Israelis who are fairly sated with memories of those who have died. In his other famous liturgically reminiscent memory poem, *El Malei Rachamim* ("God Full of Mercy," 1962), he sardonically suggests, "Were it not for the God Full of Mercy, the mercy might fill the world and not just Him";[8] similarly, here, his *Yizkor* poem knows full well that Israelis, unlike Nora's French, suffer from no lack of collective memory. If anything, Israelis miss a place for forgetting! And there seems no way to find any. Hence the wish to offload memorializing onto the environment, which Amichai lists in a progression that suggests an inexorable chain that never ends—not just mountains and buildings, but ritual objects as well, and, ultimately, the phantom stuff of decomposition and degeneration, mere dust and dung.

Taken together, we find Israeli consciousness of memory overwhelming. People and places alike continue to remember, until they themselves become objects of memory. And so it goes. Nowhere is this painful, ongoing process of memory more evident than in Aviv Geffen's song *Ani Holekh Livkot Lekha* ("I am going to cry for you"), a more recent, and similarly canonical, Yom Hazikaron song, which is also associated with the aftermath of Rabin's assassination and the national mourning for the lost cause of the Oslo peace process. In this song, the young first-person speaker says that he is about to cry for his loved one. Like many others who are sad, he goes to the sea to mourn (and cry), "which is why the sea is salty."[9] The beach, normally a vacation or leisure spot, now too has become a site of mourning. At the conclusion of the song, the speaker and the sea become as one: *K'mo hagalim anakhnu mitnaptzim el hamezach el hachayim* ("Like the waves, we crash or disintegrate into the pier, into life"). Here the Israeli mourner and the site of memory flow and crash into one another, symbolic of a national memory of life and death that seems now as repetitive and fathomless as the sea.

❦

PART II
Historical Insights

Would Jeremiah Have Recited *Yizkor*?

YIZKOR AND THE BIBLE

Dr. Marc Zvi Brettler

The death of my mother six years ago initiated me into *Yizkor*. No longer merely the prayer that others around me muttered, it became a way of forcing me to remember, four times a year, the good and the bad: the many years of Alzheimer's that robbed my mother of her very being, but also the years before, when she had been vibrant, loving, and caring. My being forced to remember is altogether in keeping with *Yizkor*, which focuses on asking God to remember, but which insists that we do the remembering as well. As such, the institution of *Yizkor* highlights Jewish tradition at its finest—a tradition that is, by and large, remarkably constructive in dealing with death, dying, and the dead.

Yizkor, which certainly could not have been recited by the biblical prophet Jeremiah, represents the creativity of Judaism at its best, because the ideas central to it are altogether the creation of the Rabbis. These

Dr. Marc Zvi Brettler is the Dora Golding Professor of Biblical Studies at Brandeis University. He contributed to all volumes of the *My People's Prayer Book: Traditional Prayers, Modern Commentaries* series, winner of the National Jewish Book Award; and to *My People's Passover Haggadah: Traditional Texts, Modern Commentaries*; *Who by Fire, Who by Water—Un'taneh Tokef*; *All These Vows—Kol Nidre*; and *We Have Sinned: Sin and Confession in Judaism—Ashamnu and Al Chet* (all Jewish Lights). He is coeditor of *The Jewish Annotated New Testament* and *The Jewish Study Bible*, which won the National Jewish Book Award; co-author of *The Bible and the Believer*; and author of *How to Read the Jewish Bible*, among other books and articles. He has also been interviewed on National Public Radio's *Fresh Air* by Terry Gross.

Rabbis inherited the biblical books, canonized them, and considered them sacred. Yet they used the Bible to uphold ideas that the Bible never itself intends. This is particularly true with *Yizkor*, a prayer with views on death and an afterlife that fly in the face of the Bible they inherited.

In the Bible, with few exceptions (we will look at them shortly), the central "afterlife" for the deceased is their shared residence in Sheol, a place underground where they all congregate, irrespective of merit or social class; in the words of Psalm 89:49, "What man can live and not see death, can save himself from the clutches of Sheol?"[1] Even kings are there (Isaiah 14). Its denizens live an uncomfortable life, removed from God: they are mere "bodies lying in the grave, of whom You are mindful no more, and who are cut off from your care" (Psalm 88:6). This divine remoteness is also reflected in the belief that "the dead cannot praise Adonai, nor any who go down into silence" (Psalm 115:17). Unlike the world assumed in *Yizkor*, no righteous biblical figure lives in the Garden of Eden, and no one, upon death, finds shelter under God's wings.

Yizkor insists on just the reverse and then cites selectively from the Bible to create the constructive illusion that its theology is ancient, a matter of biblical record. It recalls the biblical Garden of Eden; it uses biblical phrases such as "divine wings" and "bind ... in the bundle of life"; and it opens with a collection of biblical verses. A careful look at these elements, however, shows how later tradition has refracted earlier ideas, often turning them on their head.

The Rabbinic concept of a Garden of Eden is a prime example of such a transformation. In the Bible (Genesis 2–3), the Garden is simply a place where the primordial couple enjoyed their life for an undefined period of time. It is by no means the paradise that it becomes in later tradition—in fact, Adam and Eve were placed there to "till and tend it" (2:15). Only later in the biblical period (see especially Ezekiel 28:13 and Joel 2:3) does it appear somewhat idealized, but even then, it is not populated by the righteous dead, as presupposed by *Yizkor*. It is the Rabbis who offer us this notion of a Garden in which the deceased get to enjoy an afterlife of bliss.

A "bundle of life" (*tz'ror hachayim*)—eternal life, as *Yizkor* seems to imply—is a second example of the way the Rabbis borrow freely on a biblical notion but then transform its meaning. The term is found only once in the biblical text—in a blessing that Abigail offers to David in 1 Samuel 25:29: "And if anyone sets out to pursue you and seek your life, the life of my lord will be bound up in the bundle of life [*tz'ror hachayim*] in the care of Adonai; but He will fling away the lives of your enemies as from the hollow of a sling." In context, however, *tz'ror hachayim* may be better translated as "the document of the living," the idea being that David's welfare has already been guaranteed because of being duly noted in the divine record. It is the same "book of life" (*sefer hachayim*) that is referred to so often in the High Holy Day liturgy. Though never called "book of life" in the Bible, the belief in a divine record was well known (see, e.g., Exodus 32:32–33), having been borrowed from Mesopotamia. In neither culture, however, does this divine record-keeping have anything at all to do with an afterlife. It is merely a document that contains the names of those who live on the earth as we know it.

A third example is *Yizkor*'s stipulation that the dead may be protected under "divine wings" (*kanfei hash'khinah*). This reflects an appropriation of the winged Semitic sun-disk and of the Egyptian Horus falcon who protected the king. In either case, it expresses divine protection, leading the endangered psalmist to request, "Guard me like the apple of Your eye; hide me in the shadow of your wings" (Psalm 17:8). But here too, protection has nothing to do with the deceased. Without exception, the safety of God's wings denotes the blessed state of the living only—albeit, typically, the frightened and embattled living. Nowhere in the Bible do the deceased find "repose ... under divine wings."

The introductory verses to *Yizkor*, almost all from Psalms (Psalms 144:3–4, 90:6, 90:12, 37:37, 49:16, 73:26; Ecclesiastes 12:7), are a remarkable pastiche. The first four verses all emphasize the creaturehood of people who are born and who die upon the earth and who have no particular expectation of an afterlife; these four verses can, therefore, be employed without injustice to their biblical usage. The following four, however, are meant to connote such an afterlife and must therefore be taken completely out of their original biblical context. In its original biblical setting, the first such verse (Psalm 37:37) is a piece of wisdom prescribed for a happy life here on earth. It notes the bright "future" of the innocent and upright person in this world: "Mark those who are innocent and observe those who are upright, for a future awaits people of peace." This is simply the common biblical idea that the "innocent" live long lives. In the *Yizkor* prayer, however, this "future" is assumed to be the afterlife.

A similar transformation occurs with the next verse, Psalm 49:16, "For surely God will redeem me from Sheol, taking me in." The Bible refers only to the individual's hope that he will be saved from dire straits here on earth, an idea consonant with the fact that the same psalm elsewhere actually denies the existence of a differentiated afterlife: "For one sees that the wise die, that the foolish and ignorant both perish, leaving their wealth to others" (49:11). Yet in *Yizkor*, consistent with certain strands of later Jewish tradition, Sheol is reconceived as hell, so that verse 16 is redefined to mean that the righteous may escape hell.

The next verse in our *Yizkor* introduction is Psalm 73:26, "My flesh and heart fail, but God is my heart's strength and my lot forever." In the Bible, "forever" (*l'olam*) is a relative term meaning "for a long time, until death" (see, e.g., Exodus 21:6). In the context of *Yizkor*, however, the last words are understood as "and my lot is with God forever," as if "forever" includes eternal life with God even after this earthly life is over. This idea is found in Daniel 12:2–3 and builds upon one of the latest biblical texts that is so unlike what is found in earlier biblical strata:

> Many of those that sleep in the dust of the earth will awake, some to eternal life, others to reproaches, to everlasting abhorrence. And the knowledgeable will be radiant like the bright expanse of sky, and those who lead the many to righteousness will be like the stars forever and ever.

This passage in Daniel reflects the beginning of the process by which older biblical ideas would be transformed into the notion of a life after death. The dominating force behind this transformation was the Hellenistic idea of a body-soul dualism, where the soul is immortal. Overall, the Bible is unaware of this idea, although Ecclesiastes (another very late book) does wonder, "Who knows if a man's lifebreath [*ru'ach*] rises upward and if a beast's breath [*ru'ach*] sinks down into the earth?" (3:21). Apparently, the possibility of some form of life after death was at least floating around in some circles late in the biblical period.

But the various terms used to refer to the soul (or spirit) in postbiblical literature (*ru'ach*, *n'shamah*, and *nefesh*) really just mean "breath" or "life force" in the Bible. Their meaning changes dramatically only after the late biblical idea rooted in Hellenistic conceptualizations becomes mainstreamed—a process, as we saw, reflected initially in Ecclesiastes and in Daniel, but not completed successfully until the Rabbinic era. Only then are these terms understood as relating to the soul, at which time verses containing them attract dramatically new meanings. Thus, the final introductory verse of *Yizkor* reads in its biblical context, "Dirt returns to cover the earth as it was, and the lifebreath returns to God who gave it" (Ecclesiastes 12:7). A later era would see this as promising, "Dirt returns to the ground as it was, and the soul (or spirit) returns to (be with) God who gave it."

In other ways, *Yizkor* is quite at home in the biblical world and might have been recognized by biblical personages such as Jeremiah. The call to God to remember—at the very heart of the meaning of the word *Yizkor*—is very biblical. Contrary to what we naturally imagine today, biblical authors do not assume that God is omniscient; rather, they are quite certain that God needs reminding on important occasions. Sometimes, Israel's outcry triggers a divine memory (e.g., Exodus 2:24, 6:5), and according to Numbers 10:9, "When you are at war in your land against an aggressor who attacks you, you shall sound short blasts on the trumpets, that you may be remembered before Adonai your God and be delivered from your enemies." Appropriately, various biblical prayers call upon God to remember the ancestral covenant (e.g., Deuteronomy 9:27). The late biblical personage Nehemiah asks God several times to remember him, as in 5:19: "O my God, remember to my credit all that I have done for this people!" But there is no intimation in any of these texts that the speaker or worshiper expects to be remembered after he dies. Nehemiah's request is similar to that of the Babylonian king Nebuchadnezzar II, who says, "O Marduk [the head of the Babylonian pantheon], my lord, do remember my deeds favorably as good";[2] both Nehemiah and Nebuchadnezzar are asking a deity to keep their good deeds in mind so they may be rewarded with well-being in this world, not in a world to come. Thus, *Yizkor*'s central call for God to remember is well precedented; it is just that never in the Bible is there a call for God to remember the *deceased* and to improve *their* lot.

To be sure, the Bible knows that people can be remembered after they die. Such memories are altogether human. For example, the end of Psalm 112:6 notes, "The beneficent man [*tzadik*] will be remembered forever." Proverbs 10:7 is similar: "The name [*zecher* = "memory of"] of the righteous is invoked in blessing, but the fame of the wicked rots." These, however, are memories by humans, not by God.

I understand how and why certain notions of death and the afterlife changed over time: biblical traditions were reinterpreted under

Hellenistic influence, and the Rabbis, fully Hellenized in this respect, created a post-biblical Judaism by, among other things, taking the Bible out of its original context. I appreciate these transformations. In their new contexts, the biblical verses and phrases emerge with a richer and more optimistic depiction of life after death. I do not know if I find that representation more compelling than the biblical vision or if I even believe it is true. Yet, I find *Yizkor* soothing and marvel at Judaism's ability to remain creative and vibrant, deeply attached to its biblical roots, but not enslaved to them.

☙

Hazkarat N'shamot ("Memorial of Souls")

HOW IT ALL BEGAN

Rabbi Solomon B. Freehof, PhD (z"l)

A Jewish legal principal can usually be traced from the Talmud (or earlier) all the way down the chain of tradition to the present time. But a custom, a *minhag*, generally enters into the literature as an observance already well established among the people. Then when one attempts to trace its origin, we find that it is lost in mystery. Many of the best beloved and most universally observed of Jewish ceremonial life can hardly be traced to their origins. This is true of such popular ceremonies as the Orphan's [Mourner's] *Kaddish*, *yahrzeit*, bar mitzvah, the *chuppah* [canopy] at weddings, and the subject of this essay, *Yizkor*.

There is general agreement among the writers in the field of liturgy that *Yizkor* started in the Rhineland at the time of the Crusades and that this part of the service took place on Yom Kippur. Then the writers add that in Eastern Europe this prayer for the dead was extended from Yom Kippur to the closing days of the three festivals. That is about all that any writer says about it.

Yet surely so popular a service that brings such vast groups to the synagogues, many of whom rarely come at any other time, deserves a

---

Rabbi Solomon B. Freehof, PhD (1892–1990), was born in London to a family that traced its roots to Schneur Zalman of Liadi, the founder of Lubavitch Hasidism (CHaBaD). Upon moving to the United States, he attended Hebrew Union College, after which he rose to become a world-renowned authority on Jewish law, a prolific writer of responsa for Reform Jews, a prolific author and prayer-book editor, and a pulpit rabbi for much of his life at Rodef Shalom Temple of Pittsburgh.

much closer study, for it greatly needs clarification. It appears in the literature among a variety of analogous memorial observances, which are in some undetermined way related to it.

The early medieval legal compendia and books on *minhagim* [customs] seem to refer to a considerable variety of memorial prayers. There was a special memorial service for the martyrs of the Crusades and of the Black Death persecutions. The clearest references to this are in the headings of the Memor lists [memorial books listing the names of the dead]:[1]

> Therefore the whole house of Israel is in duty bound to memorialize them (*l'hazkirem*) between Passover and Shavuot on the Sabbath closest to Shavuot; and also a second time on the Sabbath between the seventeenth of Tammuz and the ninth of Av, on the Sabbath closest to the ninth of Av, which is called "the Black Sabbath" (*Shabbat Shachor*).

That this indeed became the established custom can be clearly seen from the recitation of the prayer *Av Harachamim*. This prayer, as its text indicates ("the holy communities that gave their lives in the name of God's holiness") was written for the martyrs. In Eastern Europe this prayer came to be recited on every Sabbath (with certain exceptions). But in Germany, where the custom originated, it was recited only on the two "martyr Sabbaths," the Sabbath before Shavuot and the Sabbath before the ninth of Av (cf. Heidenheim, *Siddur Safah Berurah*, and Baer, *Avodath Yisrael*, ad loc.).

As to the memorial on Yom Kippur, *Siddur Rashi*, 214 [eleventh to twelfth century, France], speaking of Yom Kippur, says: *Uposkim tz'dakah b'rabim al hametim v'al hachayim; ein poskim tz'dakah b'khol eretz ashkenaz rak hayom l'vado* ["We allot charity publicly for the dead and the living alike; but in all of Ashkenaz, we do so only on that day"]. *Machzor Vitry* [eleventh to twelfth century, France], also on the Yom Kippur service (353), has exactly the same statement and then explains: *Umah sheposkin tz'dakah avur hametim l'fi shehu yom kaparah s'lichah um'chilah lahem* ["As for our allotting charity for the dead, it is because it is a day of atonement, pardon, and absolution for them"]. In other words, it is Yom Kippur that is especially suited for this memorial and therefore it is held *only* on this day.

Roke'ach [thirteenth century, Germany] also is careful to explain that the idea of atonement makes the Yom Kippur service the only appropriate one for *Yizkor* (217): *Umah sheposkin tz'dakah avur hametim b'yom hakippurim v'lo b'yom tov* ... ["As for our allotting charity for the dead on Yom Kippur but not on holidays ... "]. Mordecai [thirteenth century, Germany] to [the Talmudic tractate] Yoma [on Yom Kippur] also refers to the Yom Kippur memorial (727): *Umah shehurg'lu lidor tz'dakah ba'ad hametim b'yom hakippurim* ... ["As for it becoming customary to vow charity for the dead on Yom Kippur ..."]. Maharil [fourteenth to fifteenth century, Germany] also speaks of the *Yizkor* on Yom Kippur and adds, however (at the end of the section on Hoshanah Rabbah [the seventh day of Sukkot]), "Every *yom tov* when we read 'Each according to the gift of his hand' (Deuteronomy 16:17, i.e., on the last day of each of the three festivals) we memorialize the dead (*mazkirin n'shamot*) and say *Av Harachamim*."

Some of the texts speak of a memorial not only on the festivals, but even on *every* Sabbath. Thus [midrash] *Tanchuma* (ed. Warsaw) to *Ha'azinu* (p. 122): "Thus it is our custom to memorialize the dead every Sabbath" (*shelo yashuvu l'gehinnom* ["so that they should not have to return to *Gehinnom*"]), and then he mentions also the regular Yom Kippur memorial service.

Besides all these, there seem to have also been congregational lists of people for whom money was donated so that their names be read out in memorial, although the sources do not specify just on which days the lists were read. Meir of Rothenberg ([thirteenth century], *Responsa*, ed. Berlin, 37) speaks of a man who left a *Sefer Torah* to the synagogue in order that his name be read (*im yirtzu hasefer torah yazkiru nishmato im sh'ar n'shamot* ["if they were happy with the Torah scroll, they might memorialize him along with the others"]). Similar bequests are mentioned in his responsa (ed. Budapest, 342 and 286). In fact such private bequests are mentioned earlier.

Sefer Chasidim [by Judah Hechasid, twelfth to thirteenth century, Germany] (ed. Warsaw, 170) speaks of a righteous man who left money to the community in behalf of the dead. This custom of leaving money for names to be included in memorial lists became a fixed custom (cf., for example, the responsa of Samuel Engel [nineteenth to twentieth century, Slovakia], 5:24).

All these statements reveal a complex set of customs. It is no wonder that one writer[2] finds some of the texts mutually contradictory and that most writers on the liturgy deal with the subject only in a general way.

At the outset, it is evident that the customs were in a continual state of development and explanation and may be classified somewhat as follows: First of all, there was, as mentioned, the communal memorial of the martyrs who were killed in the Crusades and the Black Death, as listed in the Memor-books, to be memorialized on certain specified Sabbaths. This memorial to the martyrs can be conveniently labeled as a Liturgical Communal Memorial, since it was part of the liturgy and referred to the dead that were to be honored by the entire community.

In addition to this Liturgical Communal Memorial there developed what may be described as a Liturgical Family Memorial. This is what we commonly refer to nowadays as *Hazkarat N'shamot* or *Yizkor*. This is a regular part of the liturgy on certain days and is a memorial, not for the dead of the community as a whole (i.e., for the martyrs) but for the dead of one's own family, whether martyred or not. This Liturgical Family Memorial is also vague as to origin and observance. In Western Europe the Liturgical Family Memorial was only on Yom Kippur. In Eastern Europe it was also on the last day of the three festivals.

There is also a third type of memorial, which cannot be described as liturgical, namely, as a part of the prayer book incumbent upon all worshipers simultaneously. It may be described as an Individual Memorial. A man is called up to the Torah and he has a special prayer recited for his dead. This Individual Family Memorial seems to be the one carried over into the Sephardi world from the Ashkenazi. Among the Sephardim there is the custom that an individual, whether called up to the Torah or not, asks for a prayer that is to be recited before the ark in memory or in behalf of his departed relative. This the Sephardim call *Hashkavah*.

In addition to these three, or as a variation of them, some communities have lists not of the martyrs whom the communities remember, but of the family dead, and these are read at stated occasions.

All these various modes of memorial are somehow related to each other. Though the line of evolution is very vague, as is often the case with emerging *minhagim* [customs], there seems to be one thread tying them all together, and that is the thread of giving charity, either in memory of the dead or in their behalf. This charity, called *matnat yad* (from Deuteronomy 16:17 ["the gift of his hand"]), is sometimes found with the prayer for the benefactors of the community whose names were appended to the martyr lists. It is sometimes found with the Liturgical Family Memorial, though in the present texts of *Yizkor* the theme of *matnat yad* has dropped out entirely. Then, too, in some rituals *matnat yad* at certain times of the year has no direct connection with memorial at all, either communal or family.

As we attempt to find some order among all these related observances, we must look more closely at the legal compendia and the *minhagim* books. Unfortunately, these texts themselves, as already mentioned, give a confused impression. Some of the texts, as we have noted, indicate that the dead are memorialized on certain special Sabbaths; some say it is to take place on *every* Sabbath; some say only on the Day of Atonement, and some say also on the last days of the festivals. The obvious explanation of such differing statements would be that the custom of memorializing was unfixed, unregulated, and therefore it varied from place to place as well as from time to time. This explanation, usually sufficient in the case of many other popular observances, is not quite adequate here because we find apparent contradiction within the *same literary source.* For example, Roke'ach (217) says of Yom Kippur that we give charity in behalf of the dead *only* on this day. On the other hand, Roke'ach (296), speaking of the festivals says, "On all the festivals we give charity when we read the portion 'each according to the gift of his hand'" (i.e., on the last day of the holiday). That this second statement is also related to memorials we see from Maharil, who in his *minhagim* in the section on Hoshanah Rabbah states more fully, "It is a rule that on every holiday when we read the portion 'each according to the gift of his hand,' we recall the souls of the dead [*mazkirin*] and we say *Av Harachamim.*" Do Roke'ach and Maharil mean, as they seem to mean, that there was at that time [thirteenth to fifteenth century] a regular *Hazkarat N'shamot* on the festivals as well as on Yom Kippur? Or was there some difference between the observances on the respective days? Also the heading of the various Memor collections sometimes states that the dead are to be memorialized only on two specified Sabbaths, but sometimes they call for memorializing on *every* Sabbath. Such apparent complications are found in all of the older sources, a situation that is aggravated by the firm insistence in most of these sources that the dead are memorialized *only* on Yom Kippur.

Clearly there is need to review all the available sources in order to distinguish as far as possible between various types of memorializing, between various local customs, and between the various stages of the development of the memorial observance.

The Communal Martyr Liturgy

The prayer *Av Harachamim*, written as a memorial to the martyrs, accompanied the reading of the martyr lists in the various memorial books in medieval Germany;[3] and as Heidenheim and Baer note, in most German congregations this prayer was recited on only two Sabbaths of the year, the Sabbath before Shavuot and the Sabbath before Tisha B'av. Why these two Sabbaths particularly? A study of the brief liturgical notes at the head of many of the Memor lists makes clear why this martyrs prayer was recited only on these two Sabbaths in the German usage (which was the original one). The heading on page 1 of the Hebrew text in Salfeld reads: "Sivan: The martyrs of Cologne [were slain] on the day after Shavuot and we remember them [*mazkirin otam*] on the Sabbath before Shavuot." Also: "The martyrs of Mainz [were slain] on the third day of Iyar and we remember them on the Sabbath before Shavuot." So with the martyrs of Worms. They are to be remembered on the Sabbath before Shavuot.

The butchery of Rhineland Jewry (especially the large communities of Mainz, Speyer, Worms, and Cologne) took place around Shavuot, as the dates in the Memor lists indicate. It was not deemed proper to set the memorial on the holiday itself. To do so would disturb the joy of the holiday (which was mandatory), and therefore they fixed it on the Sabbath before the holiday. This Sabbath was suitable for memorial since it was part of the Omer period, which was associated with the massacre of the disciples of Rabbi Akiva. Thus the Sabbath before Shavuot became set after the Crusades as the special memorial Sabbath at which the lists of the martyrs were read and the prayer *Av Harachamim* recited.

However, heading the lists recording later martyrs (those of the Black Death riots in 1348) an additional martyrs Sabbath is mentioned. On page 80, beginning the list of the Black Death martyrs is the following: "Therefore all the house of Israel is in duty bound to remember them [*l'hazkiram*] between Passover and Shavuot, on the Sabbath nearest to Shavuot *and also a second time* on the Sabbath between the seventeenth of Tammuz and the ninth of Av, on the Sabbath nearest the ninth of Av, the Sabbath that we call 'the Black Sabbath.'"

The Black Death massacres were not concentrated within a few days, as were the massacres of the Rhineland communities in the First Crusade. They lasted for more than a year. Thus the memorial lists do not give any day or month, as they do with the Crusade martyrs, but only the year. However, the largest massacre took place in Mainz and claimed six thousand victims. This took place in August near to Tisha B'av. It would have been natural, therefore, to place a second memorial day on the Sabbath before Tisha B'av, which was always solemn in mood because of the denunciatory haftarah reading (Isaiah 1).

The Memor book calls this Sabbath the Black Sabbath. So this Sabbath was in mood appropriate for a memorial Sabbath, whether or not it specifically commemorated the date of the greatest single Black Death massacre, that of the Jews of Mainz. At all events, it may well be that the custom of *yahrzeit* that developed in the Rhineland may have first started with the memorial for the martyrs of the Crusades, since they were remembered in the synagogue service on the Sabbath nearest the date of their death. Be that as it may, the two memorial dates that became fixed, the first from the time of the Crusades and the second from the time of the Black Death, remained in the German Jewish liturgy as the only two Sabbaths on which (in the German rite) the martyrs prayer *Av Harachamin* is recited.

The Communal Family Liturgy

The oldest extant memorial list is the one written in 1296 by Isaac ben Samuel of Meiningen.[4] The brief introduction giving the date says also that this was the day when the community (of Nuremburg) worshiped for the first time in its new synagogue. It was natural, therefore, that this chronicler should list not only the martyrs, but those deceased benefactors who made the building possible, as well as the names of other benefactors now deceased. He then lists, also, famous rabbis and leaders (among them Rabbenu Gershom [eleventh century, Germany]). He adds the rubric that these names shall be mentioned *every* Sabbath. Then follows a prayer for the martyrs.

This cannot mean that the martyr list was read every Sabbath; only the two special Sabbaths were dedicated to that purpose. Perhaps it means that merely the prayer be read: "May God remember the souls of all the communities who were slain, stoned, burned," and so on[5] and only the names of seven scholars and benefactors were to be read *every* Sabbath. If, however, the list of benefactors grew,[6] it is hardly believable that such a list was read every Sabbath. Perhaps only the seven famous names were read or perhaps the names were read on their *yahrzeit,* just as the Sabbath before Shavuot was deemed to be the *yahrzeit* of the martyrs of the First Crusade.

Since now the memorial lists and the memorial prayers were extended beyond the martyrs to include the benefactors who died a normal death, it was natural that the desire should arise for members of *every* family to memorialize by name their deceased relatives who were neither martyrs nor famous leaders nor great communal benefactors. Thus the family memorial liturgy arose, namely, our present *Hazkarat N'shamot*.

This service could hardly be put on the same two Sabbaths set aside for the martyrs, so for this family memorial, the Day of Atonement was preferred. The chief reason was perhaps the belief bolstered by a number of midrashic passages that the dead as well as the living need atonement and deliverance (this in spite of the Talmudic dictum that death itself is an atonement, Mo'ed Katan 28a) and that the living can speed the deliverance of the dead by the giving of charity. Thus in all the early references to this ritual, charity by the living is mentioned in this connection. For example, *Vitry* (353), speaking of the Yom Kippur service, says: "And we set aside charity [*poskim tz'dakah*] in public for the living and the dead, since the Talmud says there is no proper fast day without charity (Berakhot 6b)." *Siddur Rashi* 214 makes virtually the same statement. Both these early sources add that no charity is given for the dead except on the Day of Atonement.

This statement of the Yom Kippur memorial is not in contradiction to the custom of the memorializing of the martyrs on the two Sabbaths. The meaning of the statement is not that we do not memorialize the dead except on Yom Kippur (which was not so) but that no *charity* is pledged for the dead except on the Day of Atonement. The reason for this distinction between the Day of Atonement family memorial and the two special Sabbaths of the martyr memorial was that while they believed that the average dead may need the redemption through the giving of charity, the martyrs needed no redemption. Their martyrdom made them *k'doshim*, "saints." In fact there was a widespread debate as to whether it was necessary even to say *Kaddish* for the martyrs (cf. responsa of Maharil, 99). The long list of benefactors remembered for charity in the Salfeld list[7] includes a number of martyrs. The (redemptive) gifts of the benefactors are all carefully mentioned. But in the case of the martyrs, no gift of charity is mentioned (except in one case where it is said that he left prayer books). The ordinary deceased were believed to need redemption either by their own charity or that of their descendants. The martyrs did not need redemption. Hence the average dead were mentioned on the Day of Atonement and charity given; the martyrs were honored on the two Sabbaths, and no charity was given on those two occasions.

However, as we shall see later, on certain festival days when donations were given for the support of the congregations, prayers were occasionally made for the family dead. But the statement "only on Yom Kippur," and so on, was substantially correct. Gifts by the worshipers for the dead were given *as a rule* only on Yom Kippur and not on the two martyr Sabbaths.

The Family Liturgical Memorial Extended

Although all the earlier sources say positively that the memorial for relatives (*Yizkor*) was held only on Yom Kippur, the observance spread in Eastern Europe from Yom Kippur to the last days of the three festivals. It is possible to fix fairly closely when this newer custom must have begun.

Moses Isserles [sixteenth century, Poland] does not mention it at all. He speaks of *Hazkarat N'shamot* only for Yom Kippur, but at the appropriate places in the *Tur* and the *Shulchan Arukh*, at the end of the three festivals, he does not mention it at all. Evidently either he did not know of any such observance or, if he did hear of it, he did not approve of it. This is exactly the situation in *Matteh Moshe*, by Moses Mat [sixteenth to seventeenth century, Poland], the pupil of Solomon Luria. He also mentions *Yizkor* only on Yom Kippur and makes no mention of it on the three festivals. The oldest authority to speak of it is Isserles's pupil Mordecai Jaffe [sixteenth to seventeenth century, Bohemia and Poland], in his *L'vush* (*Ateret Zahav* 346:3). He says that "it is our custom to memorialize the dead even during the festivals" (quoted by *Shach* [Rabbi Shabbetai Hakohen, seventeenth century, Lithuania] to *Yorch De'ah* 237:2; also by *Ba'er Hetev* [Judah ben Shimon Ashkenazi, eighteenth century, Germany] to *Orach Chayim* [*O. Ch.*] 547:5). Since the prayer books record the three-festival *Yizkor* as the custom of Bohemia and of Poland, and since Jaffe was born and lived in Bohemia, the custom may well have started there.

However, this extended custom needed special justification, since it is certainly contrary to the mood of rejoicing that must prevail on the three festivals. Even the original custom of memorializing on Yom Kippur had needed special justification. It had been necessary to prove that the dead were benefitted by the prayers of the living. But granting that such prayers in behalf of the dead were necessary or effective, it was a simple matter to justify their use on the Day of Atonement. Isserles (in *Darkhei Moshe* to *Tur, O. Ch.* 621) cites Jacob Weil [fifteenth century, Germany], who said that we use the plural Yom Hakippurim to indicate that the day can bring atonement both to the living and to the dead. He also cites Roke'ach, who said that our remembering the dead on Yom Kippur helps to humble the heart.

But the extended use of *Yizkor* on the three festivals needed a new justification. It was no longer necessary to prove that the dead are benefitted by such prayers. This was by now long accepted as true. What was needed was to justify the recitation of memorials on the joyous festivals. It is forbidden to give a *hesped* ["sermon"] for the dead thirty days before a festival (cf. *O. Ch.* 547). Caro [Joseph Caro, author of the *Shulchan Arukh*, sixteenth century, Safed] nevertheless allows our memorializing on Yom Kippur; he says: "at the end of the year," even though it is within thirty days of the coming festival of Sukkot. But how can Mordecai Jaffe justify a memorial as he does within the festival itself? Many legalists have attempted to justify it. Hirsh Kaidanover [seventeenth to eighteenth century, Lithuania] (in *Kav Hayashar*, chap. 86) says that the three festivals correspond to the three patriarchs and we should mention them on the three holidays. Joseph T'omim [eighteenth century, Poland and Germany] in *P'ri M'gadim* (*Eshel Avraham*, 547) says that mentioning the dead on the festival is not really so mournful as going to the grave and saying *El Malei Rachamim*, which certainly would be forbidden. As recently as the past generation, there still was felt some need to justify the memorial on the festivals. Solomon Schick [nineteenth century, Hungary] (*Rashban, O. Ch.* 294) says that after all, the last day of the holiday is not truly festive; it is only the Rabbinical (calendar) addition to the holiday.

All these explanations are obviously forced. The simple fact is that the three-festival memorials became an established *custom*, and the custom was popularly accepted, as Mordecai Jaffe indicates as a matter of fact. Yet, in spite of the difficulty in justifying it, the very fact that it *did* become widespread would indicate that it must have had some fairly strong roots in the past. The earlier sources give us sufficient indications as to how this newer custom must have arisen.

The earlier sources (e.g., Roke'ach, *Yom Kippur* 217; *Vitry* 353) that insist emphatically that in all the "land of Ashkenaz" we have *Yizkor* only on Yom Kippur evidently express a strong effort to *restrict* this solemnity to this one day when it would be most appropriate. But certainly the dead were remembered on other days too. It was the widespread custom to donate or bequeath money for the memorializing of the family dead (*Sefer Chasidim* [twelfth to thirteenth century, Germany], old edition, 170; new edition, 397, 396; Meir of Rothenberg [thirteenth century, Germany], responsa edition Budapest, 342, 280; edition Berlin, 371). In the heading of one of the Memor lists,[8] the congregation is directed to remember the listed benefaction *every* Sabbath. So there were many occasions during the year when individual dead were memorialized. Then what, in relation to these numerous personal memorials, was the meaning of the first statement, so frequently repeated in the basic sources, that charity is given for the memory of the dead in all of Germany *only* on Yom Kippur?

It meant simply that *public* liturgical memorial *incumbent* upon the entire congregation (of the bereaved) took place only on Yom Kippur. During the year there could be individual memorials, but these were voluntary. The *Yizkor* on Yom Kippur was the only regular liturgical *required* memorial.

It was natural, therefore, that there arose a desire to regularize the personal voluntary memorials and to make them, as it were, official; or, more correctly, to extend the one official family memorial beyond Yom Kippur. There was a good reason why, when this extension took place, it spread to the last days of the three festivals, for these three last days already had a special function that was akin to the Yom Kippur liturgical memorial.

The Torah reading for the last day of Passover, the second day of Shavuot, and Sh'mini Atzeret was from Deuteronomy 15:19–16:17, which contains the words "Three times a year shall all your males appear before Adonai. Each according to his gift [*ish k'matnat yado*]," and so on. This scriptural reading made the last day of the three holidays a suitable occasion for soliciting gifts from each member ("all your males") for the support of the congregation. On this occasion a donor could, if he wished, also have the name of his departed relative mentioned as his gift was announced. This memorializing was permitted but was voluntary. The main purpose of the gifts was the support of the congregation.

So *Tanya Rabbati* [sixteenth century, Italy] (53 at the end of the Passover section) says: "Our custom is to pledge gifts for the *shalosh p'amim* (["three times" =] the scriptural verse 'three times a year,' etc.)

and *ish k'matnat yado*; also to mention the souls of the dead." The author makes a similar statement at the section of the last day of Shavuot (54) and Sh'mini Atzeret [the eighth day of Sukkot] (88). See also Maharil at the end of Hoshanah Rabbah; also *Siddur Yavetz* [Jacob Emden, seventeenth to eighteenth century, Germany] on the rules for the last of Passover.

These donations three times a year were called *matnat yad*, from the closing sentence of the Torah reading. The same term was applied to the regular required Yom Kippur memorial service, because then, too, gifts were given in memory of the dead. Since, therefore, the last day of the three holidays was called *matnat yad*, as was the Yom Kippur memorial, and since among the regular gifts to the congregation, gifts could also be given in honor of the dead, it was natural when the officially required *Yizkor* was extended that it was extended to these three days, even though that created some incongruity between the memorial mood and the *joyous* spirit of the festival.

Of course, even this extension of the required *Yizkor* did not abolish the individual voluntary and special memorials. Some people still gave or left money to the *chevra kaddisha* [the burial society] to read the names of the deceased on a *yahrzeit* list or to study Mishnah on the *yahrzeit* and to say *Kaddish* (cf., for example, responsa of Samuel Engel, 5:24).

This elaborate memorial system spread to some extent to the Sephardi communities. Two great Sephardi communities in the Ashkenazi world, namely, London and Amsterdam, have a memorial on the Sabbath before Tisha B'av for the victims of the Inquisition in Spain, exactly on the same Sabbath that the Ashkenazi Jews called the Black Sabbath and had chosen for the memorial to the victims of the Black Death.[9] But chiefly the Sephardim make use of the personal voluntary memorializing when a man is called to the Torah (*Hashkavah*).

Although the development of the memorial service is complicated and although the sources frequently seem confused and contradictory, the line of development is fairly clear. The first memorials were for the victims of the Crusades. Their names were read and the prayer *Av Harachamim* recited close to their common *yahrzeit*, the Saturday before Shavuot. Then the next memorial was for the victims of the Black Death. They were memorialized on the Sabbath before the ninth of Av (the Black Sabbath). Also there were memorials for benefactors of the congregation at various times during the year. All this is clear from the Memor lists and their introductory paragraphs. Soon there developed a regular liturgical memorial for members of each family. This was placed on Yom Kippur after the Torah reading. In addition, there were voluntary memorials at various individual *yahrzeit* dates, for which gifts were given or left by will. An individual memorial prayer could be asked for during the collections of the regular gifts for the support of the congregation, gifts expected from each member, which were collected on the last day of the three festivals. This collection, because of the Torah reading on that day, was called *matnat yad*, a term also applied to the regular liturgical memorial on Yom Kippur. When in Bohemia and Eastern Europe the regular liturgical memorial was extended, it was naturally extended to these three *matnat yad* days, the last day of the three festivals.[10]

Kaddish and Memorial Services

Rabbi Jakob J. Petuchowski, PhD (z"l)

[Editor's Note: Petuchowski's essay handles the *Kaddish* as well as the memorial service (*Yizkor*), because the Kaddish is the standard prayer associated with death. Traditionally, however, the *Kaddish* is not included as part of *Yizkor*— although it has usually been added in the extended memorial services of modernity. Discussion of the *Kaddish* is supplied separately in *My People's Prayer Book*, volume 6, *Tachanun and Concluding Prayers*, so we could have excluded the first half of Petuchowski's classic essay here. But given the natural affinity of the *Kaddish* to *Yizkor*, we have chosen to include it. Discussion of the memorial service per se begins on p. 99.]

Part 1: The *Kaddish*

While the *Kaddish* prayer in its several versions[1] goes back to the period of the Talmud, the custom of having the mourners recite it at the end of the service, for a period of eleven months after bereavement, is of comparatively

---

Rabbi Jakob J. Petuchowski, PhD (1925–1991), was raised in Berlin, the grandson of an Orthodox rabbi and a member of an Orthodox community, until age fourteen, when he escaped the Nazis on one of the last transports rescuing Jewish children. After a brief stay in England, he moved to the United States, and attended the Hebrew Union College, where he was ordained, earned a PhD, and served as faculty member instructing generations of students in liturgy, rabbinics, and theology. He wrote or edited more than thirty books, including the classic treatment of prayer book reform in Europe.

recent origin. The custom originated in Germany at the time of the persecutions that accompanied the Crusades. Eleazar of Worms, writing
around 1200, is still very indefinite about the custom. Isaac Or Zaru'a,
in 1220, reports that in Bohemia and along the Rhine, orphans recite the
Kaddish at the conclusion of the services, whereas that custom had not
been adopted in France. As for the *Kaddish* recited by the orphan on the
anniversary of his parents' deaths, Jacob Moellin, in the fifteenth century,
seems to be the first to record it. But, after that, both kinds of *Kaddish*
custom spread very rapidly throughout the Jewish world.[2]

The *Kaddish* is, of course, an eschatological prayer. Its reference to the
establishment of the Kingdom of God would be understood by the learned
to refer to the time when, among other eschatalogical happenings, the dead
will be resurrected. However, apart from the version of the *Kaddish* recited
at the graveside after a burial, which specifically mentions the resurrection
and life eternal,[3] no other forms of the *Kaddish* make any explicit references
to the dead. That includes the form of the *Kaddish* customarily recited by
the mourners.[4] The so-called Mourner's *Kaddish*, in its actual wording, is a
doxology [glorification or praise] addressed to God, which, when recited by
the bereaved, is meant to dramatize the theme of "Adonai hath given, and
Adonai hath taken away; praised be the name of Adonai" [Job 1:21]. That,
at any rate, would be the ideal. In practice, however, helped along by folklore and superstition, the Mourner's *Kaddish* was increasingly understood
as the kind of prayer that the living offer up *on behalf of the* dead—somewhat analogous to the Roman Catholic Mass for the Dead. Like the latter,
it was believed to be actually efficacious, so that the view quite naturally
gained ground that the more times *Kaddish* would be recited, the more
assured would be the salvation (or the rescue from hell) of the departed on
whose behalf the *Kaddish* was said. As a consequence, seeing that nobody
wants to be deficient in filial devotion and piety, the traditional service was
to witness a veritable proliferation of *Kaddish* recitations.

That the liturgical reform of the nineteenth century drastically
reduced the number of recitations of the Mourner's *Kaddish* almost goes
without saying. That was in line with abbreviating the liturgy as a whole
and omitting repetitions. But what about the *Kaddish* itself? What did
Reform do to divest the *Kaddish* of its superstitious associations and of
the notion that the *Kaddish* was a prayer that the living offer on behalf
of the dead? Theoretically, a radical Reform Movement might have done
away with the *Kaddish* altogether, just as it had eliminated a number of

customs and ceremonies that, in the mind of the people, had given rise to superstitious notions. But, in practice, Reform Judaism did nothing of the kind with the *Kaddish*. On the contrary, it provided an introduction to the *Kaddish*, and it added a paragraph to the *Kaddish*, in such a way that henceforth the *Kaddish* would express in its actual wording the meaning that people had read into it all along. Reform Judaism made the *Kaddish* a "prayer for the dead." The *Hamburg Temple Prayer Book* of 1819 was the first to do so.

Stating that "this prayer is recited only when mourners are present at the Temple," that prayer book offers the following text:[5]

כל ישראל יש להם חלק לעולם הבא. שנאמר
ועמך כלם צדיקים. לעולם יירשו ארץ: אשרי מי
שעמלו בתורה. ועשה נחת רוח ליוצרו. גדל בשם
טוב. ונפטר בשם טוב מן העולם: ועליו אמר שלמה
בחכמתו. טוב שם משמן טוב ויום המות מיום
הולדו: למוד תורה הרבה. ויתנו לך שכר הרבה. ודע
מתן שכרם של צדיקים לעתיד לבוא:
יתגדל ויתקש שמיה רבא. דהוא עתיד לחדתא
עלמא. ולאחאה מתיא. וימליך מלכותיה בחייכון
וביומיכון וגו':
אמן, יהא שמה רבא וגו':
יתברך וישתבח וגו':
על ישראל. ועל צדיקיא. ועל כל מן דאתפטר מן
עלמא הדין כרעותיה דאלהא. יהא להון שלמא
רבא. וחולקא טבא לחיי עלמא דאתי. וחסדא ורחמי.
מן קדם מאריה שמיא וארעא. ואמרו אמן:
יהא שלמא רבא וגו':
עשה שלום במרומיו וגו':

All Israel have a share in the world to come, as it is said, "And thy people shall be all righteous; they shall inherit the land forever."[6]

Happy is he whose labor was in the Torah, and who has given pleasure to his Creator. He grew up with a good name, and departed the world with a good name. And it is about him that Solomon said in his wisdom: "A good name is better than precious oil, and the day of death than the day of one's birth."[7]

Study much Torah, and they will give you much reward; and know that the giving of the reward to the righteous is in the world to come.[8]

Magnified and sanctified be the great name of Him who will renew the world and revive the dead. May He establish his kingdom during your life and during your days....

Amen. May his great name be blessed....

Blessed, praised, glorified....

May there be to Israel, and to the righteous, and to all who have departed from this world by the will of God abundant peace and a good portion in the life of the world to come, and grace and mercy from the Master of heaven and earth and say ye Amen.

May there be abundant peace etc. Amen.

He who maketh peace in his high places....

Before we trace the influence of this unprecedented form of the *Kaddish* upon the further development of European Liberal and Reform liturgy, something ought to be said about the sources whence form, wording, and ideas of this *Kaddish* were derived. For, while this version of the *Kaddish* had been without precedent in liturgical history, it was constructed out of materials contributed by both the Ashkenazi and the Sephardi rites.

First, we must note the *Hashkavah* prayer of the Sephardi rite [see Bitton, pp. 19–21, and appendix A, pp. 230–235]. This is a prayer recited for the repose of the departed as part of the Burial Service, in the house of the mourner, and on occasions when someone commemorating the anniversary of a death is called to the Torah.[9] The *Hashkavah* prayer, which asks for celestial repose to be granted to the departed, is preceded by a number of Scripture verses, which vary in accordance with the departed person's standing in the community and which are different in the cases of men and of women. Unlike the passages introducing the Hamburg *Kaddish*, which are all taken from Rabbinic literature, the verses preceding the *Hashkavah* are all from the Bible. But, apart from the fact that Ecclesiastes 7:1 ["A good name is better than precious oil, and the day of death than the day of one's birth"] happens to occur in both rituals, it is important to realize that the custom of reciting suitable passages before the "prayer for the dead" comes from the Sephardi rite. Moreover, the *Hashkavah* prayer itself contains the kind of ideas (and some of the words) that the Hamburg reformers inserted into the *Kaddish*. Quoting the text of the *Hashkavah* in Hebrew only, we render in bold type the words that found their way into the Hamburg *Kaddish*.

מנוחה נכונה בישיבה עליונה. תחת כנפי השכינה.
במעלת קדושים וטהורים: כזהר הרקיע מאירים
ומזהירים. וחלוץ עצמים. וכפרת אשמים. והרחקת
פשע. והקרבת ישע. וחמלה וחנינה. מלפני שוכן
מענה. **וחלקא טבא לחיי העולם הבא.** שם תהא
מנת ומחיצת וישיבת נפש השם הטוב (פלוני) רוח
יי תניחנו בגן עדן. **דאתפטר מן עלמא הדין. כרעות**
אלהא מרא שמיא וארעא: המלך ברחמיו יחס
ויחמל עליו: וילוה אליו השלום. ועל משכבו יהיה
שלום. כדכתיב. יבא שלום ינוחו על־משכבותם.
הלך נכחו: הוא וכל־בני ישראל השכבים עמו בכלל
הרחמים והסליחות. וכן יהי רצון ונאמר אמן:

We may note in passing that, apart from the vocabulary that the *Hashkavah* of the Sephardi rite furnished for the Hamburg *Kaddish*, the *Hashkavah* itself—although in a simplified form, and made to apply to *all* the departed rather than to individuals—found its way into many a reformed ritual (including the *Hamburg Temple Prayer Book*) as a part of the memorial service.

A second source of the Hamburg *Kaddish* is to be found in the traditional Burial *Kaddish*, which begins as follows:[10]

יתגדל ויתקדש שמה רבא בעלמא דהוא עתיד
לחדתא, ולאחיאה מתיא, ולאסקא יתהון לחיי
עלמא, ולמבנא קרתא דירושלם ולשכללא היכלה
בגוה, ולמעקר פלחנא נכראה מן ארעא, ולאתבא
פלחנא דשמיא לאתרה. וימלוך קדשא בריך הוא
במלכותה ויקרה בחייכון וביומיכון וגו':

Finally, as far as the structure of the *Kaddish* insert is concerned, the prototype is to be found in the traditional *Kaddish D'rabbanan*, which is recited after the study of passages from Rabbinic literature.[11]

על ישראל ועל רבנן ועל תלמידיהון, ועל כל
תלמידי תלמידיהון, ועל כל מן דעסקין באוריתא,
די באתרא הדן ודי בכל אתר ואתר, יהא להון ולכון
שלמא רבא, חנא וחסדא ורחמין, וחיין אריכין,
ומזוני רויחי, ופרקנא מן קדם אבוהון דבשמיא
וארעא, ואמרו אמן:

There is undoubtedly a peculiar irony in the fact that the Hamburg reformers turned this traditional prayer, which asked for spiritual grace and material welfare to be granted to the living scholars of Israel, into a prayer requesting celestial bliss for the dead. It should be borne in mind, however, that by the side of this explicit Mourner's *Kaddish*, the *Hamburg Temple Prayer Book* also retained other forms of the *Kaddish*, the "Half *Kaddish*" and the "Full *Kaddish*," in different sections of the service, thereby retaining the pure doxological character of the traditional *Kaddish*. In this, the *Hamburg Temple Prayer Book* was followed by other German reformed editions of the prayer book. It was only in the liturgy of American Reform Judaism that the *Kaddish* was lost as a doxology, when the single recitation of the *Kaddish* at the conclusion of the service was given the character of a Mourner's *Kaddish* by the adoption of the Hamburg insert, "May there be to Israel, and to the righteous, and to all who have departed." Altogether, it may be said that the Hamburg version of the Mourner's *Kaddish* exerted a greater influence on American Reform liturgy than on the development of European Liberal and Reform liturgy. In European countries outside of Germany, the *Kaddish* insert does not seem to have been adopted at all—that is, in England, France, Holland, and Sweden. In Germany itself, some rituals, of which we shall consider a number of examples below, did adopt the Hamburg *Kaddish*; others used it only as part of the memorial service. What caught on much more was the idea of an introduction to the *Kaddish*, usually in the vernacular, and not necessarily in the form of the Rabbinic passages selected by the 1819 edition of the *Hamburg Temple Prayer Book*. Thus, without changing the text of the *Kaddish* itself, it was possible to give expression to the mood of an explicit mourner's prayer.

Moreover, the *Hamburg Temple Prayer Book*, which retained the text of its 1819 version of the Mourner's *Kaddish*, although it introduced some changes in the introductory passages, in subsequent editions, remained alone in utilizing the phrases from the Burial *Kaddish* for the beginning of the Mourner's *Kaddish*. It was followed in this by the Aachen prayer book of 1853; but the Aachen prayer book used the Hamburg Mourner's *Kaddish* as a Burial *Kaddish* only,[12] and not for the conclusion of other services. At a time when Reform Judaism was beginning to tone down the traditional dogma of the resurrection, few reformers may have felt called upon to introduce specific references to that dogma into the traditional version of the Mourner's *Kaddish*, which did not contain them. However, Kirchenrat Joseph von Maier, in the prayer book for private devotion, which he published in 1848, did adopt the Hamburg *Kaddish*, complete with introductory passages and insert.[13]

However, Maier provides two separate German meditations, one to be said by mourners in the year of bereavement, and one to be said by those observing the anniversary of a death, which were meant to be read silently while the cantor recited the Rabbinic passages of the introduction—a procedure that was later adopted by other rituals as well. Also, in his German version of the Mourner's *Kaddish*, Maier paraphrases the reference to the resurrection of the dead in terms of spiritual immortality.

Geiger, in his 1854 edition of the prayer book, leaves the traditional Mourner's *Kaddish* unchanged and provides no introduction to it. However, the Hamburg introductory passages to the *Kaddish* are used in the memorial service,[14] while the *Kaddish* there remains without the Hamburg insert.

Stein's 1860 edition of the prayer book contains the Hamburg introductory passages to the *Kaddish*, omitting only the first part of the last passage, for which Proverbs 12:28 and 23:18 are substituted. Stein follows Maier in providing silent German meditations while those passages are being read aloud. The special mourner's insert in the *Kaddish* is adopted.[15]

After Stein had adopted and amended the Hamburg version of 1819 and 1841, the 1868 edition of the *Hamburg Temple Prayer Book*, in its turn, adopted the introductory passages as amended by Stein, retaining, however, the 1819 version of the opening words of the *Kaddish* itself.[16]

Two years later, in 1870, Geiger followed Stein in the choice of introductory passages and in the inclusion of the *Kaddish* insert, both at the conclusion of the Sabbath eve and at the conclusion of the Sabbath morning service[17]—representing a departure from his own 1854 ritual.

On the other hand, the prayer book of the Berlin New Synagogue, published in 1881, adopted the *Kaddish* insert for the memorial service only.[18] Its regular introduction to the Mourner's *Kaddish* on Sabbaths and festivals consists of Psalm 36:8–10,[19] one of the introductory passages of the Sephardi *Hashkavah*. This remained in all subsequent editions of the Berlin prayer book.

In his 1882 edition of the prayer book, Stein reprinted his 1860 version—with one interesting change. The opening words now read: *Kol yisra'el. Kol tzaddikei v'chasidei ha'olam yesh lahem chelek la'olam haba,* "All Israel, all the righteous and the pious of the world, have a share in the world to come."[20]

Vogelstein, in 1894, follows Geiger's 1870 version.[21] But Stein's 1882 attempt at "universalizing" the franchise of candidates for the world to come, in the introduction to the *Kaddish*, is pushed beyond the logical limits in Seligmann's 1910 edition of the prayer book. For Sabbaths and festivals, Seligmann has a German introduction to the Mourner's *Kaddish*, which bears no resemblance to the tradition initiated in Hamburg. The *Kaddish* itself has the Hamburg insert. But for the conclusion of the weekday services, both evening and morning,[22] Seligmann takes over Stein's introductory passages, omitting the last, and changing the first to read as follows: *Chasidei umot ha'olam yesh lahem chelek la'olam haba,* "The pious of the nations of the world have a share in the world to come."

Now, it is obvious that, if the pious of *all* peoples have such a share, the pious Israelites would automatically be included in that definition; and, in his 1912 *Denkschrift*, Seligmann makes the point that it is self-evident (*selbstverständlich*) that he means Jews to be included. Unfortunately, language occasionally imposes its own logic; and in Rabbinic Hebrew, *chasidei umot ha'olam* never includes Jews, but specifically the pious among the gentiles. The concept is based on Tosefta Sanhedrin 13:2, where, however, the noun used is *tzaddikim* rather than *chasidim*. However, the Tosefta passage is popularly quoted in the very phraseology that Seligmann uses to introduce the *Kaddish*.[23] Thus, any Jew familiar with Rabbinic literature who reads Seligmann's introduction to the *Kaddish* can only conclude that there is no room for Jews in the world to come!

While the above is not directly relevant to the theme of the *Kaddish*, we found it necessary to pay some attention to it, if only to alert future liturgists of Reform Judaism to the danger inherent in overstating one's universalism. We now revert to the fate of the Hamburg *Kaddish*.

The *Einheitsgebetbuch* [*Union Prayer Book*, Germany's attempt at a prayer book for all congregations] of 1929, which on purpose and by design reflects the more prevalent liturgical forms of German liberal Judaism, provides, in its appendix, a number of German introductions to the *Kaddish*, none of them, however, based on the Hamburg passages. The Hamburg *Kaddish* insert is regularly printed whenever the Mourner's *Kaddish* is called for, but it is separated from the rest of the text and marked, "In some congregations." Of the two memorial services contained in that volume, one includes the *Kaddish* insert, and the other does not. It may thus be seen that, with some notable exceptions including Stein, Geiger, and Seligmann, European Liberal and Reform liturgy—unlike the Reform liturgy of America—failed to follow the Hamburg example in making the text of the Mourner's *Kaddish* conform to the popular understanding of that prayer. This much, though, can be said for the influence of the Hamburg Temple in the matter of the *Kaddish*: the recitation of suitable introductory prayers or meditations in the vernacular became the standard procedure in practically all non-Orthodox synagogues in the Old World as well as in the New.

And Hamburg's example was followed also in another matter connected with the departed: the memorial service.

Part 2: The Memorial Service

The history of the memorial service in the traditional synagogue is complicated, and the reports frequently seem confused and contradictory. A helpful sifting of the sources has been undertaken by Rabbi Solomon B. Freehof, who traces the institution of the memorial service back to the times of the Crusades [see Freehof's essay in its entirety, pp. 77–89 in this volume].[24]

But, regardless of the involved history of the institution, the texts included in the traditional Ashkenazi memorial service (on the Day of Atonement, according to the German rite, and also on the last days of the three Pilgrimage Festivals, according to the Polish rite) were very few and simple. They consisted of the *Yizkor* prayer, recited silently by the survivors in memory of the departed, including the promise of a donation to be made on behalf of the repose of the departed; the *El Malei Rachamim* prayer, of similar contents, but recited aloud by the cantor; and the *Av Harachamim* prayer, commemorating the victims of the Crusades.[25] Whatever else is printed, even in Orthodox prayer books today, as part of the memorial service, by way of psalms and other readings, already represents the influence of the Reform Movement in Judaism. Thus, the late Chief Rabbi Joseph H. Hertz, who reprints the memorial service arranged by Chief Rabbi Hermann Adler (in which *Yizkor* is preceded by a number of verses from the Psalms and Ecclesiastes, and followed by a newly composed prayer), says in a note, "It has for several centuries been customary to commemorate the dead on the last day of Festivals, and especially on the Day of Atonement. In recent generations, such prayers have become an important feature of the Festival Service."[26] What the Orthodox chief rabbi so coyly covers by the phrase "in recent generations" is, of course, the liturgical endeavor of nascent Reform Judaism. Writing about the development of the modern form of the memorial service, as distinct from the few traditional prayers we have mentioned above, Max Joseph correctly saw its origin in the German congregations using a reformed liturgy.[27] But when Joseph also ascribed the introduction of the first modern memorial service to Kirchenrat Maier, in Stuttgart and other congregations of Württemberg, "around the middle of the nineteenth century," he was dating the beginning of the new form of the memorial service some decades too late. It was, in fact, the *Hamburg Temple Prayer Book* of 1819 that, as far as we have been able to ascertain, was the first prayer book to contain a specific "Memorial Service" (*Totenfeier*) for the Day of Atonement.[28]

The memorial service of that prayer book begins with a German hymn. This is followed by a rather lengthy prayer, which is really more of a philosophical argument demonstrating immortality than an actual prayer. We are quoting a few excerpts from it here:

> Great Spirit, whose ways are beyond searching out!
> Ruler over life and death! Thou didst call forth the
> infinite universe out of nothing. Thine almighty word
> did adorn it with magnificence and beauty. Thy breath
> breathed into it living beings of innumerable shapes;
> and man towers supreme above all. Thou hast created
> him in Thine own image, and Thou hast given him the
> power of command over the work of Thy hands. Thou
> didst kindle within him the divine spark of reason, so
> that he might recognize Thy might and greatness in all
> creation. Yet in Thy wise providence, it hath pleased
> Thee to apportion a finite time unto all Thy creatures;
> and thus didst Thou set a limit also for man.... But
> Thou, Almighty, hast not created Thy works in order
> to give them over to destruction. Nothing is destroyed.
> Nothing will be lost which was created by Thy creative
> hand. Everything dies in order to be newly formed: not
> a mote of dust will lose its being, seeing that Thy cre-
> ative breath hath formed it. How, then, should man,
> the masterpiece of all creatures, be annihilated by death?
> How wouldst Thou, who only createst, but destroyest
> nothing, destroy the spirit living in man, which is a part
> of Thine own being? No! Thou raisest the spirit unto
> Thyself, and only the fragile shell which contained the
> divine spark, only the body which is mortal, rests in the
> lap of the earth, and will turn into the dust out of which
> it was created....
> Through death, a purer and better life begins for us in
> the blissful abodes of peace. No cover of earth limits the
> pure spirit.... Death is a gate which leads from darkness
> into pure light, ... where the soul, saturated by pure joy,

will cast its glance into eternity, and will acknowledge
more deeply and more ardently the perfection of the
Eternal, and proclaim Thy praise in the choir of the
spirits, O Thou Unsearchable One! ...

This is followed (in Hebrew) by Psalms 144:3–4, 90:6, 90:3; Deuteronomy
32:29; Psalms 49:18, 37:37, and 34:23.

After this, there is, for silent devotion, a German adaptation (and
elaboration) of the traditional *Yizkor* prayer:

Of thee, O my beloved father (my beloved mother) I
think in this solemn hour, and of the love, the care, and
the fidelity with which thou didst guide me as long as
thou wast with me on earth. Thou didst depart from
me, and leave me behind; but I remember the teachings
which thou gavest me, and my heart is deeply touched,
and beats loudly and warmly towards thine immortal
spirit, which dwells aloft with its Heavenly Father. O
that the Almighty may have received thy soul into His
fatherly protection, united with those who live forever,
basking in the glory of the divine greatness and majesty,
and hovering over me until my spirit, too, will be associated with thine, and meet, in the kingdom of purest
light, those who wandered virtuously on this earth, and
who were so dear and beloved to me. And Thou, O
Heavenly Father, think Thou of the pious gift which I
vow to the benefit of this house, and devote to the dear
memory of the departed. O that the willing sacrifices of
my mouth may be acceptable unto Thee.

A similar prayer is provided on behalf of other departed relatives.

After those silent meditations, the service continues with an abbre-
viated form of the Sephardi *Hashkavah* in Hebrew, including the preliminary Scripture verses. This is followed by the introduction to the
Mourner's *Kaddish* and the Mourner's *Kaddish* itself, in the form initiated by this prayer book. The service concludes with another German
hymn.

In the 1841 edition of the *Hamburg Temple Prayer Book*, the memorial service is even more elaborate. But the same pattern prevails—not only in subsequent editions of the *Hamburg Temple Prayer Book*, but in all reformed rituals published after that time. There are variations in detail. Some continue to make reference to the donations vowed on behalf of the departed, others omit any reference of that kind. Some versions of the memorial service have the survivors address the departed in the second person, others let the survivors speak to God about the departed. Such matters could be of profound theological import, and a difference in nuance could represent important dogmatic divergences. Yet the overall impression one gains is that the liturgists producing those prayers and meditations were far less concerned with theological niceties than they were with comforting the mourners and turning the memorial service into a didactic occasion for the contemplation of life, death, and immortality.

As the inclusion of memorial services even in modern Orthodox prayer books (where, however, they are never quite as elaborate as in the reformed rituals) shows, this innovation of Reform Judaism, first introduced in the Hamburg Temple, was an immediate success. A. Wiener, the rabbi of Oppeln and, by the standards of those days, something of a religious radical, remained largely unheeded when, in a criticism of Geiger's version of the memorial service, he urged:

> It is not at all fitting for us to speak, in our prayers, about the ways and the manner of immortality as though we were intimates and confidants of God, completely initiated into that obscure mystery.... Such confident assertions about the hereafter, especially when voiced in a skeptical age like ours, often achieve the very opposite effect from the one intended. Our statements about it must be very modest and very cautious. Our expressions must be carefully chosen.... Particularly with regard to that kind of prayer, we cannot urgently enough recommend the words of Ecclesiastes 5:1. ["Be not rash with thy mouth, and let not thy heart be hasty to utter a word before God; for God is in heaven, and thou upon earth; therefore let thy words be few."][29]

Perhaps the modern type of memorial service became so popular because, in many cases, one's attachment to the memory of one's parents may be stronger than one's devotion to Judaism and will certainly outlast it. At any rate, experience has shown that the memorial service will bring people into the synagogue who worship on no other occasions throughout the year. Max Joseph, writing in 1928, may have been a little premature in his apprehensions; but, when one surveys the Reform liturgy for memorial services and delves into its motivations, the words of Max Joseph could well have a sobering effect. He wrote:

> The intention to arouse religiosity and devotion to Judaism by means of the feelings of filial piety is bound to miss the mark to the extent to which the contemporary generation is no longer able to look back upon parents who were pious and permeated by their Judaism.[30]

Yizkor

A MICROCOSM OF LITURGICAL INTERCONNECTIVITY

Dr. Eric L. Friedland

The First Modern *Yizkor*

At the heart of the elaborate memorial service (*Hazkarat N'shamot*)[1] on Yom Kippur in most synagogues throughout the world is the familiar *Yizkor* prayer recited in silence by the individual worshiper in memory of deceased kindred and loved ones. The non-Orthodox variations on this prayer are many. The multiple variations derive from different points of origin and influences, intercommunally, intertextually, and intergenerationally. The transmutations of the one-paragraph *Yizkor* prayer can be said to form a microcosm of the manifold development of the Jewish liturgy at large, over a long stretch of time and often enough within a single

---

Dr. Eric L. Friedland is professor emeritus, after serving as Sanders Professor of Judaic Studies in a consortium of three universities and a United Methodist seminary in the Greater Dayton area for thirty years (1968–1998). During that time up to now he has written extensively on Progressive Jewish liturgies, American, European, and Israeli. Capturing his wholehearted interest at this time are 1) the works of the Israeli philosopher Shmuel Hugo Bergman (1883–1975), who was ever in search for the larger religious meaning, and 2) a highly novel collaborative interfaith effort with Dr. Wa'el Azmeh, a gifted Syrian Muslim study partner. Profoundly deaf from birth, Friedland is continually rejoicing in what he is presently able to hear with the wondrous help of a cochlear implant.

generation. Because of the overabundance of material, we have a chance to look at only a sampling of these modifications. The highly innovative memorial service in the premier Reform prayer book, the Hamburg Temple's pivotal *Seder Ha'avodah* (*Ordnung der öffentlichen Andacht*, Hamburg, 1819), will serve as our jumping-off point, notably in relation to the following concerns:

- The use of Hebrew or the vernacular
- Predilection for Sephardi or Ashkenazi usage, or both
- Placement of the service
- Entreaties for the deceased or to them
- Assumptions with respect to the hereafter
- Pledges on behalf of the departed

Meanwhile, we will see how these concerns—and contemporary ones— were handled in rites that took shape in the succeeding two centuries— that is, right up to our own time.

The epoch-making *Hamburg Temple Prayer Book* may strike us today pretty much like a modern-day Conservative/Masorti one insofar as the structure and layout are indisputably the traditional ones and the text preponderantly in Hebrew. This even though the pagination is from left to right. For the Day of Atonement, those *piyyutim* that are kept are principally drawn from the Sephardi rite; newly composed hymns in German as a rule take the place of the discontinued *piyyutim*. Replacing the personal Confession during the *Amidah* is, for instance, a frank, long, and eloquent admission of wrongdoing, again in German. In the Sephardi tradition there is technically no *Yizkor* as such, but rather what is known as *Hashkavah* (Requiem),[2] which the Reform Hamburg rite as good as reproduces. The *Hashkavah* is made up of two key parts: *Mah Rav Tuv'kha* ("How precious is Thy lovingkindness") and *M'nuchah N'khonah* ("Perfect repose"—see Bitton, pp. 19–21). In the Sephardi rite, the entire service may appear either between the additional service (*Musaf*) and the afternoon service (*Minchah*) or between the afternoon service and the concluding service (*N'ilah*), either of which sequence came to be adopted in virtually all non-Orthodox prayer books throughout the nineteenth century, in Europe and in America.[3] Another variation is the placement of the *Hashkavah* during the Yom Kippur eve service. The only non-Orthodox *machzor* to imitate this latter practice is the moving monolingual memorial service during *Ma'ariv* on Yom Kippur in Isaac Mayer Wise's *Minhag Amerika* (Cincinnati, 1866).[4]

The Language of the Modern *Yizkor*

What makes the Hamburg *Totenfeier* unlike any other is that the opening part of the service is entirely in German,[5] including what would have been the culminating *Yizkor* prayer itself. Noteworthy throughout are the earnest spirituality and *Innerlichkeit* (a religious interiority typical of German piety, both Christian and Jewish) and a sure conviction with respect to a life beyond the grave "in a realm of pure light." While Progressive *machzorim* have in most cases been bilingual, there have been the rare few that have been solely in the vernacular—to mention just four: the radical, yet highly influential *Reformgemeinde* of Berlin (ending, interestingly, in *Herr der Welt* ["Master of the World" = *Adon Olam*]);[6] Abraham Geiger's generally tradition-leaning *D'var Yom B'yomo* (Frankfurt am Main, 1891; with an all-German Mourner's *Kaddish* and a *Shiviti* [Psalm 16:8–9] as the concluding hymn); the masterly treatment[7] in Cäsar Seligmann's *Gebetbuch für Neujahr und Versöhnungstag* (Frankfurt am Main, 1904; drawing to a close with the Mourner's *Kaddish*); and Hebrew Union College–trained Joseph Krauskopf's free-spirit, cutting-edge re-creation *The Service Manual* (Philadelphia, 1892; terminating in a wholly revamped *Kaddish*).[8] The advantage of conducting a memorial service all in one language is the opportunity given the worshipers to commune with their lamented loved ones in an intense, barrier-free, and intimate manner. While nearly the entire Hebrew text of the *Hamburg Temple Prayer Book* is rendered rather literally in the German, its *Yizkor* substitute is a wholly new—and quite poignant—entreaty fixed on those who have gone the way of all flesh. Here is Rabbi Jakob J. Petuchowski's precise rendition of the *in memoriam* for one's parents [see also Petuchowski, pp. 90–103]:[9]

> Of thee, O my beloved father (my beloved mother), I think in this solemn hour, and of the love, the care and the fidelity with which thou didst guide me as long as thou wast with me on earth. Thou didst depart from me and leave me behind; but I remember the teachings which thou gavest me, and my heart is deeply touched, and beats loudly and warmly towards thine immortal spirit,

which dwells aloft with its Heavenly Father. O that the Almighty may have received thy soul into His fatherly protection, united with those who live forever, basking in the glory of the divine greatness and majesty, and hovering over me until my spirit, too, will be associated with thine, and meet, in the kingdom of the purest light, those who wandered virtuously on this earth, and who were so dear and beloved to me. And Thou, O Heavenly Father, think Thou of the pious gift which I vow to the benefit of this house, and to the dear memory of the departed. O that the willing sacrifices of my mouth may be acceptable unto Thee.

A similar prayer follows for other relatives and friends. Three key points might be noted:

- The prayer is trained on the departed themselves (e.g., "I think of thee, my beloved father").
- The hope is voiced that the worshiper may join the dearest and nearest in paradise.
- A donation is pledged to the synagogue in their memory.

Addressed to God or to the Deceased?

In some ways more traditional and in others more liberal, the second, 1845 edition of the *Hamburg Temple Prayer Book* undergoes a significant adjustment in its *Yizkor* vernacular surrogates. They are no longer pitched to the deceased. Instead, God becomes once again the sole recipient of prayer. The ending as regards the promise of a charitable donation (*die fromme Spende*) remains the same. We see this oscillation or ambiguity between addressing God, on the one hand, and speaking head-on to the souls of dead relatives and friends, on the other, going on for at least another hundred years.

In any event, I would venture to say, such creative liberties as were taken with the *Yizkor* text in the Hamburg rite could indeed be ventured largely because the original passage was familiar to only a segment of the congregation—that is, the Ashkenazi contingent—and was nonexistent in the ritual on which the majority of the temple members had been reared as Sephardim.

Yizkor Couched Anew

Virtually all nineteenth-century American non-Orthodox liturgies followed in the footsteps of their German antecedents.[10] Somewhat an exception was the gracefully lean and hebraically literate *Order of Prayer* (1855) for Congregation Emanu-El of New York City skillfully wrought by its founding rabbi, Leo Merzbacher. While the sequence and text of his memorial service are on the whole patterned after the Hamburg Temple version, *Yizkor* in its traditional wording (with "may his [her] soul be bound up in the bond of eternal life *with the souls of Abraham, Isaac and Jacob, Sarah, Rebekah, Rachel and Leah, and with the rest of righteous men and women*")[11] remains its fulcrum of the service. On the English side, what appears to be an entirely new prayer is none other than Merzbacher's shortened rendition of the *Yizkor* stand-in from the 1819 *Hamburg Temple Prayer Book*![12] As an indication of his literary skills in the Hebrew language, Merzbacher brings in this fine composition of his own that contains its quota of biblical allusions, a novel *Yizkor* on behalf of the benefactors of the congregation who have passed on:

יזכור אלהים נשמות כל הישרים והישרות אשר
הטיבו עם בני קהלתנו ונאספו אל עמיהם והניחו
אחריהם ברכה (...מזכיר בשם...) מנוחתם כבוד
שמם ייכון לעד וזכרם ממנו לא ימוש אשרי כל
הולך בדרכם. אמן:

May the Lord remember the souls of all the righteous and good who lived as benefactors in our midst, and have been gathered to their people, and left a blessing to their name.

They rest in glory with imperishable renown, and their memory shall not depart from us.

Happy are those who walk in their path. Amen!

Reformulated, Yet Orthodox

British Orthodoxy was always in a class by itself, in that it was under the jurisdiction of a chief rabbi who served as the key religious representative

of the Jewish community in the eyes of the government, a miniature counterpart to the archbishop of Canterbury, "the Primate of all England."
Inasmuch as it was every inch English as it was Orthodox Jewish, the
United Synagogue (constituted in 1870 by Act of Parliament) was
always up on developments both throughout the British Empire (later,
Commonwealth) and on the Continent. It noted liturgical changes taking place mostly under the auspices of Reform/Liberal Judaism, starting,
to be sure, with the dissident West London Synagogue's *Forms of Prayer*,
which drew much inspiration from the *Hamburg Temple Prayer Book*.
Hence, congregations under the aegis of the United Synagogue saw fit
to embrace "modern" features, such as decorum during worship, choral
harmony, and new prayers, so long as they were not deemed violating
halakhic norms. Hence, the cornerstone of the memorial service, *Yizkor*,
was reworded by Chief Rabbi Hermann Adler in a more elevated, mildly
demythologized vein:

יזכור אלהים נשמת...שהלך לעולמו (שהלכה
לעולמה). אנא תהי נפשו (נפשה) צרורה בצרור
החיים ותהי מנוחתו (מנוחתה) כבוד שובע שמחות
את פניך נעימות בימינך נצח:

> May God remember the soul of.... who has gone to his
> (her) repose. May his (her) soul be bound up in the bond
> of life. May his (her) rest be glorious, with fullness of
> joy in Thy presence, and bliss for evermore at Thy right
> hand.[13]

The perdurability of this revised text is uncanny inasmuch as it has caught
on throughout the world by way of another, non-Orthodox stream
of Judaism, the Conservative Movement. The United Synagogue of
America[14] issued not long afterward (1927) its stately *Festival Prayer Book*,
which adopted, as for most of its prayer texts and poetic translations, the
revised *Yizkor* of the British [Orthodox] United Synagogue. This version
became axiomatic in all subsequent Conservative prayer-book revisions—
and through them in Reform, Liberal,[15] and Reconstructionist[16] prayer

books ever since. While settling on Adler's emendation for the Hebrew text, Morris Silverman, usually given to paraphrase, chose to pen for his *High Holiday Prayer Book* (Hartford, Connecticut, 1951) a brand-new prayer on the English side that is personalized wherein the deceased are hailed and spoken to directly, as is God in the last paragraph. It might be noticed that the language, if a touch stilted, is not all that far removed in content from the pre-Shoah German Liberal *machzorim*. The most recent *Machzor Lev Shalem* (New York, 2010) uses the same English formula for everyone. Sadly, it is laconic, nondescript, and impersonal. A redeeming feature is the one heartbreaking yet wise prayer—the only one of its kind—by Robert Saks in a sidebar, "A *Yizkor* Meditation in Memory of a Parent Who Was Hurtful."

Spurred by Adler's innovative *Yizkor* (which they wisely appropriated), the Conservatives drew up a short and sweet, yet soul-stirring new one for those who perished during the Holocaust. Sadly, none of their imitators in the other movements of modern Judaism saw fit to ratify it as well.[17]

יזכור אלהים נשמות כל־אחינו בני ישראל שמסרו

נפשם על־קידוש השם. אנא יישמע בחיינו הד

גבורתם ומסירותם ויראה במעשינו טוהר ליבם

ותהיינה נפשותיהם צרורות בצרור החיים ותהי

מנוחתם כבוד. שובע שמחות את־פניך נעימות

בימינך נצח. אמן:

May God be mindful of the souls of all our brothers, departed members of the house of Israel who sacrificed their lives for the sanctification of the Holy Name and the honor of Israel. Grant that their heroism and self-sacrificing devotion find response in our hearts and the purity of their souls be reflected in our lives. May their souls be bound up in the bonds of eternal life, an everlasting blessing among us. Amen.

Pledges

While retaining Hermann Adler's lofty formula, the Harlow 1972 *machzor* introduced into the *Yizkor* prayer the phrase *Hin'ni noder [noderet] tz'dakah b'ad hazkarat nishmatah* (paraphrased as "In loving testimony to her life I pledge charity to help perpetuate ideals important to her"), no doubt because this is a good opportunity, given the masses of people in attendance, to fund-raise for the synagogue and charitable causes.[18] By contrast, the Israeli Masorti (Conservative) siddur, *Va'ani T'fillati*, leaves out the phrase. We may speculate that the none-too-subtle monetary appeal would be seen by the native Hebrew speaker as a tad opportunistic and mercenary. Or perhaps the kind of halakhic scruples expressed by Sacks below lie behind the hesitation to revive the importunate phrase. Meanwhile back in England, the most recent rebirth of the long-lived *Singer's Prayer Book*—that is, *The Authorised Daily Prayer Book*, originally under the sanction of the aforesaid Chief Rabbi Adler in 1890—renamed *The Koren Siddur*, edited by the former chief rabbi Jonathan Sacks, furnishes the qualifying phrase *Ba'avur b'li neder she'eten tz'dakah* ("I pledge without formal vow to give charity in ... memory"). No explanation is given in the notes. This is undoubtedly done in tacit recognition of the gravity with which unfulfilled vows have historically been considered in classical Judaism from at least as far back as the days of Ecclesiastes 5:4 ("It is better not to vow at all than to vow and not fulfill").

Contemporary Trends

What are some of the trends we are seeing nowadays that either build on the 1819 Hamburg liturgical template or that depart markedly from it? Bilingualism remains. There is much less of a declamatory or disquisitional nature. Dogma is demoted; a much wider variety of views is espoused. Instead of lengthy discursive prayers, we may encounter more poems and ruminations, almost always by Jews[19] of whatever standpoint. More extensive use is made of the psalms,[20] mostly for their evocative quality than for any authoritative, final-word disclosure concerning the mysteries of life or what may lie beyond. The reshaping and enrichment of the memorial service, particularly in the British Reform *Forms of Prayer for Jewish Worship* (London, 1985) and Liberal *Machzor Ruach Chadashah* and the American Reconstructionist *Kol Haneshamah* (Elkins Park,

Pennsylvania, 1999), is a realistic assessment of where Jews are today, spiritually, psychologically, and emotionally—in all their wondrous heterogeneity—that is at the same time a courtesy. The array of literary passages, prayers, and music is, in palpable contrast to what was in vogue during the past two centuries, profuse. Ironically, the *Yizkor* prayer itself as a result pales by comparison and is made, with the barest minimum of variation, the same for all of the deceased, whether parent, child, spouse, sibling, or friend.[21] From a climax it has turned, in effect, into an anticlimax. A drastic example is the rubric in the French Liberal *Mahzor Anénou* (Paris, 1999): "*On observe quelques minutes de silence pour la méditation personelle*"—with no hint of a scripted *Yizkor* text! It is now an occasion for private musings about one's loved ones. Or, to put it in another way: starting two hundred years ago with the *Hamburg Temple Prayer Book*, all our non-Orthodox High Holy Day liturgies have shared a good deal and without stint as pertains to the interhuman nexus, God, death, immortality, and memory. So fortified and so heartened, the worshiper may these days candidly and freely pronounce her or his own *Yizkor*.

⌒ຕຕຕ໐

"Service for the Souls"

THE ORIGIN OF MODERN MEMORIAL SERVICES, 1819 TO 1938

Dr. Annette M. Boeckler

A separate and elaborate *Yizkor* service for Yom Kippur and festivals is a gift of nineteenth-century German liberal Judaism to today's Reform, Liberal, Conservative, Masorti, and even Orthodox Jewish denominations. Until the nineteenth century the memorializing of a dead relative was something quite unspectacular and short, called in Ashkenazi congregations *hazkarat n'shamot* ("bringing into memory the souls") or simply *mazkir* ("bringing into memory"), and in Sephardi congregations *hashkavah* or *ashkavah* ("laying to rest").[1]

In Ashkenazi synagogues, the custom was to pledge a donation (*tz'dakah*) in memory of the deceased. One would silently say the Hebrew prayer *Yizkor* ("May He [God] remember"), which included the vow to give charity and a blank place to insert the sum; then the *chazzan* would chant *El Malei Rachamim* and/or a prayer in memory of martyrs, starting with *Av Harachamim*. Because Yom Kippur has traditionally associated *tz'dakah* with repentance, it was regarded as an especially suitable time for giving charity in the memory of a loved one. In Sephardi congregations,

Dr. Annette M. Boeckler is lecturer for liturgy at Leo Baeck College in London and manager of its library. She studied theology, Jewish studies, and Ancient Near Eastern Studies in Germany and Switzerland and *chazzanut* both privately (with cantor Marcel Lang, *z"l*, and cantor Jeremy Burko) and at the Levisson Instituut in Amsterdam. She contributed to *All These Vows*—Kol Nidre and *We Have Sinned: Sin and Confession in Judaism*—Ashamnu *and* Al Chet (both Jewish Lights).

the custom occurred on other occasions as well. On the anniversary of someone's death, one might ask to have the deceased remembered after an *aliyah*—with the assumption that a donation would subsequently be made to the synagogue. During the nineteenth century, these two customs were elaborated, enlarged, and mixed, to the point where their original character was completely changed.

Prussian *Totensonntag* ("Sunday for the Dead") and the Jewish *Totenfeier* ("Service for the Dead")

In 1817, Eduard Kley and C. S. Günsburg, the editors of the very first German liberal prayer book published in Berlin (the *Hamburg Temple Prayer Book* was published later, in 1819), introduced their work by expressing deep gratitude for the Jewish condition and the place of the synagogue in celebrating it:

> Five years have now passed since the Eternal One our God, has given to us the great sign of his love and mercy, that He turned the heart of his anointed one, our wise, pious, and righteous king, toward us for good, filled him with his Holy Spirit, so that he took from us the heavy burden that weighed upon us for more than eighteen hundred years, and that he by his merciful sunlike gaze on us removed the unworthy shackles of humiliation and we regained the human right to be free humans and citizens.... Where else could the beautiful sense for fatherland and king be ignited, than in the house of God?[2]

The authors were looking back at the defeat of Napoleon on October 18, 1813, at the battle of Leipzig, an event that was commemorated annually as a "day of liberation." German territories had slowly emerged from these "liberation wars" with newfound regard for themselves as a single political unit, with memorial celebrations of victory serving as a unifying factor. October 18 was duly marked with sermons everywhere, including the Hamburg Temple, as we see from the opening words of this 1825 example by Rabbi Gotthold Salomon:

> For the twelfth time now this meaningful majestic moment is repeated, when Adonai walked in the fields of Leipzig as

a hero and war comrade, inspiring the zeal, noiseful, jubi-
lant, victorious,[3] his greatness and glory revealing to the
nations of the earth. And for the eighth time this memo-
rable day is celebrated here, in these walls.[4]

The Hamburg Temple was in fact officially opened—deliberately—on
the "Day of Liberation," October 18, 1818.[5]

All of this is connected with *Yizkor* because King Frederick William
III of Prussia, the above-mentioned "anointed one, our wise, pious, and
righteous king," who played an active role in creating a new order of service for Protestant churches, ordered on April 24, 1816, that Protestants
should from now on hold an annual memorial service on the last Sunday
of the liturgical year to remember the dead of the liberation wars. This
Sunday became known as *Totensonntag* ("Sunday for the Dead")[6] and
was outfitted with theological reflections on eternal life (leading to it
later being also called *Ewigkeitssonntag*, "Sunday of Eternity"). Protestant
churches outside of Prussia quickly adopted this custom, which soon
added recollection also of those who had died within the congregation in
the course of the past year and finally all deceased relatives of congregants.
Their names were read aloud during the service to which their relatives
were specifically invited—and came. Still today, this is regarded as an
important event in German Protestant churches.

These religious commemorations of the dead were both common-
place and important, especially in the Prussian capital, Berlin, where
Israel Jacobson had established a private synagogue in 1815. Leading
Protestant theologians, like F. D. E. Schleiermacher, pastor at the main
Prussian church (the Dom in Berlin) and author of several sermons for
Totensonntag, were regular visitors in Jacobson's synagogue. So too was
Eduard Kley, himself, one of the two editors we saw above. In 1817, Kley
left Berlin for Hamburg and initiated, in the same year, the founding of
the "New Israelite Temple Association," which led to the building of the
Hamburg Temple on "Liberation Day" 1818 and the publication of the
first Reform prayer book to be used in services a year later. Bar mitzvah
was replaced by "confirmation," modeled after Prussian Protestant custom, and a memorial service called *Totenfeier* ("Service for the Dead")
was introduced. Like the liturgy of the Protestant *Totensonntag* ("Sunday
for the Dead"), the latter focused on eternal life and eternity in honor of
the dead.

The *Totenfeier* of the *Hamburg Temple Prayer Books*

The Jewish version of the memorial service in the *Hamburg Temple Prayer Book* of 1819 is celebrated on Yom Kippur just following *Musaf*[7]—picking up the theme of the traditional Yom Kippur service, which inserts the *Avodah* service and its accompanying martyrology into *Musaf.* The new memorial service thus enlarges the martyrology.

It starts with an unspecified congregational chant, which is followed by a long prayer by the prayer leader that presents a kind of philosophical treatise in prayer form about the eternal life of the soul (the German word used is *Geist*, which can also mean "intellect," "spirit," or "consciousness").[8] The prayer proposes that God, the creator of everything, made human beings higher than other creatures, but even humans are mortal—they are like grass. God's works, however, are eternal, so there must be something human that is eternal too. It is the *Geist* that is created in God's image and that returns to God. The souls of our parents and relatives are thus with God; only their bodies, the mortal shells of their souls, have died. With death, a new and even higher way of existence begins for those who lived an ethically good life. "Death is the gate that leads us out of darkness into clear light, where a new sun illuminates us." We should therefore look forward to the hour of our own death with calmness and joy. The prayer ends with the plea "Take us into the shadow of your wings, because You are the source of life and in your light we behold light."

Then the choir takes up these philosophical insights, singing in Hebrew a combination of biblical verses starting with the words *Adonai Mah Adam* ("God, what are humans?"—see p. 129). This is followed by a silent meditation, for which German texts are provided, starting with the words "I remember my dear father/mother/brother or other relative ... ," thus creating a new text focusing on memory, but without the traditional *Yizkor* vow to donate *tz'dakah*. The aim of the text is pure memory.[9]

The prayer leader then chants two further biblical quotations starting with *Mah Rav Tuv'kha* ("How great is your goodness") followed by the prayer *M'nuchah N'khonah* ("Proper repose")—an abridged version of the core text of the Sephardi *Hashkavah*. This is followed by a *Kaddish* in memory of the deceased, an altogether new version that abridges the *Kaddish* that is said at a graveside or after finishing the study of a Talmud tractate—a lesser known *Kaddish* of Jewish tradition and the only one that expressly mentions resurrection of the dead. In line with the prayer book's turn toward modern thought, however, it omits the traditional lines about the rebuilding of Jerusalem, the completion of the Temple, and the coming of the messiah, even though it retains reference to resurrection itself (*m'chayeh hametim*), a traditional phrase that is kept in the *Amidah* as well. It introduces this *Kaddish* with three very short Rabbinic texts, taken again from the Sephardi liturgy, all on the theme of the necessity to believe in an afterlife.[10]

Quite clearly, this new liturgical creation draws heavily on Sephardi texts and uses the Sephardi structure of the *Hashkavah*. This should not surprise, as the Hamburg Temple, having a Sephardi *chazzan*, introduced several other Sephardi features as well, among them Sephardi congregational tunes instead of Protestant hymn melodies, and Sephardi pronunciation for the Hebrew instead of the Ashkenazi one.

The form of this new memorial service was retained in further editions of the *Hamburg Temple Prayer Book*, but the introductory German text and its theology changed in the course of the years. In the second edition (1841), the introductory text contains not only philosophical thoughts about the eternity of the *Geist*, now also called "soul," but also has a stronger focus on ethics and justice. On this day, it teaches, where we ponder our sins, we also reflect on our vanity: "We are like a fragile shard, a fleeting shadow, a fleeing dream"; and we should therefore call to mind the final judgment: "How often is the wicked person happy, whereas the one, who keeps your [God's] word, is severely bent down." Death will bring the same end to both, but the souls of those who have trusted in God will rise upward and receive their due reward.[11] The purpose now is not just to remember the dead but also to provide moral strength and comfort to the living.

The *Totenfeier* in the sixth and last edition (1904) begins with two strophes of "Why are you downcast, my soul" (*Seele, was betrübst du dich*) as introductory song (see pp. 119–120). The German prayer now focuses completely on the memory of lost relatives. Any references to eternal soul or future justice are gone.

The decision to place this *Totenfeier* after *Musaf* was intentional. As we saw, it takes up the theme of death from the martyrology in the *Musaf Amidah*. In addition, the editors perceived how *Minchah* and especially *N'ilah* adopt an atmosphere of hope looking forward.[12] The new memorial service thus provides a transition from *Musaf* to the hope and confidence expressed in the last two services of the day.

The Orthodox Response

This Hamburg innovation was the starting point of extraordinary liturgi-cal creativity, leading finally to what we know today as the "*Yizkor* ser-vice." It spread quickly even to Orthodox synagogues—first in Hamburg, then elsewhere. Because the Orthodox development is less various, we turn to it first, before studying the variety of German liberal versions.

A thin supplement booklet (eight pages) to the prayer book for the Orthodox congregation in Hamburg, printed in 1844, contains *Shir Hakavod* ("Song of Glory") and *Hazkarat N'shamot*. Because this is within a separate booklet, one cannot say when it was used. *Shir Hakavod*, the main title of the book, is actually the name of a prayer that is said at the end of *Musaf* every Shabbat (see *My People's Prayer Book*, vol. 10, *Shabbat Morning*, pp. 177–93). The memorial service here consists basically of the three traditional *Yizkor* texts (*Yizkor* itself, *El Malei Rachamim*, and *Av Harachamim*; see p. 136)—including the promise of a donation for a father, mother, both parents, and/or relatives. A *Kaddish Yatom* ("Mourner's *Kaddish*") is handwritten (by a scribe in the style of Torah writing) on one of the last pages of this booklet.[13]

More transparent in terms of usage are Orthodox *machzorim* for Yom Kippur printed later in the nineteenth century. They, too, have an expanded memorial service for Yom Kippur, not the brief memorial that we associate with traditional liturgies prior to the modern era, but a fuller version as in Hamburg—usually within the Torah service (follow-ing the haftarah or the prayer for the government) or just after it (roughly where the traditional practice of *Yizkor* is embedded). A Berlin edition of the Orthodox siddur *S'fat Emet*, edited by J. Bleichrode (1906), for example, starts with some of the liberal introductory verses (in Hebrew): *Enosh k'chatzir* ("Human beings are like grass") and *Adonai Mah Adam* ("Adonai, what is man?") before the traditional *Yizkor* vow. *Adonai Mah Adam* quite frequently opens these memorial services, which include the traditional Ashkenazi Hebrew texts of *Av Harachamim*, *Yizkor*—without the vow, however—and *El Malei Rachamim*. Often verses from Psalm 16 are quoted, and sometimes also other psalms belonging to a house of mourning or funeral (such as Psalm 91 or Psalm 23). Even if it is placed in the usual place within the Torah service, these are now singled out as an independent liturgical unit with a special heading.

The Liberal Development of the *Seelenfeier*

Liberal synagogues created new German texts and experimented with the placement of the new service during Yom Kippur.

In 1848 the Hamburg memorial prayer had been introduced in Stuttgart in a prayer book for private devotion.[14] For public synagogue use, a *machzor* was published in 1861. Its *Seder Hazkarat N'shamot* (*Gebet für das Seelenheil der Hingeschiedenen*, "Prayer for the salvation of the souls of the deceased") begins with a German translation of *Mah adam* read by the rabbi, followed by a congregational hymn ("Choral"): "*Seele, was betrübst du dich*" ("Why are you downcast, my soul"), a creative elaboration of Psalm 42:6—written probably by Leopold Stein (1840). The text (which appears now along with music) casts some of the ideas of the Hamburg opening philosophical tractate on eternity into poetic form. In the nineteenth and early twentieth century, it will become the most commonly used opening chant, including in the North American *Union Prayer Book* (1894):

Seele, was betrübst du dich,	Why art thou cast down, my soul,
was ist dir so bang in mir!	Why disquieted in me?
Fühlst du nicht des Vaters Nähe,	Feel'st thou not the Father nigh,
der uns all' im Herzen	Him whose heart contains
trägst?	us all?
lebt kein Gott dir in der Höhe,	Lives no God for thee on high,
der da liebet, wenn er	Loving while His judgements
schlägt?	fall?
Aufwärts schau!	Look above!
Gott vertrau!	God is love!
Seele, was betrübst du dich!	Why art thou cast down my soul?
Himmelwärts	To the skies
heb' das Herz:	Turn thine eyes;
jede Thräne, die da fällt,	Every tear on earth that flows,
zählt der Lenker seiner	God the world's great Ruler
Welt.	knows.
Seele, was betrübst du dich,	Why art thou cast down my soul?
Was ist dir so bang in mir!	Why disquieted in me?

Hat dich Alles denn
  verlassen?
Stehest du denn ganz
  allein?
Kannst du nichts mit Lieb'
  umfassen,
Nennst du nichts auf Erden
  dein?
    Gott bleibt dir
    Für und für.
Seele, Seele, zage nicht!
    Fest und treu
    Gott dich weih':
Seine Treue niemals
  trügt,
Seine Liebe nie versiegt.

Seele, was bebrübst du dich,
Was ist dir so bang in mir!
Riß der Tod dir von dem
  Herzen
Heißgeliebte Wesen ab?
Sahest du sie unter
  Schmerzen
Sinken in das finstre
  Grab?
    Bannt der Tod.
Seele, sey getrost im
  Herrn!
    Weine nicht!
    Denn im Licht
Wandelt die verklärte Schaar,
Selig, selig immerdar.[15]

Was thy head in sorrow
bending
  'Neath the dreaded reaper's
  blight,
When thy loved ones were
descending
  In the darkness of death's
  night?
    Have no fear!
    God is near!
Be consoled, my soul, in God,
    Tears take flight,
    For in light
Walk thy dead on Heaven's
shore,
Blessed, blessed, evermore!

Why art thou cast down, my soul?
Why disquieted in me?
  Ever shall thy dead be living—
    From the darkness of the
    tomb
  God, thy Father, mercy-giving,
    Takes them to his heavenly
    home.
      Wilt thou trust
      God, the Just?
  Soul, my soul, be strong in
  God.
      God's with thee
      Eternally!
Then thy hopes shall be fulfilled
And thy heart's pain shall be
  stilled.[16]

The Stuttgart memorial service then provides a meditative prayer read by the rabbi. On a day devoted entirely to prayers for forgiveness and mercy, he pleads, how can we not think about those through whom we received all the good that God has granted us? All that we are and have, we owe to our parents: our lives, our faith, our knowledge. As we think about our loved ones, may their memory be for a blessing, meaning, may we continue their good work and be found worthy of them.

Then two passages in Hebrew starting with the word *yizkor* are read in silence in memory of a deceased father or mother. The Hebrew is the traditional *Yizkor* vow; the German translation, however, is not literal and omits mention of donations. This is followed by an unusual prayer addressed to the deceased relatives themselves—a remarkable example of a Jewish version for an intercession of the dead for the living.

> May you, my dear ones, look down from heaven in kindness and love, as you did before God took you away from me. Be pleased with my gratefulness, that I offer you today for all your loving parental care. Forgive me what I sinned against you in childish inconsiderateness. Remember me before God, pray for me and those with me, that God may keep away all pain and suffering. And when I myself will be called and get to my eternal resting place, then may your love welcome me.

The rabbi then asks God to remember all the faithful and just men and women of the community, including benefactors and supporters of the congregation, whose names are read aloud. Then follow the Hamburg texts *M'nuchah N'khonah* ("Proper repose") from the Sephardi *Hashkavah* and the introductory Rabbinic quotes for the *Kaddish* that we saw in Hamburg. Unlike Hamburg, however, the graveside *Kaddish* is replaced with a *Kaddish D'rabbanan* (the "*Kaddish* of the Rabbis" that accompanies study) that traditionally also is said by mourners. The timing of this service is different from Hamburg, too, in that it is postponed until just before *N'ilah*.

The Opening Reflections and Their Changing Theology

By the second half of the nineteenth century, vivid liturgical creativity is expended on other liberal versions of a memorial service for Yom Kippur. The term that became most common was the one introduced by Abraham Geiger: *Seelenfeier* ("Service for the Souls"), an abbreviation for the linguistically correct term *Seelengedaechtnisfeier* ("Service for the Memory of the Souls").

The services vary in their theology, which is expressed in the rabbi's prayers and in the German meditations. Most contain reflections on the vanity of life and the immortality of the soul (*Geist*).[17] "Yes, our faith teaches us about an eternal home ... an eternal life of the soul which death cannot touch, and to which the grave is only the dark, mysterious gate."[18] Most books also offer reflections to inspire memory and comfort[19]—a moving meditation about parental sacrifice and love, for instance. And they present moral conclusions from the fact that life is finite: we should live humbly; we should not set our hearts to material things; we should focus on our tasks and not waste time; we should live conscious of the fact that we may die unexpectedly. Some books also add spiritual implications that might follow from a moment of memorial: thinking about death makes us aware of our dependency on God. Others reflect about the apparent lack of justice in the world, with the expectation that future judgment will put right the things that look unjust now. The chosen themes are inspired by the *Un'taneh Tokef* (God's judgment, humanity's vanity, trust in God's faithfulness—see *Who by Fire, Who by Water—Un'taneh Tokef*), Greek philosophy (eternity of the soul), and the psychological need of memory and comfort.

The opening reflection is then followed by a choice of certain elements to guide the thought and memories, of which several are still in use in congregations of all denominations today.

The Typical Elements (in alphabetical order)

1. *Adonai Mah Adam* ("God, what are humans?"): A patchwork of quotes from Psalms 144:3–4, 90:3, 90:6; Deuteronomy 32:29; Psalms 49:18, 37:37, and 34:23—first introduced in Hamburg's opening philosophical reflection as a summary of the ideas of eternal

life. It may have been inspired by Solomon ibn Gabirol's hymn of the same name, chanted in the Sephardi service after the Yom Kippur *Musaf Amidah*.[20] Some books include only some of these Hamburg verses, but Psalm 144:3 always opens the meditation.

2. *Av Harachamim* ("**Father of mercy**"): A response to Jewish martyrdom during the Crusades.

3. *El Malei Rachamim* ("**God, full of compassion**"): Another prayer for Jewish martyrs, this one from the 1648 Chmielnicki massacres in Ukraine.

4. *Enosh k'chatzir* (**Psalm 103:15–17**): This psalm quotes God's thirteen attributes (verse 8) and God's mercifulness (verse 13). Some of its motives ("human beings are like grass") were familiar from *Un'taneh Tokef*. It became popular in the memorial service, first in Berlin but quickly elsewhere, because of a very moving choir composition by Louis Lewandowski (1821–94).[21]

5. *Kaddish*: Different versions of the *Kaddish* were used in the German liberal memorial services. A few used the graveside *Kaddish*, following the Hamburg Temple tradition. Others used *Kaddish D'rabbanan* ("Rabbis' *Kaddish*," the form of the *Kaddish* recited after study) or *Kaddish Yatom* ("Mourner's *Kaddish*").

6. *Kol Yisrael*: A selection from the Sephardi liturgy at the end of the Yom Kippur *Musaf* service (before *Ein Keloheinu*), citing verses from Rabbinic texts (Mishnah Sanhedrin 10:1; Talmud, Berakhot 17a; Mishnah Avot 2:16) that express the Jewish belief in eternal life. In the Hamburg Temple, it introduced the *Kaddish*.

7. *Mah Rav Tuv'kha*: A patchwork of quotes from the Sephardi *Hashkavah* liturgy (Psalms 31:20, 36:8–9, 149:5; *Ashrei* [Psalm 145]; Proverbs 3:13; and Ecclesiastes 7:1 for a man or Proverbs 31:30–31 for a woman).

8. *M'nuchah N'khonah*: An abridged version of the core of the Sephardi *Hashkavah*, a prayer for the rest of the soul, in which the name of the deceased is mentioned. The content is similar to the Ashkenazi *El Malei Rachamim*.

9. *Seele, was betrübst du dich* (see above): A congregational hymn written specifically for the memorial service, probably by Leopold Stein (1840), for which different melodies were in use.[22] The Anglo-American version begins with "Why art thou cast down, my soul?"

10. *Shiviti or Lachen samach libi* (**Psalm 16:8/9–11**): A psalm traditionally used in a house of mourning. Although Louis Lewandowski (1821–1894) composed a melody for verses 9–11,[23] the tune that became popular for verses 8–11 was composed by Solomon Sulzer (1804–1890).

11. *Yizkor*: The standard prayer but abridged to omit the vow to give *tz'dakah* and altered into a meditation intended to prompt memories of the deceased not by God but by the worshipers.

Style and Atmosphere

As important as *what* was said in these services were considerations of *how* to say it. Almost all liberal German prayer books accompanied the spoken and musical offerings with a moment of silence, in which to cherish memories of the deceased or meditate on words in the prayer book, often inspired by the traditional *Yizkor* text. These texts for silent meditation give an interesting insight into nineteenth-century social roles: fathers are remembered as active, having worked for our good and been our teachers; mothers appear as sacrificing themselves, caring and loving. Sometimes also the Hebrew text of the *Yizkor* is printed in an abridged version leaving out the *tz'dakah* vow. Prayer books often recommended that during this time of "silent memory," the organ might be played softly in the background.

After the silence (with or without soft organ play) allotted for personal meditation, some services called for the naming aloud of community benefactors and/or congregational members who died during the past year.

The German liberal memorial service generally featured concert-like choir and cantor performances, featuring expressive music of the European Romantic Period that created a variety of powerful emotions.

It became a widespread custom in Ashkenazi congregations that those whose parents are still alive rush to leave the sanctuary just before *Yizkor*, to return at its end or even only after it. They congregate outside or in other rooms of the synagogue, waiting and chatting. This custom sometimes leads to fierce emotional debates between the advocates of both sides. The reasons given for leaving are partly based on medieval suspicion transferred into the modern *Yizkor* service:[24] ghosts of death are around (especially *satan*) who could do harm to those whose parents are still alive.

The "evil eye" could bring mischief, meaning those who mourn may envy those who don't, or even the gaze of someone whose parents have died may harm the parents of his fellow.[25] Those with parents still alive would pay just empty lip service but would not honestly mean what they pray. Partly the arguments given are psychological: When the mourners stay among themselves, this lifts the holiness of the special occasion and creates a special intimate atmosphere. Non-mourners are not able to share the prayers said during *Yizkor*. Many people feel uncomfortable when addressing the issue of death and feel happier to skip the depressing mood of *Yizkor*. Children, who would see their parents sad, would share their sadness and thus not be able to enjoy the festive day.

The most important reason in the nineteenth century may have been that children should not see their parents crying. Showing emotions was something not common or desired in nineteenth-century Germany, and this may have been a reason for younger people to be made to leave. Against these emotional reasons it has to be stressed that there is no halakhic or rational reason to leave; rather, it is important for anybody to reflect about the fragility of life and also to share mourning and comfort as a whole congregation. Furthermore, the memorial is often not only for deceased relatives, but also for friends and teachers. In some congregations, *Yizkor* therefore begins with a comment by the rabbi or service leader about what the custom is in that particular congregation. When one is used to one custom, it feels very strange to act differently.

The Point of Time during Yom Kippur

The placement of the memorial service within the day's liturgy varied. Some congregations followed tradition in placing it within the morning Torah service: either before *Ashrei* and *Y'hall'lu* (Berlin New Synagogue),[26] following the traditional Sephardi placement of its *Hashkavah* memorial, or immediately after the Torah service ended (Geiger and liturgies based on him),[27] following Ashkenazi tradition. In the latter instance, it followed the sermon, which was central to German worship and could introduce the memorial service. As we saw, however, Hamburg began the custom of placing it between *Musaf* and *Minchah*,[28] in order to build on the martyrology of the *Musaf* service. Another choice in some places was within the Torah service of *Minchah*, before *Y'hall'lu* and after closing the ark.[29] This strategy helped abridge the overly lengthy *Shacharit* service but kept the tradition of associating *Yizkor* with the moment of reading Torah. It also may have helped bring people to the synagogue for *Minchah*, by which time most liberal Jews had usually abandoned the synagogue for the day. Finally, the memorial service can be found before *N'ilah* (Berlin Reform, Frankfurt, and others),[30] thus playing with the ideas of the end of life and the end of the day as metaphors for end and new beginning; this choice also attracted people to synagogue in the afternoon, albeit after *Minchah*.

How unfixed the developments in Germany remained can be seen from the *Einheitsgebetbuch* (the German equivalent of a "*Union Prayer Book*") from 1929 (second edition, 1931). Unable still to reach agreement on a unified form, the editors include an appendix[31] with "*Seelenfeier* A" according to the custom in Frankfurt, "*Seelenfeier* B" according to the Berlin customs, and "*Seelenfeier* C" with the Geiger/Joel-Breslau customs. The *Einheitsgebetbuch* also provides page numbers of different places during Yom Kippur where the *Seelenfeier* is to be inserted: within the *Shacharit* Torah service, after the haftarah and before the sermon; before or within the *Minchah* Torah service; after *Minchah*, framed by a poem by Yehuda Halevi (*Yah Shimcha*); and before *N'ilah*.

The third edition of the *Einheitsgebetbuch* (1938)—a rare edition today, as the reprints for German immigrant congregations after the war were made from the second edition—offers a version basically identical with "*Seelenfeier* B" of the previous editions but added *Shiviti* before *Kaddish*. It appears at the end of the Torah service in the afternoon service (*Minchah*), before *Ashrei* and the returning of the scroll.[32]

৩৩৩৩

PART III
The Liturgy

The Traditional *Yizkor* Service

Translation and Commentary by
Dr. Joel M. Hoffman

Adonai Mah Adam
("God, What Are Humans ... ")

[1]God, what are humans that You should acknowledge them, mortals that You should consider them? [2]Humans are like a breath, their days like a passing shadow. [3]In the morning they blossom, renewed; at night they fade and wither. [4]So teach us to count our days that we might gain wisdom.

¹יְיָ, מָה אָדָם וַתֵּדָעֵהוּ, בֶּן
אֱנוֹשׁ וַתְּחַשְּׁבֵהוּ.
²אָדָם לַהֶבֶל דָּמָה, יָמָיו כְּצֵל
עוֹבֵר.
³בַּבֹּקֶר יָצִיץ וְחָלָף, לָעֶרֶב
יְמוֹלֵל וְיָבֵשׁ.
⁴לִמְנוֹת יָמֵינוּ כֵּן הוֹדַע, וְנָבִא
לְבַב חָכְמָה.

---

[1]*Humans*: Hebrew, "person," commonly, if wrongly, translated more narrowly as "man." We use the plural here to avoid "him/her" and other awkward phrasings. The underlying issue is that Hebrew has both singular and plural forms that are gender-neutral, while in English we are limited to the plural if we don't wish to specify gender.

[3]*They*: From Psalm 90, in which the words originally compare people to grass that "blossoms, is renewed," and so on.

[4]*Wisdom*: Literally, "a wise heart." But in Hebrew the "heart" (*levav*) refers both to emotion and to intellect, making the English translation "heart" a poor choice.

⁵Mark those who are innocent and observe those who are upright, for a future awaits people of peace. ⁶For surely God will redeem me from Sheol, taking me in. ⁷My flesh and heart fail, but God is my heart's strength and my lot forever. ⁸Dirt returns to cover the earth as it was, and the spirit returns to God who gave it.

שְׁמׇר־תָּם וּרְאֵה יָשָׁר, כִּי ⁵
אַחֲרִית לְאִישׁ שָׁלוֹם.
אַךְ אֱלֹהִים יִפְדֶּה נַפְשִׁי מִיַּד ⁶
שְׁאוֹל, כִּי יִקָּחֵנִי, סֶלָה.
כָּלָה שְׁאֵרִי וּלְבָבִי, צוּר לְבָבִי ⁷
וְחֶלְקִי אֱלֹהִים לְעוֹלָם.
וְיָשֹׁב הֶעָפָר עַל הָאָרֶץ ⁸
כְּשֶׁהָיָה, וְהָרוּחַ תָּשׁוּב אֶל
הָאֱלֹהִים אֲשֶׁר נְתָנָהּ.

⁵*Mark*: From the Hebrew *shamar*, which often means "to guard." Here, in parallel with "observe," "mark" makes more sense.

⁵*Future awaits people of peace*: Or perhaps, "people's future is peace."

⁶*Redeem me from Sheol*: "Sheol" is part of the psalmist's imagery of death, as is the notion of being "redeemed" from it (see J. Hoffman, pp. 162–165).

⁶*Taking me in*: Or "taking me up."

⁷*Heart*: Here we use "heart" for the Hebrew *levav* because the Hebrew refers to the actual organ. Later in the line, we are forced to use "heart's strength," to preserve the poetic contrast, even though just "strength" would be more accurate in English.

⁸*Dirt*: Commonly, "dust."

Yizkor Elohim
("May God Remember ... ")
For a Father

[1]May God remember the soul of my father and teacher ... who has gone to his eternal rest. [2]In return for my pledge of charity on his behalf, may his soul be bound up in the bundle of life with the souls of Abraham, Isaac, and Jacob, Sarah, Rebecca, Rachel, and Leah, and with the other righteous men and women in paradise. Amen.

יִזְכּוֹר אֱלֹהִים נִשְׁמַת אָבִי [1]
מוֹרִי ... שֶׁהָלַךְ לְעוֹלָמוֹ.
בַּעֲבוּר שֶׁאֲנִי נוֹדֵר צְדָקָה [2]
בַּעֲדוֹ, בִּשְׂכַר זֶה, תְּהֵא נַפְשׁוֹ
צְרוּרָה בִּצְרוֹר הַחַיִּים עִם
נִשְׁמוֹת אַבְרָהָם יִצְחָק וְיַעֲקֹב,
שָׂרָה רִבְקָה רָחֵל וְלֵאָה, וְעִם
שְׁאָר צַדִּיקִים וְצִדְקָנִיּוֹת
שֶׁבְּגַן עֵדֶן. אָמֵן.

[1]*Eternal rest*: Literally, "his *olam*," often translated either "world" or "eternity," because the Hebrew word refers to both unending space and time. Here we prefer "eternal rest," the English phrase that is commonly used in connection with death (see J. Hoffman, pp. 162–165).
[2]*Bundle*: Commonly, "bond." But the point of the Hebrew is that the verb and noun match closely. In spite of the similarity of sound between "bound" and "bond," the two words mean different things. In English, things are bound into a bundle, not into a bond.
[2]*Paradise*: Literally, "the Garden of Eden" (see J. Hoffman, pp. 162–165).

For a Mother

[3]May God remember the soul of my mother and teacher ... who has gone to her eternal rest. [4]In return for my pledge of charity on her behalf, may her soul be bound up in the bundle of life with the souls of Abraham, Isaac, and Jacob, Sarah, Rebecca, Rachel, and Leah, and with the other righteous men and women in paradise. Amen.

³יִזְכּוֹר אֱלֹהִים נִשְׁמַת אִמִּי מוֹרָתִי ... שֶׁהָלְכָה לְעוֹלָמָהּ. ⁴בַּעֲבוּר שֶׁאֲנִי נוֹדֵר צְדָקָה בַּעֲדָהּ, בִּשְׂכַר זֶה, תְּהֵא נַפְשָׁהּ צְרוּרָה בִּצְרוֹר הַחַיִּים עִם נִשְׁמוֹת אַבְרָהָם יִצְחָק וְיַעֲקֹב, שָׂרָה רִבְקָה רָחֵל וְלֵאָה, וְעִם שְׁאָר צַדִּיקִים וְצִדְקָנִיּוֹת שֶׁבְּגַן עֵדֶן. אָמֵן.

For a Husband

[5]May God remember the soul of my dear husband ... who has gone to his eternal rest. [6]In return for my pledge of charity on his behalf, may his soul be bound up in the bundle of life with the souls of Abraham, Isaac, and Jacob, Sarah, Rebecca, Rachel, and Leah, and with the other righteous men and women in paradise. Amen.

⁵יִזְכּוֹר אֱלֹהִים נִשְׁמַת בַּעְלִי הַיָּקָר ... שֶׁהָלַךְ לְעוֹלָמוֹ. ⁶בַּעֲבוּר שֶׁאֲנִי נוֹדֶרֶת צְדָקָה בַּעֲדוֹ, בִּשְׂכַר זֶה, תְּהֵא נַפְשׁוֹ צְרוּרָה בִּצְרוֹר הַחַיִּים עִם נִשְׁמוֹת אַבְרָהָם יִצְחָק וְיַעֲקֹב, שָׂרָה רִבְקָה רָחֵל וְלֵאָה, וְעִם שְׁאָר צַדִּיקִים וְצִדְקָנִיּוֹת שֶׁבְּגַן עֵדֶן. אָמֵן.

For a Wife

[7]May God remember the soul of my dear wife ... who has gone to her eternal rest. [8]In return for my pledge of charity on her behalf, may her soul be bound up in the bundle of life with the souls of Abraham, Isaac, and Jacob, Sarah, Rebecca, Rachel, and Leah, and with the other righteous men and women in paradise. Amen.

יִזְכֹּר אֱלֹהִים נִשְׁמַת אִשְׁתִּי[7] הַיְקָרָה ... שֶׁהָלְכָה לְעוֹלָמָהּ. בַּעֲבוּר שֶׁאֲנִי נוֹדֵר צְדָקָה[8] בַּעֲדָהּ, בִּשְׂכַר זֶה, תְּהֵא נַפְשָׁהּ צְרוּרָה בִּצְרוֹר הַחַיִּים עִם נִשְׁמוֹת אַבְרָהָם יִצְחָק וְיַעֲקֹב, שָׂרָה רִבְקָה רָחֵל וְלֵאָה, וְעִם שְׁאָר צַדִּיקִים וְצִדְקָנִיּוֹת שֶׁבְּגַן עֵדֶן. אָמֵן.

For Martyrs

[9]May God remember the souls of the blameless holy ones who were killed, slaughtered, burned, drowned, or strangled sanctifying God's name. [10]In return for our pledge of charity on behalf of their memory, may their souls be bound up in the bundle of life with the souls of Abraham, Isaac, and Jacob, Sarah, Rebecca, Rachel, and Leah, and with the other righteous men and women in paradise. Amen.

יִזְכֹּר אֱלֹהִים נִשְׁמוֹת[9] הַקְּדוֹשִׁים וְהַטְּהוֹרִים שֶׁנֶּהֶרְגוּ, שֶׁנִּשְׁחֲטוּ וְשֶׁנִּשְׂרְפוּ, וְשֶׁנִּטְבְּעוּ וְשֶׁנֶּחְנְקוּ עַל קִדּוּשׁ הַשֵּׁם. בַּעֲבוּר[10] שֶׁנּוֹדְרִים צְדָקָה בְּעַד הַזְכָּרַת נִשְׁמוֹתֵיהֶם, בִּשְׂכַר זֶה, תִּהְיֶינָה נַפְשׁוֹתֵיהֶם צְרוּרוֹת בִּצְרוֹר הַחַיִּים עִם נִשְׁמוֹת אַבְרָהָם יִצְחָק וְיַעֲקֹב, שָׂרָה רִבְקָה רָחֵל וְלֵאָה, וְעִם שְׁאָר צַדִּיקִים וְצִדְקָנִיּוֹת שֶׁבְּגַן עֵדֶן. אָמֵן.

El Malei Rachamim
("God, Full of Compassion ... ")
For a Man

[1]God, full of compassion, dwelling on high: under divine wings, among the holy and blameless who shine with the radiance of the sky, grant perfect repose to the soul of ... , who has gone to his eternal rest. [2]In return for the pledge of charity on behalf of his memory, may he rest in paradise. [3]Therefore, may the master of mercy protect him under his protective wings forever, and bind his soul in the bundle of life. [4]God is his inheritance. [5]May he rest on his bed in peace. And let us say: Amen.

[1]אֵל מָלֵא רַחֲמִים, שׁוֹכֵן בַּמְּרוֹמִים, הַמְצֵא מְנוּחָה נְכוֹנָה תַּחַת כַּנְפֵי הַשְּׁכִינָה, בְּמַעֲלוֹת קְדוֹשִׁים וּטְהוֹרִים כְּזֹהַר הָרָקִיעַ מַזְהִירִים, אֶת נִשְׁמַת... שֶׁהָלַךְ לְעוֹלָמוֹ. [2]בַּעֲבוּר שֶׁנָּדְרוּ צְדָקָה בְּעַד הַזְכָּרַת נִשְׁמָתוֹ, בְּגַן עֵדֶן תְּהֵא מְנוּחָתוֹ. [3]לָכֵן בַּעַל הָרַחֲמִים יַסְתִּירֵהוּ בְּסֵתֶר כְּנָפָיו לְעוֹלָמִים, וְיִצְרוֹר בִּצְרוֹר הַחַיִּים אֶת נִשְׁמָתוֹ. [4]יְיָ הוּא נַחֲלָתוֹ. [5]וְיָנוּחַ עַל מִשְׁכָּבוֹ בְּשָׁלוֹם, וְנֹאמַר אָמֵן.

[1]*Divine*: Literally, "of the *Shekhinah*" (see p. 42).
[1]*Repose*: We avoid "rest" here in English because we'll need "rest" for a different Hebrew word as part of "eternal rest," immediately below.

For a Woman

[6]God, full of compassion, dwelling on high: under divine wings, among the holy and blameless who shine with the radiance of the sky, grant perfect repose to the soul of ... , who has gone to her eternal rest. [7]In return for the pledge of charity on behalf of her memory, may she rest in paradise. [8]Therefore, may the master of mercy protect her under his protective wings forever, and bind her soul in the bundle of life. [9]God is her inheritance. [10]May she rest on her bed in peace. And let us say: Amen.

[6]אֵל מָלֵא רַחֲמִים, שׁוֹכֵן בַּמְּרוֹמִים, הַמְצֵא מְנוּחָה נְכוֹנָה תַּחַת כַּנְפֵי הַשְּׁכִינָה, בְּמַעֲלוֹת קְדוֹשִׁים וּטְהוֹרִים כְּזֹהַר הָרָקִיעַ מַזְהִירִים, אֶת נִשְׁמַת... שֶׁהָלְכָה לְעוֹלָמָהּ. [7]בַּעֲבוּר שֶׁנָּדְרוּ צְדָקָה בְּעַד הַזְכָּרַת נִשְׁמָתָהּ, בְּגַן עֵדֶן תְּהֵא מְנוּחָתָהּ. [8]לָכֵן בַּעַל הָרַחֲמִים יַסְתִּירֶהָ בְּסֵתֶר כְּנָפָיו לְעוֹלָמִים, וְיִצְרוֹר בִּצְרוֹר הַחַיִּים אֶת נִשְׁמָתָהּ. [9]יְיָ הוּא נַחֲלָתָהּ. [10]וְתָנוּחַ עַל מִשְׁכָּבָהּ בְּשָׁלוֹם, וְנֹאמַר אָמֵן.

Av Harachamim
("May the Father of Mercy ... ")

[1]In his great mercy, may the father
of mercy who dwells on high in
mercy attend to the righteous, the
upright and the honest, the holy
communities that gave their lives
in the name of God's holiness.
[2]Beloved friends in life, even in
death they were not parted.
[3]Swifter than eagles, stronger than
lions, they did their Master's will,
their Rock's desire. [4]Our God will
remember them favorably among
the other righteous of the world,
and will avenge his servants'
spilled blood, as it is written in the
Torah of Moses, the man of God,

אַב הָרַחֲמִים שׁוֹכֵן מְרוֹמִים.
בְּרַחֲמָיו הָעֲצוּמִים. הוּא
יִפְקֹד בְּרַחֲמִים. הַחֲסִידִים
וְהַיְשָׁרִים וְהַתְּמִימִים.
קְהִלּוֹת הַקֹּדֶשׁ שֶׁמָּסְרוּ
נַפְשָׁם עַל קְדֻשַּׁת הַשֵּׁם.

הַנֶּאֱהָבִים וְהַנְּעִימִים
בְּחַיֵּיהֶם וּבְמוֹתָם לֹא
נִפְרָדוּ. מִנְּשָׁרִים קַלּוּ
מֵאֲרָיוֹת גָּבֵרוּ. לַעֲשׂוֹת
רְצוֹן קוֹנָם וְחֵפֶץ צוּרָם:
יִזְכְּרֵם אֱלֹהֵינוּ לְטוֹבָה.
עִם שְׁאָר צַדִּיקֵי עוֹלָם.
וְיִנְקוֹם נִקְמַת דַּם עֲבָדָיו
הַשָּׁפוּךְ: כַּכָּתוּב בְּתוֹרַת
מֹשֶׁה אִישׁ הָאֱלֹהִים.

[1]*In his great mercy*: For more information and translation notes, see *My People's Prayer Book Vol. 4, Seder K'riat Hatorah (The Torah Service)*, pp. 179, 181–182.

5"Nations of the world, make his people joyful, for He avenges the blood of his servants, renders vengeance to his foes, and forgives his land, his people." 6And by your servants the prophets it is written, 7"I will cleanse their blood which I have not yet cleaned. 8Adonai dwells in Zion." 9And in the holy writing it is also said, 10"Why should the nations say, 11"Where is their God?' 12Before our eyes let the vengeance of your servants' spilled blood be known among the nations." 13And it is also said, 14"The one who demands blood remembers them; He does not forget the cry of the humble." 15And it is said, 16"He judges the nations, filling it with bodies, crushing heads across the land. 17He will drink from the stream by the path, and therefore raise heads."

הַרְנִינוּ גוֹיִם עַמּוֹ כִּי דַם 5
עֲבָדָיו יִקּוֹם. וְנָקָם יָשִׁיב
לְצָרָיו וְכִפֶּר אַדְמָתוֹ עַמּוֹ.
וְעַל יְדֵי עֲבָדֶיךָ הַנְּבִיאִים 6
כָּתוּב לֵאמֹר. וְנִקֵּיתִי דָּמָם 7
לֹא נִקֵּיתִי. וַיְיָ שֹׁכֵן בְּצִיּוֹן: 8
וּבְכִתְבֵי הַקֹּדֶשׁ נֶאֱמַר. לָמָּה 10 9
יֹאמְרוּ הַגּוֹיִם אַיֵּה אֱלֹהֵיהֶם. 11
יִוָּדַע בַּגּוֹיִם לְעֵינֵינוּ. נִקְמַת 12
דַּם עֲבָדֶיךָ הַשָּׁפוּךְ: וְאוֹמֵר. 13
כִּי דֹרֵשׁ דָּמִים אוֹתָם זָכָר. 14
לֹא שָׁכַח צַעֲקַת עֲנָוִים:
וְאוֹמֵר. יָדִין בַּגּוֹיִם מָלֵא 16 15
גְוִיּוֹת מָחַץ רֹאשׁ עַל אֶרֶץ
רַבָּה: מִנַּחַל בַּדֶּרֶךְ יִשְׁתֶּה 17
עַל כֵּן יָרִים רֹאשׁ.

ௐ

PART IV
Interpretations and Reflections

What Happens When We Die

INTIMATIONS OF IMMORTALITY

Rabbi Lawrence A. Englander, CM, DHL

As the years go by, I find that it takes me longer and longer to get through the *Yizkor* prayers. More members of my family have died, and I want to pause and remember something about each of them. More of my friends, too, have left this life, and I still cherish the relationships I had with them. It takes some time to recount all their names—and even longer to express my feeling for them.

When I was younger, during *Yizkor* services I used to wonder: Where do people go after they die? Are they aware of what is happening to us on earth? Can we still communicate with each other in some way? Now my musings concentrate upon another question: where is the justice in death? Our lives come to a halt without giving us a chance to tie up loose ends, and we can't help but wonder what will happen to everything we have worked for. As Kohelet mused, "Alas, the wise person dies, just like the fool" (Ecclesiastes 2:16).

To respond to these questions, most religions have a doctrine of the afterlife. In Rabbinic tradition, this doctrine centers around the *olam haba*, which can be translated as "the world to come" or "the life to

---

Rabbi Lawrence A. Englander, CM, DHL, has been rabbi of Solel Congregation of Mississauga, Ontario, since its inception in 1973. He is author of *The Mystical Study of Ruth*, former editor of the *CCAR Journal*, and a contributor to *We Have Sinned: Sin and Confession in Judaism— Ashamnu and* Al Chet (Jewish Lights).

141

come." According to theologian Neil Gillman,[1] the Rabbis combined two themes that they found in Greco-Roman philosophy: the resurrection of the body and the immortality of the soul. Thus many Jews today believe that our bodies will be restored to new life in the days of the messiah, and even more believe that the soul continues to exist after the body's death. In the mystical tradition of the Kabbalah, we find the additional teaching that, after death, each soul becomes reincarnated to create another human life. These beliefs have given comfort to mourners by assuring them that their loved ones continue to live on, even aware, perhaps, of what is happening in this world.

Caring deeply about these views, I have arrived at my own perspective on the Jewish theory of *olam haba*. I base it on three scientific insights.

The first relates to a scientific discussion regarding the origin of consciousness in the universe. One side claims that the universe is made up of matter and energy and that consciousness develops as an "epiphenomenon," a by-product of the evolution of increasingly complex life forms. The other side, however, suggests that mind or consciousness is hardwired into the universe. As the American scientist George Wald writes, "Mind, rather than emerging as a late outgrowth in the evolution of life, has existed always, as the matrix, the source and condition of physical reality.... *The stuff of which reality is composed is mind-stuff.*"[2] Following this latter argument, I conclude that just as there is *physical* energy in the universe, so too, we must allow for the possibility of *psychic* energy. This possibility remains speculative because, as yet, we have no instruments with which to measure it.

What we already know about physical energy yields the second insight. It is based on the first law of thermodynamics: energy can be neither created nor destroyed but can be transferred from one form to another. For example, when we bang a nail with a hammer, the kinetic energy of the hammer becomes transferred to the nail in the forms of motion and heat. If we apply this law to psychic energy, it gives us reason to argue that it, too, remains a constant. In other words, human consciousness—what our Jewish tradition calls the soul—is immortal.

This brings us to the third insight. In any living organism—and most certainly in human beings—mind is not a simple entity. Rather, consciousness is related to a complex system of nerve impulses taking place within a network of cells. In the same way, we can regard the soul as a community of psychic parts that parallels the material components that we see, touch, and feel as the body. When body and soul function in harmony, there is life and health. When these energy communities disintegrate, the result is death. It follows that death is the dislocation of the materiality we call body from the psychic components we call soul. But because energy is indestructible, both physical and psychic energy remain, albeit in different forms.

Let me clarify what I am saying with the following metaphor. When someone dies—let's call her Rivka[3]—the body gives off physical energy in the process of decomposition. The soul energy, for its part, returns to a central reservoir of life—a cosmic soup, if you wish—thereby conserving all of Rivka's "psychic cells." As another life begins, it is as if a ladle dips into that soup to create a new soul. Some of those cells will come from Rivka, but the new soul community that is formed will be unique. That is why no two human beings are alike, because we each possess a distinct combination of psychic cells.

For me, this view is more attractive than imagining that my body will suddenly emerge from the ground in some distant age. But my view also involves a sacrifice. What makes each of us a living person involves the combination of body cells and soul cells. The sensations we experience and the emotions we feel all come to us through the body. Moreover, the particular characteristics of our bodies play a large role in forming our personalities. Because the body decays away after death, and because the soul becomes dispersed to form other lives, I believe that none of us will persist as a distinct identity after death; nor will we remain conscious of what happens on earth.

Nevertheless, I believe that there is a way in which Rivka does continue to live, both in this world and in the *olam haba*. In this world, the experiences, insights, and virtues accumulated in her soul cells will return to enrich new lives. And as long as Rivka herself is remembered by others, as long as we think and speak of her, she will continue to live. That is why it is a custom of Jewish scholars to cite authorities in the present tense: not to say "Rashi said" but rather "Rashi *says*." This is due to a Talmudic teaching that each time we state an insight in the name of a teacher, that person's lips vibrate from the grave.[4]

But memory eventually fades, and even our greatest deeds are ultimately buried in the sands of time. Most of our names will disappear from memory within one hundred years. Is there someplace we go where we are never forgotten? I believe there is. A passage in the Mishnah states that each time a person dies—no matter how good or evil, no matter how famous or obscure—the *Shekhinah* feels pain as if a limb had been severed.[5] God grieves with us when a loved one dies, knowing that no one like this person will ever exist again. Yet the memory of this beloved soul is stored forever in the memory of God and thereby becomes a part of the divine yearning for completion. Each life, stamped indelibly upon God's memory, plays its own role in bringing the world a step closer to messianic fulfillment.

In the liturgy of the Days of Awe, we pray that we may be inscribed in the book of life. What I am suggesting is that all human beings write their own book during their lifetime, beginning a new chapter with each New Year. When this life comes to an end, the book is stored in the divine library, where God preserves and reads every single volume. Although we may last but a short time in this world, in the *olam haba* we remain cherished in the memory of God—*Yizkor Elohim*.

A story from the Talmud[6] may bring this idea into focus. There lived a saintly man named Rabbi Baroka. Because of his righteous conduct, he once received a heavenly visit from the prophet Elijah. At the time, he was strolling through the marketplace. He asked Elijah, "Is there anyone here who merits a special portion in the world to come?" The prophet pointed to two men doing juggling acts in a corner of the square. Rabbi Baroka went over to them and asked, "What is your occupation?" They replied, "We are jesters. When we see people depressed, we cheer them up; and when we see two people quarreling, we work hard to make peace between them." The names of those two jesters have long been forgotten, but their model of compassion remains an inspiration for us today. Might it also be possible that their antics have left a smile imprinted upon the face of God?

᧩ᚹᛞᛞᛞᚹ᧩

The Age of Amusement

Rabbi Edward Feinstein

The gentleman died and his family asked me to officiate his funeral. So we agreed to meet, his children and I, to prepare the service. Sitting around the spacious dining room table I asked them, "Tell me about your father." After a long silence one of the sons volunteered, "Dad loved golf."

"Golf is good," I responded. "What else did he love? What were his passions?"

"Golf," they all agreed, "just golf."

"Just golf? What did he dream of? What were his values, his causes?"

"Well, he always wanted to live on a golf course ... "

So I prepared a eulogy all about golf. (It's not so hard to do: eighteen is *chai*.) All the while, I felt the tragedy: How can a human life be so small ... reduced to a game, to golf?

Henry David Thoreau proclaimed that "men today live lives of quiet desperation." He's wrong. Today we live lives of amused distraction. The philosopher Søren Kierkegaard proposed that no one could live the aesthetic, pleasure-seeking life forever because it must eventually grow dull. The pleasure seeker falls into a cycle of addiction. To hold our interest, each pleasure needs a bigger one to follow. This is the lament of Kohelet in Ecclesiastes, "I said to myself, Come I will treat you to merriment. Taste mirth! That, too, I found was futile" (2:1).

Rabbi Edward Feinstein is senior rabbi of Valley Beth Shalom in Encino, California. He is an instructor in the Ziegler Rabbinical School of American Jewish University and the Wexner Heritage Program. He is the author of *Tough Questions Jews Ask: A Young Adult's Guide to Building a Jewish Life* (Jewish Lights) and *Capturing the Moon*, and the editor of *Jews and Judaism in the 21st Century: Human Responsibilities, the Presence of God, and the Future of the Covenant* (Jewish Lights). He contributed to *Who by Fire, Who by Water*—Un'taneh Tokef and *We Have Sinned: Sin and Confession in Judaism*—Ashamnu *and* Al Chet (both Jewish Lights).

American culture has accomplished what neither Kierkegaard nor Kohelet could conceive. We have cultivated a culture of such powerful distractions, entertainments, diversions, that today one actually can fill a lifetime with amusement ... with golf.

When I was a kid, there were seven channels on the TV. Once you surveyed those seven and found nothing interesting, you turned the set off. Today, there are enough TV channels that you can spend the entire evening not actually watching anything, but just flipping through the channels—surfing the dial. And if not TV, there are all the treasures of the Internet. A thousand years ago, Western culture knew an age of faith, so the church was the central architectural feature of a town. Five hundred years ago, we began an age of industry, and the factory was the town's notable structure. In today's age of amusement, the mall and its cineplex is a town's most important public place.

Paul Tillich, the Protestant theologian, argued that every person has a God. "God" he defined as each person's "object of ultimate concern." But what if the object of ultimate concern is precisely not to have an object of ultimate concern? What kind of human being does that leave?

In the age of amusement, *Yizkor* is dangerous. *Yizkor* reminds us of our finitude—the startling truth that not one of us has an infinite number of tomorrows. *Yizkor* demands that we make something eternal of our lives; it compels our attachment to matters of eternal significance. *Yizkor* forces us to focus on the meaning and purpose of life, to align our personal lives with narratives that outlast a single life. The spirit of *Yizkor* embarrasses us. It undermines amusement ... it gets in the way of golf.

There comes a moment when the diet of amusement ceases to satisfy and nourish. There comes a time when we discover that life is difficult, that it is a struggle to live with integrity and pursue justice. With all its tears, *Yizkor* is the spark that may yet kindle a search for wisdom. With all its sadness, *Yizkor* may reawaken courage. Gathering in the lives of those who came before us—with all their blessings and all their shortcomings—may give us the resolution to bind ourselves to lives of higher purpose and accept God's call to "choose life."

༺༻

Remembering through Forgetting

Yizkor as Unshared Experience

Rabbi Shoshana Boyd Gelfand

"As long as we are alive, our memories remain wonderfully volatile. In their mercurial mirror, we see ourselves."[1]

I am not a neuroscientist. Nonetheless, I am intrigued by the light that research on brain plasticity may shed on theology and religion. I am especially fascinated by how the human brain processes information to provide us with a continuous sense of self through memory.

From the Bible onward, Jewish literature has focused intently on the subject of memory, and because memory and identity through time are so central to being a Jew, Jewish tradition has been extraordinarily sensitive to what scientists are now discovering about the brain. It is as if the Rabbis intuitively grasped certain fundamental truths that are only now being fleshed out and elaborated by modern brain research.

The verb *lizkor* ("to remember") appears no fewer than 228 times in the Bible, referring to elements as diverse as Shabbat, Miriam's leprosy,

---

Rabbi Shoshana Boyd Gelfand received her rabbinic ordination in 1993 at The Jewish Theological Seminary in New York. She has served as chief executive of the United Kingdom Movement for Reform Judaism and prior to that was vice president of the Wexner Heritage Foundation in New York. Currently she is director of JHub, an operating program of the London-based Pears Foundation. She contributed to *All These Vows*—Kol Nidre and *We Have Sinned: Sin and Confession in Judaism*—Ashamnu *and* Al Chet (both Jewish Lights).

and Amalek's attack on the Israelites.[2] The Torah repeatedly refers *mitzvot* back to the rationale "because you were slaves in Egypt," thereby drawing on collective memory to promote contemporary behavior in general and empathy for others in particular.

But Jewish tradition understood that simply mentioning past events, and even commanding the abstract remembering of them, are not enough to solidify a memory. Embedding memory indelibly in the brain requires intentional action. As Joshua Foer notes in his account of his bid to become 2009 USA Memory Champion:

> In Judaism, observance and remembering are interchangeable concepts, two words that are really one.... For Jews, remembering is not merely a cognitive process, but one that is necessarily active. Other people remember by thinking. Jews remember by doing.[3]

So our holiday rituals are not only vehicles for sharing communal celebrations, but also a mechanism to revisit our deepest values through shared memories: the Exodus from Egypt, the revelation at Sinai, the creation of the world. None of us was physically present at these events, but reenacting them in communal rituals embeds them as part of our collective autobiographical memory. The assertion that we all stood at Sinai is not just some whimsical notion. It is a profound statement that all Jews are bound together in a communal sense of memory.

This focus on communal memory makes the *Yizkor* ceremony all the more striking; it is the exception that proves the rule, for *Yizkor* is the one moment in the liturgical calendar when individual, not communal, memory is what matters. Instead of collectively conjuring our communal past, each of us stands personally consumed by our own singular memories of relatives and friends who have died. Unlike a funeral or shivah, where our individual memories are shared publicly as a collective mosaic of the person we are remembering, *Yizkor* provides a communal space for individual reflection and inward memorializing. Yet Jewish tradition provides no express reason behind this liturgical anomaly. Why is it that a religion so fully dedicated to communal memory makes this regular exception when it comes to *Yizkor*?

Neuroscience tentatively provides a reason. Here is Joshua Foer again:

Memories are not static. Somehow, as memories age, their complexion changes. Each time we think about a memory, we integrate it more deeply into our web of other memories, and therefore make it more stable and less likely to be dislodged. But in the process, we also transform the memory, and reshape it—sometimes to the point that our memories of events bear only a passing resemblance to what actually happened.[4]

Apparently, the very act of remembering alters the memory itself!

Neuroscientist Eric Kandel goes even further. Long-term memories, he says, actually change their molecular structure over time. One class of memory molecules, prions, are a class of anomalous proteins. They seem to be virtually indestructible, yet surprisingly "plastic" in their ability to change shape easily. As Jonah Lehrer describes it:

Every time we conjure up our pasts, the branches of our recollections become malleable again. While the prions that mark our memories are virtually immortal, their dendritic details are always being altered, shuttling between the poles of remembering and forgetting. The past is at once perpetual and ephemeral.[5]

Neuroscience is describing what we all know from experience: memory is inaccurate, malleable, imperfect. In recalling a memory, we do not replay an exact mental recording of an actual event. Rather, we draw on our subjective experience of that event, and the very act of doing the recalling physically alters the brain so as to change the memory itself. Ironically, the very act of remembering changes what is remembered. This may be the key to understanding why Jewish tradition created a memorial ritual that is profoundly individual.

In contrast to the *Yizkor* liturgy, the Jewish rituals of death and mourning encourage us to share our memories publicly. At the funeral, we listen to eulogies; then, during the seven days of mourning (shivah), we show visitors our photographs and other documentation as external props for conjuring the presence of the person who has died. Our collective memories create a composite of the person who has recently disappeared from our midst. The psychological logic behind this memorializing practice is unmistakable: having just experienced a loss, we seize whatever precious imprint we have of the person who has died as a treasure to hang onto. During shivah, we work together to solidify our impression of the person we have lost.

Yizkor works differently. It is not intended as a time to reflect our memories accurately; rather, it is designed to allow those memories to adapt. Without the corrective of actual physical evidence or the balance provided by others' recollections, *Yizkor* provides us our own private *ongoing* relationship with a loved one. It encourages an evolution of that relationship as opposed to allowing it to be frozen in time. Remembering someone over and over again enhances the parts of that relationship that prove sustaining but allows us to forget those characteristics that are not.

In some ways, *Yizkor* ("Remembering") should more accurately be called *Yishkach* ("Forgetting"), as forgetting is a necessary part of the process by which we maintain meaningful memories. The most poignant literary example of this selective forgetting comes from the famous story by Jorge Luis Borges, "Funes the Memorious." The main character, Funes, has a photographic memory that allows him to recall every detail of every moment in his life. But his total recall allows him no leeway to have actual workable memories:

> Without effort, he had learned English, French, Portuguese, Latin. I suspect, nevertheless, that he was not very capable of thought. To think is to forget a difference, to generalize, to abstract. In the overly replete world of Funes there were nothing but details, almost contiguous details.[6]

In our daily life, we successfully forget most of the mundane details of our encounters with others and focus instead on the meta-level of experiencing them as whole persons, thereby providing richness and depth beyond the detail (precisely what eludes the tragic character of Funes). In like manner, after they die, we cannot focus on every single detail of a loved one's life at the expense of a larger whole. Through the selective perception of *Yizkor*, we allow static memories to adapt and develop—the people we remember may be gone, but our relationship with them continues to evolve.

Strikingly, the very structure of our brain processes memories in such a way as to permit this natural process. In the words of Joshua Foer:

As neuroscientists have begun to unravel some of the mysteries of what exactly a memory is, it's become clear that the fading, mutating, and eventual disappearance of memories over time is a real physical phenomenon that happens in the brain at the cellular level.[7]

The purpose of *Yizkor* is to allow us to access the person we have lost and to keep the relationship alive. Reciting *Yizkor* collectively would prevent this active and ongoing reconstruction of those whom we have lost. It would not allow our brains to do their natural work of reshaping and altering memory. By reciting *Yizkor* individually, without the corrective of others, we interact with our own memories, allowing the cells of our brain to mutate the memories as they are recalled; our memories change as we remember. So even though we cannot have an actual relationship with the person we have lost, we can have a dynamic relationship with our memory of them. Our memory literally keeps them alive in the sense that they continue to change and develop through our changing perception of them. While we can't hold them in our arms, the Jewish practice of *Yizkor* provides a way in which they can be recollected and revived in our minds through the gift of memory.

෴

Hard to Plan the Day

Rabbi Edwin Goldberg, DHL

We live in a democracy of time. Scholar or ignoramus, aristocrat or wage slave, everyone receives the same 168 hours a week. They are nonnegotiable and, unlike cellphone minutes, definitely do not "roll over" if not used well. The English poet Samuel Johnson said that nothing concentrates the mind of a condemned man like the sighting of a rope. Likewise, the *Yizkor* prayers remind us of our departed dear ones, but they also speak to us of our own finitude. One could easily wish to avoid *Yizkor* for this very reason! The bestselling *Denial of Death* by Ernst Becker makes the point very clearly in the title alone: our society would rather not think about death at all.

Recently, a congregant approached me and said she could not stop thinking about a teaching I had once shared with her from the writings of Franz Kafka: "The meaning of life is that it ends." On the one hand, this recognition frightened her; at the same time she understood how precious time is because it is finite.

Kafka's sober insight supports my belief that the most important message in the traditional *Yizkor* liturgy comes from Psalm 90:12: "Teach us to number our days, that we may attain a heart of wisdom." Time is the ultimate limited and non-reusable resource, so that numbering our days should make us feel even worse. Yet we are told that in such numbering we will find wisdom. Can it be true?

Rabbi Edwin Goldberg, DHL, serves as coordinator of the Central Conference of American Rabbis (CCAR) editorial committee on the forthcoming CCAR *machzor*. He has a doctorate in Hebrew letters from Hebrew Union College–Jewish Institute of Religion and is the senior rabbi at Temple Sholom of Chicago. He is author of *Saying No and Letting Go: Jewish Wisdom on Making Room for What Matters Most* (Jewish Lights). He contributed to *We Have Sinned: Sin and Confession in Judaism*—Ashamnu *and* Al Chet (Jewish Lights).

This much does make sense to me: reminding myself every day that I have only 168 hours a week—the same as a billionaire—helps me act more intentionally. I make better choices. I also recall the wisdom that E. B. White shared upon retiring from his career at the *New Yorker*:

> If the world were merely seductive, that would be easy. If it were merely challenging, that would be no problem. But I arise in the morning torn between a desire to improve the world and a desire to enjoy the world. This makes it hard to plan the day.[1]

Hard to plan the day—wisdom becomes necessary if we want to plan. The memorial prayers on Yom Kippur give us more than a reminder to contemplate our eventual demise. They also supply a reason to plan a better use of the time in between today and the journey to—as Shakespeare put it—"the undiscovered country."

I think the citation from the Bible should be read backward: not just, "Teach us to number our days, that we may attain a heart of wisdom," but, "We can find wisdom only if we learn that our days are numbered." To state it more simply: only when I take seriously the limited hours available to me each week—168—can I make decisions on how I use my time with wisdom. If time is a precious resource, then, like any expensive commodity, it must be invested wisely. Those who would never operate a business or run a family without a financial budget would do well to remember that a budget of time is just as valuable, if not more so.

I like to say that I would much rather give a friend or family member my credit card than the password to my Google calendar. We can always settle up on the money borrowed, but time "borrowed" can never be repaid. Horace Mann once put this announcement in the lost-and-found column of a newspaper: "Lost somewhere between sunrise and sunset, two golden hours, each set with sixty diamond minutes. No reward is offered, for they are gone forever."

Of course, one can also overplan and therefore act with little wisdom. Rabbi Chayim of Zans used to teach this parable:

> A poor country woman with little to eat and too many children to feed once happily found an egg. She called the children and announced that they would be well served by the egg as long as they planned everything just

so. Instead of eating the egg, they should give it to the neighbor so that their hen could sit on it until it hatched. Next, once the chick was born, they should wait for it to grow into a hen and hatch more chickens. Soon after, with the money from the chickens, they should buy a calf and then wait until it calves. With the money from the calves, they might buy a field. All this planning made the woman so excited that she dropped the egg and it broke on the floor.

The message of the parable: we should not waste too much time planning, for then life will slip by us. Or as John Lennon sang, "Life is what happens to you while you are busy making other plans."

When we understand that our days are numbered, we can plan to use them wisely, while at the same time not confuse the planning for the actual experience.

It has been said that time flies, but we are the navigators. How we use time is a choice before us, if we are aware enough to recognize the choice. *Yizkor* reminds us to make a plan for our time, although not to let the plan detract from our experience of the present.

I once read of a rabbinical school professor with a gold pocket watch. On the inside were the words, "It's later than you think." A watch is an ironic place for such wisdom, as its second hand ticks down the moments until our inevitable demise. Will such words frighten us or inspire us? That, really, is the question.

So yes, the central message of *Yizkor* is this: *Teach us to number our days, that we may attain a heart of wisdom.* You may not want to think about your death at all. Perhaps you have no desire to number your days, in which case your life will be partially wasted. You will never learn to live well; you will never learn a heart of wisdom. We are foolish if we live in denial of the one certain and unavoidable event in our lives.

A number of years ago I heard a new medical term. I was told that a seriously ill man was "pre-terminal." Evidently this means he was not yet terminal, but it was expected that soon he would be. That left me thinking: Can't that really be said about each and every one of us? When it comes right down to it, aren't we all "pre-terminal"?

E. B. White had it right. Awareness of the choices the world offers plus recognition of our limited lack of time can lead to lives of joy and meaning, if we learn from experience as we go to make sure that we are using our time well.

This much I know: those with a plan are wiser than those without a plan. So maybe Hillel deserves the last word: *If not now, when?*

அண்ண

Why Art Thou Cast Down?

Rabbi Andrew Goldstein, PhD

Since retiring, after a forty-year rabbinate in one congregation, I have been fortunate to take High Holy Day services in Dublin, Ireland. As the Dublin Progressive Jewish Congregation uses *Machzor Ruach Chadashah*, which I coedited, the services are easy to lead—so long as I mention the taoiseach and not the queen of England in the prayer for the government.

Three reflections come to mind as I review my lengthy experience with *Yizkor* over the years. The first is prompted by a visitor who chanced upon our Yom Kippur service in Dublin a couple of years ago. She arrived just as we were nearing the end of the morning and then continued to sit, bewildered when, a few moments later, the service ended and the vast bulk of the congregation left the sanctuary and the building. She looked crestfallen to the point of being almost in tears as I approached her.

It turned out that she was an American on a cruise ship that had docked in Dublin. She had deliberately come to the synagogue only for *Yizkor* and I had ended the morning without reciting it, since in our service, it is normally included only later in the day. As we shall see later, that placement has been commonplace among Progressive congregations for over a century. She, however, was used to its being said in the morning, the usual place in Orthodox synagogues.

That was all she wanted of the Day of Awe: just *Yizkor*! I took her into my office, where I said a few memorial prayers and recited *El Malei*

Rabbi Andrew Goldstein, PhD, is the rabbinic advisor to the European Union for Progressive Judaism and coeditor of *Machzor Ruach Chadashah*. He contributed to *Who by Fire, Who by Water*—Un'taneh Tokef, *All These Vows*—Kol Nidre, and *We Have Sinned: Sin and Confession in Judaism*—Ashamnu *and* Al Chet (all Jewish Lights).

Rachamin for her parents. Then off she went, back to her cruise ship, no doubt feeling satisfied at having done her duty.

As I say, traditionally, the memorial service has its place following the reading of Torah in the morning. Surely the Reform practice of moving it to late afternoon, as it is beginning to get dark, is emotionally more fitting. To be slightly flippant, by 12:30 p.m. most worshipers begin to tire and find their stomachs rumbling. I can't imagine how it can be satisfying for them, let alone for those who (like the woman on the cruise) come just for *Yizkor* and find it consisting of a few prayers only, quickly said, and then dispensed with so the rest of the service can proceed apace. By late afternoon, by contrast, worshipers who have spent much of the day in shul are getting a second or third wind, and those who have returned after a long break are ready for a buildup to the emotional climax of the day: the afternoon service, which is a useful prelude to the memorial service, which (in turn) then moves smoothly into *N'ilah*—a three-act conclusion to the Day of Awe.

Elsewhere, this volume explains the details of how *Yizkor* was extended to become a service of its own and moved from morning to late afternoon as well. It was truly an early Reform (in Germany and then America) innovation, going back to the "memorial service" (*Totenfeier*) for Yom Kippur in the *Hamburg Temple Prayer Book* of 1819.[1] There were exceptions, to be sure—in his *Minhag Amerika*, Isaac M. Wise placed it in the *Kol Nidre* service,[2] and a couple of other editors moved it back to its earlier morning slot.[3] But normally, it was moved to the afternoon. The Hamburg community that pioneered the change still kept *Musaf* and so could move it there. Most Reform congregations dispensed with *Musaf* on theological grounds—it was so closely associated with the ancient sacrificial rite, and its content even requested the Temple's restoration. So the memorial service was usually included between the afternoon and concluding services, a location that became the norm in Reform and Liberal *machzorim* all over the world.

Dr. Eric L. Friedland explains the popularity of the extended memorial service, particularly among the many immigrants who arrived with the Great Migration of 1881–1924. So many of them had left behind in Europe their parents and families, whether alive or in the grave; the lengthened service assuaged their guilt at abandoning them and, maybe, their own homesickness as well.[4]

My second rumination goes back to my childhood and youth when our Yom Kippur worship featured the *Liberal Jewish Prayer Book*, volume 2, composed by Rabbi Dr. Israel I. Mattuck in 1923. Although much altered from its source, it was based on the *Union Prayer Book*, which Dr. Mattuck brought with him when he arrived from America in 1910 as the first rabbi of the Liberal Jewish Synagogue in London.

Included in his memorial service was a hymn, which I quote in full, if only to provide a fully appreciative sense of the florid English style in which it had been composed. It is Mattuck's adaptation of the version in the *Union Prayer Book*, which has a long and varied history going back to the Hamburg Temple *Gesangbuch* ("hymnal"), where it appeared as "*Seele, was betrübst du dich!*"[5]

> Why art thou cast down, my soul?
> Why disquieted in me?
> Feel'st thou not the Father nigh,
> Him whose heart contains us all?
> Lives no God for thee on high,
> Loving while his judgements fall?
> Look above!
> God is love!
> Why art thou cast down, my soul?
> To the skies
> Turn thine eyes;
> Every tear on earth that flows,
> God, the world's great Ruler, knows.
>
> Why art thou cast down, my soul?
> Why disquieted in me?
> Was thy head in sorrow bending
> 'Neath the dreaded reaper's blight,
> When thy loved ones were descending
> In the darkness of death's night?
> Have no fear,
> God is near!
> Be consoled, my soul, in God,
> Tears take flight,
> For in light

Walk thy dead on heaven's shore
Blessed, blessed, evermore!

Why art thou cast down, my soul?
Why disquieted in me?
Ever shall thy dead be living—
From the darkness of the tomb
God, thy Father, mercy giving,
Takes them to his heavenly home.
  Wilt thou trust
  God, the just?
Soul, my soul, be strong in God.
  God's with thee
  Eternally!
Then thy hopes shall be fulfilled
And thy heart's pain shall be stilled.

When Rabbis John Rayner and Chaim Stern composed *Gate of Repentance* (1973),[6] the successor to Dr. Mattuck's prayer book, the hymn was omitted. The first objection was its archaic language. One of the hallmarks of the new liturgy was its rejection of such old-fashioned English, and "Why art thou ... Feel'st thou.... 'Neath the dreaded reaper's blight" just would not do. I can't recall (for I was a young member of the editorial committee) whether attempts were made to retranslate the hymn; after all, it had appeared in various versions since its origin in Hamburg in 1819. But perhaps not, because of the second objection: its theology, which was, in any case, unacceptable. It speaks of a God who is close to the mourner ("Father nigh, / Him whose heart contains us all"), but a God Almighty nonetheless who decrees death as a judgment upon us ("Loving while his judgements fall"), and a very definite belief in life after death ("Ever shall thy dead be living— / From the darkness of the tomb / God, thy Father, mercy giving / Takes them to his heavenly home").

No doubt many did and do find these assertions difficult to make. And phrases like "God is love" may be too Christian. Yet, in my experience, so many mourners who, at other times, are cool rationalists, seem to find comfort in traditional words and beliefs when they face the death of loved ones, especially if sung to a haunting melody. Just think of the popularity of *Kol Nidre*, the traditional words of which are so difficult to take, yet whose music stirs even the most atheist of souls.

Such was the popularity of the hymn that in my synagogue we continued to sing it for years after we started using *Gate of Repentance*. Sheets of paper with the hymn (and a couple of other pieces from the previous memorial service) were distributed, and "Why art thou" was sung with gusto and, I suspect, nostalgia for the past. But isn't *Yizkor* about remembering the past and keeping our memories from it alive?

Though the music that was probably used when the hymn first appeared in Hamburg, possibly by Lewandowski,[7] does not appeal to me, we sang the words to a melody by Sigmund Schlesinger (1835–1906). Born in Germany, he came to America in 1860 and set about writing "American Jewish" music for his own synagogue, Congregation Shaarei Shomayim in Mobile, Alabama, where he was organist and choirmaster for thirty-six years until his death.

It still bothers me that, even though I was coeditor of the new Liberal Judaism High Holy Day prayer book, *Machzor Ruach Chadashah*,[8] I could not find a way to resurrect my much-loved hymn. But English nowadays must be gender neutral, so "Father nigh" didn't stand a chance. A better poet and liturgist might have written a new hymn in modern English to go with Schlesinger's haunting melody, but singing hymns in English seems an anathema to today's Liberal Jewish worshipers, in any case.

Israel Mattuck, though born in Lithuania and educated in America, introduced several very English touches to his prayer books. My third reflection recollects the very best example of this love of English literature: Mattuck's inclusion in his memorial service of sonnet 146 by William Shakespeare:

> Poor soul, the centre of my sinful earth,
>   Fool'd by these rebel powers that thee array,
>   Why dost thou pine within and suffer dearth,
>   Painting thy outward walls so costly gay?
>   Why so large cost, having so short a lease,
>   Dost thou upon thy fading mansion spend?
>   Shall worms, inheritors of this excess,
>   Eat up thy charge? Is this thy body's end?
>   Then, soul, live thou upon thy servant's loss,

And let that pine to aggravate thy store:
Buy terms divine in selling hours of dross;
Within be fed, without be rich no more:
So shalt thou feed on death, that feeds on men,
And death, once dead, there's no more dying then.

"Why art thou cast down" did set the mood for *Yizkor*; Shakespeare brought a smile to the face!

Where Do People Go When They Die?

Dr. Joel M. Hoffman

"Where do people go when they die?" It's a question that haunts us as we remember our loved ones, and also as we consider what might await us when our own life draws to an end. It is among the most frequently asked questions, and among the most important, which is why it is all the more frustrating that an answer is so elusive.

"What happens after I die?" We don't know. "Will I be reunited with my spouse?" We don't know. "Will death be better for me if I live a good life?" We don't know. "Are my parents watching over me?" We don't know. In place of answers, we have a wide variety of metaphors that represent a combination of guessing and hoping.

Perhaps the most common is "rest in peace," a phrase that's reminiscent of Isaiah 57:2, where "peace" and "resting" are used in reference to "righteous" and "pious" people when they die. (The actual phrase "rest in peace" comes from the Latin *requiescat in pace* from the Catholic Order of the Mass.) Though the wording isn't exactly the same, the sentiment

---

Dr. Joel M. Hoffman lectures around the globe on popular and scholarly topics spanning history, Hebrew, prayer, and Jewish continuity. He has served on the faculties of Brandeis University in Waltham, Massachusetts, and Hebrew Union College–Jewish Institute of Religion in New York. He is author of *And God Said: How Translations Conceal the Bible's Original Meaning* and *In the Beginning: A Short History of the Hebrew Language*, and has written for the international *Jerusalem Post*. He contributed to all ten volumes of the *My People's Prayer Book: Traditional Prayers, Modern Commentaries* series, winner of the National Jewish Book Award; to *My People's Passover Haggadah: Traditional Texts, Modern Commentaries*; and to *Who by Fire, Who by Water*—Un'taneh Tokef and *We Have Sinned: Sin and Confession in Judaism*—Ashamnu *and* Al Chet (all Jewish Lights).

seems similar. Death, at least for the righteous, is like a peaceful rest. When people die, they go to sleep. The line from Isaiah even includes a bed upon which the dead rest.

It seems to have been a common sentiment. The Roman philosopher Cicero (first century BCE) quotes Quintus Ennius, a Roman writer from a century or so earlier, as hoping that "the body rest free from evil." And Ovid (about a hundred years later) likewise hopes that the "bones rest gently."

Similar in nature are the respectful "final resting place" and even the sardonic "sleep with the fishes." Death is like sleep: generally painless and devoid of feeling.

Inherent in the hope for a peaceful sleep is the observation that life itself can be painful. Death can be an end to life that comes too soon, like bedtime for children who don't want the joy of being awake to end. Or it can be like the end of a hard day, a welcome respite from suffering.

The Bible offers another image of where people go in death: to a pit, *Sheol* in Hebrew. In 1 Samuel 2:6, for example, Hannah's prayer includes the observation that God "kills people" and "revives" them, that is, "brings people down to Sheol" and "brings people back up." Here people don't sleep quietly in death; they descend to live in a pit forever (or at least until they are resurrected). And the pit is dreary and dark, far removed from the angels of heaven.

Furthermore, Sheol is an extension of life. When Jacob learns that his son Joseph is dead, he laments that he will "go down to his son in mourning, down to Sheol" (Genesis 37:35). And Ezekiel writes that warriors bring their weapons of war, their swords and their shields, with them to Sheol (Ezekiel 32:27). Sheol, perhaps like sleep, is a new stage of existence. But unlike in sleep, people in Sheol continue in the direction established for them in life.

While Sheol is hardly a common Western concept, its implications are nonetheless widely accepted. On the one hand, the dying settle their affairs before death and make other preparations to "die in peace." From the other side of things, the living make amends with the dying. This second aspect, in particular, is predicated on the notion that the last moments of life will impact the quality of death. Death, as Jacob feared, can embody sorrow, or it can offer peace.

A variation on Sheol suggests that it is a way station for something else. This is why the psalmist in Psalm 49 (quoted at the start of the

Yizkor service) can be sure that God will redeem him from Sheol, taking him in.

Both of these metaphors present death as a continuation of life. In the first, the body, or the bones, or the person, sleeps. In the second, the whole person moves to a new home. Plato (fourth century BCE), though, thought that "death is the separation of the soul from the body." Judaism incorporated this concept of a mortal body and an immortal soul. For example, the morning liturgy thanks God for a "pure soul" that will live on after death.

The very word "soul" embodies the metaphor that our existence is (at least) twofold, including a temporary physical body and an eternal ethereal soul.

Plato refines his notion when he says that death releases the soul from the "baneful corpse" to which it was tied. Modern societies express similar sentiments in the common consolation that the deceased are "in a better place now." This alleged better place is the exact opposite of the Bible's Sheol. The dead cry out to be redeemed from the miserable Sheol, while, by definition, a better place is better than what the living have now.

These two options—a better place after death and a worse one—lie at the core of two of the most widespread metaphors regarding death: heaven and hell. In the most common scenario, good people merit heaven, while evil people are punished with hell.

Taken together, these answer the question "Where do people go when they die?" (either to a good place or a bad place) and also posit a curious purpose for death: it is a reward-and-punishment system designed to encourage good behavior and discourage bad. Though this system of eternal reward and eternal punishment did not make its way into mainstream Judaism, it is perhaps the most common modern Western view.

Maybe the most interesting metaphor comes from 1 Samuel 25:29, where, if David is attacked, he will be "bound up in the bundle of life." There the phrase refers to David being kept alive. The "bundle of life" is akin to God's book of the living.

But the phrase is better known from the *Yizkor* service, where it is the dead, not the living, who will be bound up in the bundle of life. In one sense, this shift represents a view—similar to Sheol in nature if not in detail—that life continues in death in what has become known as the "world to come."

In a broader sense, though, the phrase alludes to an all-encompassing bundle of life that includes us along with our descendants and our ancestors. As we remember the dead, we hope that they find their rightful place in the grand march of time, along—as the prayer says—with the family of Abraham and Sarah, just as we who remember them will someday do the same.

౷౷౷

Remembering
Abraham Geiger

Rabbi Walter Homolka, PhD, DHL

In a world of forgetting, Judaism is all about memory. How often are we urged to remember what God did for us "with a strong hand and an outstretched arm" (e.g. Exodus 6:6)? The very essence of God's faithfulness and love is that "God remembered His covenant with Abraham and Isaac and Jacob" (Exodus 2:23–25). "This is my Name forever, and this is my remembrance from generation to generation" (Exodus 3:15). The same is true for our teachers—especially if they have opened a new understanding of Jewish existence for us, in the light of the Enlightenment and of civil emancipation. The Enlightenment challenged medieval assumptions by opening new intellectual vistas of the mind; the second expanded Jewish possibilities far beyond anything medieval men and women could have imagined.

One such great and decisive leader is Rabbi Abraham Geiger (1810–1874), after whom our rabbinical seminary in Germany is named today. The beginnings of modern education for rabbis and of Jewish theology in the modern vein are closely linked to him. More than a century after Geiger began, Leo Baeck described his contribution by saying, "The past was discovered and with it the essence of the present was won; a new generation that was conscious again of its Judaism was gradually created."[1]

Rabbi Walter Homolka, PhD, DHL, is the rector of the Abraham Geiger College for the training of rabbis, the executive director of the Zacharias Frankel College, and a professor of Jewish studies at the University of Potsdam in Germany. He is author of many books, including *The Gate to Perfection: The Idea of Peace in Jewish Thought*, coauthor of *How to Do Good & Avoid Evil: A Global Ethic from the Sources of Judaism* (SkyLight Paths), and a contributor to *We Have Sinned: Sin and Confession in Judaism— Ashamnu and Al Chet* (Jewish Lights).

By Geiger's time, civil emancipation had given Jews citizenship status, but at the cost of subordinating rabbinical legal authority to the mandates that constituted the law of the land, thereby turning the rabbi into a civil servant. The yielding of this power may have begun as early as 1820, when Ruben Samuel Gumpertz (1769–1851), a banker and one of Berlin's community's elders, made clear to the state authorities that the rabbi—after relinquishing all judicial authority—was no more than a "guardian of the kosher" and thus did not compare to Christian clergy. As Gumpertz described it:

> In the community, in which they [the rabbis] were honored with their trust and for which they were called to serve, their activities are now limited to deciding upon matters of ceremonial law, to judging permissible and impermissible foodstuffs, to informing the butchers of the laws pertaining to butchering, to inspecting that which belongs to such, and to issuing certificates regarding the outcome of such inspections. Hence, in the most important areas, the functions of the rabbi differ completely from those of the Christian clergy. For the rabbi does not circumcise; his attendance of weddings is not required; he does not keep church registers; he preaches only upon exception; he does not administer religious instruction; he does not take care of the schools; he does not comfort the dying; in short, he is nothing more than a man to whom the Jewish community trusts to be versed in the holy texts and the laws, and of whom one asks for advice or decisions concerning matters of conscience about whatever one deems necessary....
>
> With good reason and fittingly, one could currently call the rabbi a ... guardian of the kosher, for his functions refer primarily to decisions regarding permissible and impermissible foodstuffs....[2]

Against this assessment of the rabbi as essentially a ritual specialist, Geiger pursued a goal that he had learned from his teacher Leopold Zunz (1794–1886): "To fashion out of Judaism a new and freshly animated Jewry."[3]

In 1835, Geiger published the first volume of his periodical *Wissenschaftliche Zeitschrift für jüdische Theologie* (*Scientific Journal for Jewish Theology*). In its opening essay, he charged rabbis with the duty to weld together "the inherited with the demands of the present." Rabbis would have to become representatives of Jewish theology:

> And, the theologians, what do they offer with regard to hope? ... We dare claim that they alone—when they are completely entrusted with the whole wondrous historically assembled building of our religion and when, at the same time, they stand at the forefront of contemporary times—that they alone can advance the redemption of Israel through learned and practical effectiveness. That in the last fifty years they did not do so, but rather that their untimely struggle was highly ruinous, is recognized. But God now gives us men who have the excellence of mind to think knowledge of the times through which they must steer and of the goal toward which they should steer. We need [them] to demonstrate how Judaism has evolved over time to what it has become, [and] not to shy away from arguing against a faith stuck in the past.[4]

In a further programmatic essay from 1838, Geiger argued for an alliance of theologians and community rabbis: in the liberating environment of academic freedom, a commission of Jewish theologians would develop the concepts inherent in Judaism's religious heritage; the community rabbis would then be entrusted with the realization of these concepts in practice. As his son and biographer Ludwig Geiger (1848–1920) wrote:

> His essay "Die zwei verschiedenen Betrachtungsweisen. Der Schriftsteller und der Rabbiner" ["The Two Different Points of View. The Writer and the Rabbi"] provides for a scrupulously thought-out expression of the newly won insights, and it illustrates how two different worlds can be brought closer to one another.[5]

The term *Schriftsteller* ("writer") in the essay's title referred to the Jewish-theological writer as a "priest of the true science who reveals the ... coherence of ideas in his times."[6] But this revelation was, for Geiger, a matter of great pragmatic and strategic consequence, because only by seeing how authentic Jewish ideas of the past could be relevant to the present could rabbis address that present. Writing in 1837 to his friend Joseph Dernburg, Geiger decried "[the] lack [of] a rabbi in a larger community

... who knows how to win over the intelligent part of the community; and who addresses the masses accordingly without fear."[7] Ideally, perhaps, congregational rabbis would be theologians as well as practitioners, but Geiger was forced to differentiate the two roles because of the absence of academic rabbinical education in his time and the impossibility of imagining academic excellence linked to practical community service—what we take for granted today as simply a matter of course.

To achieve this academic excellence, rabbis of Geiger's generation needed to give themselves over to scholarly research of Judaism but could do so only with difficulty, given the widespread absence of such study when it came to Judaism. The "science of Judaism" (as it was then called) was altogether absent from the yeshivot (or seminaries), which were still bastions of premodernism, and would not be included in German universities until the 1960s. Looking back in 1933, Max Dienemann portrayed the problem when he observed, "In addition to the obligatory tasks of their office, [rabbis] had to take on a task which normally would have entailed whole faculties with staffs of researchers." From the narrowness of premodern life, these rabbis were asked to expand their horizons so as to include "a broadening of outlook and a heightening of scholarship, expanding in scope to encompass all of cultural life."[8] It went practically without saying that such a rabbi would have to have received a doctorate; the common form of address "*Herr Doktor*" was a matter of course.[9]

By the dawn of the twentieth century, therefore—as a result of Abraham Geiger's concept of the modern rabbinate—rabbis increasingly saw themselves as community workers who were also academic scholars—the product of the involuntary transformation of rabbinical seminaries into the Jewish academic equivalents to Christian theological faculties. But such faculties did not yet exist! Hence Geiger's greatness, which was to call for the establishment of such a Jewish theological faculty, as early as 1830: "If a Jewish seminary were established at a university where exegesis, homiletics, and even Talmud and Jewish history were taught in true religious spirit, then this would be the most fruitful and instructive institution!"[10] Six years later, he repeated his impassioned plea.[11] And shortly thereafter, Ludwig Philippson directed an "appeal toward all Israelites of Germany for subscriptions toward the founding of a 'Jewish faculty' and a Jewish seminary for Germany."[12]

In 1870, Geiger developed a detailed curriculum for such an institution. It called for "two departments" corresponding, roughly, to academic study on one hand and practical experience on the other. He was most intent on preserving the integrity of the school being planned by demonstrating (even in name) its academic and theological essence. Believing that the name embodies the mission, he asked that "it be denoted as a Jewish theological faculty." The problem was that "whereas Christianity's various confessions have theological faculties at the center of the sciences ... Judaism lacks such provisions." Not that the state would be required to grant Jews equality in that regard—this was Germany in the nineteenth century—but Jews themselves would establish the Jewish equivalent. "We wish," he said, "independently to close the present gap through the establishment of a Jewish theological faculty [that would] remain closely linked to the whole current of the sciences."[13]

This was 1870. Geiger was sixty years old. He lived to see the foundation of the Hochschule für die Wissenschaft des Judentums in Berlin in 1872, and he died in 1874. One year later, in 1875, Hebrew Union College was founded in Cincinnati by Isaac Mayer Wise.[14]

In 1933, a catastrophic time of utmost darkness for German Jews began; subsequently the rabbinical seminaries were closed,[15] and Abraham Geiger's demand for equality of rabbinical training in Germany as a litmus test for Jewish emancipation became nothing but a footnote in history. Now, that footnote has been recovered; the dream has been revived. We are experiencing a renaissance of Jewish life in Germany, symbolized most fully by the founding in 1999 of the Abraham Geiger College, a rabbinical seminary with Geiger's vision at its center. True to that vision we will integrate rabbinic studies as a department at Potsdam University in 2013. Jewish theology will become an academic subject in Germany at last, equal to the training of pastors, imams, and priests.

Thus, Jewish life in Germany today pays tribute to the achievements and teachings of former generations. We aim to remember not only the times of darkness and tragedy, but also the long-lost dreams and hopes of leaders such as Abraham Geiger, who showed us how best to formalize rabbinic education in modern times. With pride, we at the Abraham Geiger College at the University of Potsdam say today with confidence, "We train rabbis for Europe."

> May God remember the soul of Rabbi Abraham Geiger—
> swifter than eagles and stronger than lions to do your will.
> May he be kept among all the righteous women and men
> in paradise.

An Ongoing Conversation with Empty Chairs

Rabbi Delphine Horvilleur

Yizkor: The Service of Remembrance

Year after year, as the Yom Kippur *Yizkor* service draws near, the synagogue fills up. Even in congregations where only mourners are invited to stay, the crowded sanctuaries suddenly leave no empty space. In our synagogue, for example, not a single seat remains unoccupied. It seems obvious to me, however, that even though each seat is taken, empty chairs are everywhere. They are the ones that our beloved dead no longer fill.

These seats, which have new owners, seem to mourn the loss of those intimate encounters that they once had with their former occupants. *Yizkor* is the sacred summons of the empty spaces in our existence, the haunting presence of the absent ones, the time when emptiness fills the crowded sanctuary.

Rabbi Delphine Horvilleur is the rabbi of congregation MJLF (Mouvement Juif Libéral de France) in Paris. She was ordained at Hebrew Union College–Jewish Institute of Religion in New York in 2008 and is one of two women rabbis in France. She is the creative director of Le Café Biblique, a pluralistic group of Jewish study, and chief editor of *Tenou'a* (www.tenoua.org), a French magazine of Jewish thought. She contributed to *Who by Fire, Who by Water*—Un'taneh Tokef, *All These Vows*—Kol Nidre, and *We Have Sinned: Sin and Confession in Judaism*—Ashamnu *and* Al Chet (all Jewish Lights). She is the author of *En Tenue d'Eve* (Grasset), a renewed understanding of modesty and women's bodies in Jewish thought.

In her poem *Ma chambre* ("My room"), the nineteenth-century French poetess Marcelline Desbordes-Valmore faces her beloved's empty chair and writes:

> Vis-à-vis la mienne
> Une chaise attend:
> Elle fut la sienne,
> La nôtre un instant;
> D'un ruban signée,
> Cette chaise est là,
> Toute résignée,
> Comme me voilà!

"In front of my chair, awaits another one. It used to be yours, ours for a while; signed with a ribbon, it stands there; resigned as I am!"

But, can we so simply just *resign* ourselves to the loss of loved ones? Can we truly surrender to their absence and learn to live with it—to live, that is, without them?

For many poets and artists, no image encompasses loss better than an empty seat. For Judaism, too, this is how the absence is ritualized: during shivah, traditionally, mourners abandon their chairs and sit on the ground, stunned with grief. There too, empty chairs symbolize absence and loss.

Yizkor: "May God Remember"

Anyone who has experienced loss and mourning in a Jewish way knows the word *yizkor*. But not everyone explores its etymology. Interestingly, the very same root that gives us *zekher*, "memory" (*zayin chaf resh*), gives us also *zakhar*, "masculine." We are told in the very first chapter of Genesis (1:27) that God created humanity, "masculine and feminine," *zakhar un'kevah*.

The ability to remember seems for the Hebrew language to be somehow related to a quality of maleness that is symbolically conceived as being the active power, the fertilizing agent in existence. This shared etymology may seem at first counterintuitive, because we tend to see memory as passive, a trace left on our mind by history or past encounters. We envision its process as data storage in our brains or the deep and inerasable engraving of our past upon our soul.

The Hebrew language suggests, on the contrary, that the ability to remember is anything but passive. Memory is an active process and the seed of new beginnings. Neuroscience and biology seem to agree nowadays with this perception.

Neuroscientists who study memory acknowledge that memory is far more than the capacity to store information in our brain. Instead, it depends on our cerebral ability to build new connections with past experiences. We can remember only if our brain constantly creates new neuronal bridges, thereby redesigning our ongoing understanding of what the past actually was. Without this active rebuilding process, we forget. Memory is always under construction, always reenacted—as is the very past that memory continually reenacts and reconstructs.

We are not just talking about the memory of entire past events that we carry as pictures, sounds, or other sensory records in our brains. Biologists acknowledge the far subtler phenomenon of *cellular* memory that stands, for instance, at the core of immunization theory. When you get a vaccine, your body is exposed for the first time to a "pathogenic agent" that belongs to (or shows similarities with) the virus that it is intended to ward off. This miniscule exposure inaugurates a cellular reaction in which the cells involved change in structure. If your body encounters the same agent in the future, these altered cells that govern your immune system recognize the threat and react properly to defend itself. Your cells keep track of their past encounters. But their ability to remember is only a by-product of their ability to change. Cellular memory is the product of cellular transformation: they can react only because they have changed.

The French immunologist and philosopher Jean-Claude Ameisen argues[1] that this biological phenomenon could actually be extrapolated to define memory processes in general. According to him, the person who remembers an event cannot, by definition, be the same person who experienced it to begin with. Or, to say it differently: the fact that you remember meetings with a friend (for example) means that the friend affected you in such a way that you are then no longer the very same person you were when you actually had the meetings. You only remember because *what* you remember changed you at the time, and the only way you will continue to remember is by continuing also to change.

Memory, then, is an active and living process. As we build new connections with our past, the relationship we commemorate is reenacted and kept alive within us. It stays alive as long as it is remembered, as long as a living process actively fertilizes the mourner's mind to enable memory.

Mourners often say that they will remember the person they lost as long as they live. Science teaches us that the opposite is also true: we are alive, constantly reshaping ourselves and our understanding, as long as we remember.

This acknowledgment may be one of the sacred messages of the *Yizkor* service. On Yom Kippur, we are commanded to "mortify ourselves." For an entire day, through fast and introspection, we face our own mortality and dive into our deaths by playing the dead. But equally, we are the living who seek to reunite with those who are really dead. *Yizkor* arrives with the opportunity to summon our beloved ones who have left and to remember them. As we remember them, we should marvel at the fact that the relationships we had with them remain alive as long as we are alive to do the remembering.

When *Yizkor* begins, these living relationships fill the space of the crowded sanctuary. The chairs around us will not be empty as long as an ongoing conversation takes place inside us with the ones who left.

⌀⟁⟊⟆

Ode to Mortality

Rabbi Karyn D. Kedar

Yizkor. We sit in a crowd of mourners. We have come because we take upon ourselves the obligation to honor our dead. We should say *Kaddish.* They would want us to be here. We need to be here. We come so not to be alone as we wonder and ponder and search. It is all so temporary. There is never enough time to love, to fight, to forgive. There is never enough time to truly know another, to be good at intimacy, to be better at love. As much as we try, relationships are imperfect. *Yizkor.* We have come to remember it all. The beauty, the guilt, and the regret, the ever-present sense that this is all we have. We cannot escape the imperfect nature of our character, the flaws in our relationships, the squandered opportunities to reconcile, to love, to live.

Yizkor. We come with an unspoken agreement to be vulnerable, to feel, to weep. We settle into our seats, take the time to breathe and to remember. Our minds wander as we listen to the sounds of people immersed in thought and to the melodies and feel, truly feel, loss and melancholy. We feel the beating of our heart. We feel the ache.

Yizkor. We come to speak with God. Shadows abound. Shadows that hide what is rarely said. The words of our prayers speak of death and mortality, a conversation we do not usually allow ourselves to have aloud. And so we pray. We offer God words of longing or of anger, or we even speak in stark silences. "God, what are humans that you should acknowledge them, mortals that you should consider them?" (Psalm 144:3). Never has the need for a life of meaning and purpose been so profound. And as much as we sincerely yearn to connect, the human condition is

---

Rabbi Karyn D. Kedar teaches matters of the spirit to groups throughout the U.S. She is senior rabbi at Congregation B'nai Jehoshua Beth Elohim in the Chicago area, and the inspiring author of *The Bridge to Forgiveness: Stories and Prayers for Finding God and Restoring Wholeness; Our Dance with God: Finding Prayer, Perspective and Meaning in the Stories of Our Lives,* and *God Whispers: Stories of the Soul, Lessons of the Heart* (all Jewish Lights).

solitary. It is in the midst of our grief that we cannot help but think of ourselves. We allow ourselves to question. We wonder. Does it matter? What in this life is truly of consequence? What will they say of me when I am gone? Did I matter?

And God? What of God? What of faith?

Yizkor. We are compelled to remember. Today of all days we agreed not to run, not to try to escape our mortality. "Humans are like breath; their days like a passing shadow. In the morning they blossom, renewed; at night they fade and wither" (Psalms 144:4, 90:6). And so we remember that we are like breath, like a passing shadow. We are limited by our humanity, by our finitude. We can never know the true nature of life or death. We can never know when the day will come for us or for those we love. We can never know how to perfect what fails us. There is so much we will never know.

We ask that mortality become our teacher. Uncertainty teaches us humility; ambiguity tempers our arrogance; and in the yielding to life's great mystery, we attain a measure of wisdom.

Yizkor. Every morning that we are granted another day of life, we are invited to the miracle of awakening. We are invited to awaken to the beauty of the universe, to awaken to possibility and abundance. To be awake to the daily miracles that are so terribly obvious and to which we are so often oblivious. We must not sleep. Let us accept the invitation to awaken our minds and spirits to the life that we have been granted, however small, however imperfect, however short. "So teach us to count our days, that we may gain wisdom" (Psalm 90:12).

Yizkor. Let mortality teach us to reach beyond the loneliness of self-centeredness. In this moment of remembering we surrender to a great presence, to something grander than our own lives, larger than our own existence, more sacred than our own finite being.

"Mark those who are innocent and observe those who are upright, for a future awaits people of peace" (Psalm 37:37).

Let our sorrow teach us compassion. Let our tears compel us to ease the pain of another. Let our sense of mortality make our lives stand for something great. When we love our neighbor, we transcend. When we love the stranger, we transcend. When we remove the obstacle before the blind, we transcend. When we pursue peace, we transcend. When we hold the world as a vessel of grace, we transcend. And behold, it is our bodies that enable us to walk through this world with hands that heal and arms that embrace and minds curious for understanding and solutions. We walk through this world with eyes that see possibility and ears that hear the voice of another and mouths that speak with benevolence. It is our physical nature that gives us the potential to enlighten and love and care. This is how we make life better, safer, stronger.

Yizkor. Graciousness is our immortality. Kindness is our immortality. When we act as if we are in the image of God, we animate the divine spark within us and around us. Animation is our immortality. And when the divine spark is animated, we live in light, the force that creates goodness and beauty. The creative spirit is our immortality. A memory of blessing is our immortality. We so desire to live a life that is blessed. The soul is our immortality.

There is power in righteous acts. Compassion is the antidote for despair. Hope allows us to reach for eternity.

"For surely God will free me from Sheol, taking me in" (Psalm 49:16).

Yizkor. How powerful is the obligation to remember our dead. And how powerful do we become when we sustain moments of vulnerability, when we linger in fragility. How powerful is the human spirit that longs for meaning and purpose. That seeks to touch the edge of the sky. How powerful is the experience of transcendence. And faith? *Yizkor.* "My flesh and my heart fail, but God is my heart's strength and my lot forever" (Psalm 73:26).

There is little more than this: one precious life where love is legacy and kindness is redemptive and creativity is immortality and memory is sacred.

"Dirt returns to cover the earth as it was, and the spirit returns to God who gave it" (Ecclesiastes 12:7).

ᏬᎻᏮ

What Is *Yizkor* For?

Catherine Madsen

Does it matter how you felt about your parents?

At this point my parents are still living. Particularly with my mother, I can still go from mutual love and affection to wild exasperation in an instant. I don't know what it will be like when our store of shared memories and trains of thought is entirely in the past: when there can be no more apologies or explanations or retorts. When no one else remembers this trip or this holiday or this concert or this dog; when the belongings I have missed and coveted since I left home are in my house; when my own perspective on my childhood is the only one left. I don't know what it will be like to say *Yizkor* for my parents.

I am pretty sure my feelings will clash with those supplied by the *machzor*.

As a liturgical occasion, death is as uncompromising as it gets: whatever we say about it is answered by the same implacable silence. Liberal *machzorim* have a hard time facing the silence; they offer *Yizkor* services thick with explanations and emotional prompts. But how can anyone generalize your response to your own parents' absence? The early experiences that formed you, and the lifelong attempt to understand or transcend or reinforce them, are as private and particular as anything you will ever know. Can liturgists possibly imagine their way into that privacy?

The emotional prompts change with time; a quick tour of supplemental *Yizkor* readings over several decades reveals certain generational

---

Catherine Madsen is the author of *The Bones Reassemble: Reconstituting Liturgical Speech; In Medias Res: Liturgy for the Estranged*; and a novel, *A Portable Egypt*. She is librettist for Robert Stern's oratorio "Shofar" (on the CD *Awakenings*, Navona Records NV5878), and bibliographer at the Yiddish Book Center. She contributed to *Who by Fire, Who by Water*—Un'taneh Tokef, *All These Vows*—Kol Nidre, and *We Have Sinned: Sin and Confession in Judaism*—Ashamnu *and* Al Chet (all Jewish Lights).

shifts in rhetoric and sensibility. The Silverman *machzor* (1939) is rhap-
sodic in the manner of some forgotten nineteenth-century novel:

> With what love [our parents] tended the young lives
> entrusted to their care! With what beauty life blossomed
> under their tender guidance and understanding devotion!
> Untiring were their endeavors to direct their children on
> the path of virtue and kindness. Ever mindful were they of
> their welfare, ever anxious for their happiness.

Mahzor Hadash (1978) adapts a lengthy reading originally co-written by
Mordecai Kaplan, Eugene Kahn, and Ira Eisenstein, with flowery sentiments about "a heritage of tender memories" and a catalog of idealized
family relationships: the "beloved parents who watched over us, nursed
us, guided us, and sacrificed for us," the "husband or wife with whom
we were truly united," the siblings who "shared in ... the youthful adven-
ture of discovering life's possibilities," and so on. Next to these examples,
the Harlow *machzor* (1972) is comparatively restrained, but still entirely
positive: "This day we remember those who enriched our life with love
and with beauty, with kindness and compassion, with thoughtfulness and
understanding."

Passages like these cry out for counterexamples and scenes from real
life. Nobody emerges from childhood without certain scathing memories
of a parent's anger or misunderstanding or weakness. The *Yizkor* service
is not designed to evoke or dwell on such memories, but it can withstand
them; it need not preemptively deny them. Loss is not diminished and
mourning is not compromised by an honest look at one's parents and their
world. D. W. Winnicott's concept of the "good-enough mother" suggests
that the sum of a parent's efforts is generally adequate to compensate for
the failures. Admittedly the definition of "good-enough" is elastic, and
may vary a good deal with one's circumstances; Zadie Smith's novel *NW*
presents a northwest London housing project where "Caldwell people felt
everything would be fine as long as you didn't actually throw the child
down the stairs. Non-Caldwell people felt nothing would be fine unless
everything was done perfectly and even then there was no guarantee." The
same fault lines characterize adult children's sense of how "good-enough"
their parents were, but some degree of ambivalence is nearly inevitable.

In later *machzorim* a new mood (perhaps a non-Caldwell mood)
begins to emerge. The North American Reform *Gates of Repentance*

(1984), with a literary finesse well beyond the previous examples, presents a long introspective meditation that culminates in remembering one's dead, but whose evocation of the fragility of life has more in common with the *Un'taneh Tokef* than with the standard *Yizkor* service. (Unusually, it begins with two pages in the first-person singular, with the contemplation of one's own fate and the need to "set my house in order," before proceeding to the more traditional psalms and prayers.) *Kol Haneshamah* (Reconstructionist, 1999) retains a few sentimental evocations of "treasured moments and images" involving people "with whom we lived and laughed and loved," but also includes eighteen pages of poems by authors ranging from Yehuda Amichai to Adrienne Rich, representing painful and ambivalent emotions toward several kinds of loss, including a suicide. The recent Conservative *Mahzor Lev Shalem* (2010) introduces a supplemental reading by Robert Saks for the use of children of abusive parents.

This "*Yizkor* Meditation in Memory of a Parent Who Was Hurtful" is worth a closer look. The death even of a cruel parent is difficult: the vulnerability of the human body, the pity of its helplessness. But the damage done by a parent who really did throw the child down the stairs, or committed some equivalent atrocity, is not undone by the parent's later suffering. Saks writes:

> My emotions swirl as I say this prayer. The parent I remember was not kind to me. His/her death left me with a legacy of unhealed wounds, of anger and of dismay that a parent could hurt a child as I was hurt.
>
> I do not want to pretend to love, or to grief that I do not feel, but I do want to do what is right as a Jew and as a child.
>
> Help me, O God, to subdue my bitter emotions that do me no good, and to find that place in myself where happier memories may lie hidden, and where grief for all that could have been, all that should have been, may be calmed by forgiveness, or at least soothed by the passage of time.
>
> I pray that You, who raise up slaves to freedom, will liberate me from the oppression of my hurt and anger, and that You will lead me from this desert to Your holy place.

As a first effort, the prayer opens a necessary discussion and invites further refinements. "My emotions swirl" is a vague and vaporous phrase for a state of mind likely to be both more definite and more precarious, and "not kind" is euphemistic, but Saks has a good grasp of the basic situation of the survivor of child abuse. He recognizes that forgiveness may be possible in some cases but can never be imposed as an obligation, and the aim of escaping the slavery of bitterness and resentment is sound therapy. But when Saks writes, "I do want to do what is right as a Jew and as a child," why does "what is right" consist wholly of working on one's feelings? The *Yizkor Elohim* prayer traditionally includes a pledge to give *tz'dakah*. Might this element of Jewish mourning and memory be especially salient to the ambivalent or angry mourner?

Certainly there is no reason to suppose that Jews of earlier generations were blind to their parents' imperfections. While the traditional premodern *Yizkor* liturgy assumes a decorous level of respect for one's parents, it also recognizes that they were human, no doubt with sins as well as merits written next to their names in the book of life. The phrase *ut'hi m'nuchato kavod*, which occurs in *Yizkor Elohim* in some *machzorim*, is interestingly double-edged, representing both a supplication and a doubt. Harlow renders the phrase as "May he rest eternally in dignity and peace" and *Kol Haneshamah* as "And may his rest be honorable." Apparently a parent's honorable rest is no sure thing. The earliest understanding of the prayer's pledge of *tz'dakah* was purgatorial: the donation to the living was meant to shorten the punishment of the dead. The child reciting *Yizkor* was not meant to ignore the parent's sins but to redeem them.

A literal translation of the pledge—*ba'avur she'ani noder tz'dakah ba'ado*—might be "[May God remember the soul of my father] *because* I pledge *tz'dakah* on his behalf." Liberal *machzorim*, not wishing to suggest this chain of cause and effect, supply other rationales for giving *tz'dakah* on this occasion. Harlow (whose translation is retained in *Mahzor Lev Shalem*) interpolates explanatory phrases into the rather bare-bones Hebrew text: "*In loving testimony to his life,* I pledge *tz'dakah to help perpetuate ideals important to him.*" *Mahzor Hadash* says, "*In tribute to his memory* I pledge to perform acts of charity and goodness," and suggests in a supplemental reading that "by giving to others the love which our departed gave to us, we can partly repay the debt we owe them." *Gates of Repentance* omits the pledge of *tz'dakah* altogether. *Kol Haneshamah* mentions *tz'dakah* in a footnote but omits it from the prayer.

Modern rationalist Jews may dismiss with some distaste the idea of praying their parents out of *Gehinnom* (though the child of an abusive parent might prefer to leave him or her in *Gehinnom* for a good long time). But the tradition of *tz'dakah* does not depend on one's cosmological framework. The chance to rectify the parent's sins is earthly and practical. The child of good-enough parents might donate to causes they supported; the abused child might donate—in the abuser's memory or despite—to the National Alliance on Mental Illness. How do you pray for a cruel parent to be bound up in the bond of life? Perhaps by giving life to someone else, whose life is in jeopardy as yours was.

It strikes me that the Hebrew is naked of emotional content for a reason: its purpose is not to tell you what to feel but what to do. People know what they feel about their dead; the liturgist need not supply them with adjectives or attitudes. The point of *Yizkor* is to generate an act: to establish a reflex, a neural pathway, from your own loss to someone else's survival. Bereavement obligates you. If feeling for your parents inevitably floods back when you pray God to remember them—if praying God to remember them compels *you* to remember them—the point of *Yizkor* is to generate *tz'dakah* given with the whole force of memory.

✦

"Empty-Handed before Adonai"

Rabbi Jonathan Magonet, PhD

Though a prominent part of the Yom Kippur liturgy, *Yizkor* services are also generally held among Ashkenazi Jews on the final days of Pesach and Sukkot and on the second day of Shavuot. They are to be accompanied by charitable donations, a practice based on Deuteronomy 16:16–17, "They shall not appear before Adonai empty-handed, but each with his own gift according to the blessing that Adonai your God has bestowed upon you."[1] On a literal level, the donation would suffice to fulfill the requirement "not to appear empty-handed." Metaphorically speaking, we today fill our hands on *Yizkor* with memories and what we have made of them.

Despite *Yizkor*'s powerful popular appeal, its timing on Yom Kippur (for most progressive congregations, at least) presents a minor problem. The tradition places it after the Torah and haftarah readings in the morning service—it is not, in fact, even an independent service of its own, but just an appendage of the larger service for which everyone has gathered. Modern practice in non-Orthodox communities, however, makes it into a liturgy of its own and locates it later in the day, often just before *N'ilah*, when there is more likelihood of a congregation returning for the closing of the day. A rabbinic urban legend recounts the experience of a young rabbi, frustrated at the departure of so many of the congregation after the

Rabbi Jonathan Magonet, PhD, is emeritus professor of Bible at Leo Baeck College in London, where he was principal (president) from 1985 to 2005. He is coeditor of three volumes of *Forms of Prayer* (the prayer books of the British Movement for Reform Judaism) and editor of the eighth edition of *Daily, Sabbath and Occasional Prayers*. He contributed to *Who by Fire, Who by Water*—Un'taneh Tokef, *All These Vows*—Kol Nidre, and *We Have Sinned: Sin and Confession in Judaism*—Ashamnu *and* Al Chet (all Jewish Lights).

morning Torah service. Without advance warning, he announced at the end of the morning service that they were now going to read the memorial prayers even though hardly anyone was around. The following day he was invited to see the president of the synagogue, and the next morning he was on the first train out of town to look for a new job.

As an editor and composer of liturgies for the non-Orthodox world, I have found it helpful to ask how any particular liturgical element functions within the overall structure of the service. What might have been its original purpose? How did it fulfill that purpose? And if it no longer does so, how might it be newly constructed so as to fulfill that purpose in the new situation of modernity in general and of the community that would be using it in particular? *Yizkor* raises just such questions.

For many people, *Yizkor* is real in ways that the rest of the High Holy Days are not because it touches so personally on losses we have experienced and on the feelings that are evoked by those losses. These feelings may not always be appropriate or healthy; they may be tinged with guilt—or at least, confusion—as old memories, sometimes quite uncomfortable ones, are rekindled. But *Yizkor* has the benefit of taking place at some distance in time from the actual death. Therein lies part of the key to its function.

The immediate aftermath of a death provides its own set of rituals, graded in intensity. Mourning begins with seven days of shivah, marked by daily visits from family and friends; the next twenty-three days are then added to constitute thirty days in all, the *sh'loshim*, when the mourner gradually returns to normal activity; we then count ten more months, to get the eleven months during which *Kaddish* is recited daily (non-Orthodox practice sometimes stipulates a whole year). During the crucial first few days and weeks of shock—the shivah and even the *sh'loshim*—the mourner is enveloped in communal care and support and is largely spared the responsibilities and realities of daily life. It has even been suggested that sitting shivah is, in some symbolic sense, like being dead oneself, literally cut off from life. The next ten months of gradual return to life, with all the ritual obligations of the year of mourning, continue to acknowledge the reality of the loss and offer a way to discharge our duty to the dead. But the very fact that there is a formal limit set upon the mourning period allows us—in fact, forces us—to pick up the pieces of normal life again. To mourn beyond the eleven months (a year, for those who extend the period) is in some way to be inappropriately complaining to God that the loss has taken place. Indeed, according to one strand of Jewish legend, our dead live in purgatory during these eleven months while their life is evaluated and judged, but afterward they go to heaven. So to carry on mourning longer than the eleven months is to suggest that they do not deserve to go there!

By contrast, we have *Yizkor*, divorced from the immediate experience of death and repeated annually. It must serve an altogether different purpose from those ritualized ways of remembering that mark the immediate year of mourning. On one level *Yizkor* is simply a gesture of respect and honor to the memory of those who have died—it may have less to do with the mourner directly than with the deceased, who are not allowed to drop out of sight with time. But it has come also to provide an opportunity to view one's own life against the context of the relationship we once had with the deceased. That element of distancing allows us a certain detachment from the people whose death we remember and offers us the chance to focus on the dimension of our own lives in process. This deflection onto ourselves as mortal creatures struggling with life against the certainty of death someday comes through in the white gown, the *kittel*, which may serve as the shroud in which one day we ourselves will be buried. In a symbolic way we examine our lives on Yom Kippur as if from the grave, cut off from the life of the outside world. *Yizkor* thus becomes a powerful reminder of the limits of our own life and of how little time we have on earth; how brief may be our relationship with those we love or who are important to us, and how few the opportunities we have to be with them. It asks us, like the rest of this penitential season, to consider how we use that time allotted to us.

Hence the significance of the questions facing modern liturgists: Does the *Yizkor* liturgy as we have it fulfill that function? Does it support, and even encourage, such a quest?

These were the questions that guided us in composing the *Yizkor* service for the United Kingdom Reform community. We responded by offering a selection of Hebrew texts on the theme of the transience of life, but interwoven with newly composed self-reflective meditations on our own mortality:

> We live our life, yet scarcely know its nature, for from a mystery we come and to this mystery we return. Even in life it is our companion, for from the moment we are born

we begin our journey to the grave, which swallows our
plans and buries our hopes, indifferent to our success and
failure....

We live restlessly, confusing things of eternity with
things that pass. Our eyes are not satisfied with seeing,
nor our ears with hearing. Our desires are insatiable. Like
Moses on Mount Nebo, we behold the Promised Land
from afar, but may not enter it. We struggle for goals
we can never attain and only with death do our struggles
cease. Like children falling asleep over their toys, we let go
our grasp on our possessions, and death overtakes us....

Let us have courage and while in this world, keep hold
of things that do not die; of all that is untouched by passing years; of all that does not shatter or decay; of memories
uncorroded by shame or self-reproach or recrimination; of
our awareness of God in prayer....

We think of those who have gone before us and jour-
neyed from us into the everlasting life from which they
came. Time has dulled our pain, it has not erased their
memory. We have experienced suffering, we have seen
death, and we seek God's presence in them....[2]

We also considered the fact that *Yizkor* features the ritualized memorial not just for our own relatives and friends who have died but also for
many unknown others, former members of the congregation, for example. A further function of *Yizkor*, therefore, is to extend our ties to a larger
human community, all of whose members assemble to share the universal
experience of loss and mourning. But here, we face another stumbling
block: the sheer magnitude of unknown names that may be read aloud at
such great length. The occasional awkwardness as someone stumbles over
a poorly handwritten name may even offer a welcome human intrusion
into the seemingly endless and sometimes mind-numbingly relentless
repetitions of the liturgical engine of the day.

The *Yizkor* service fits well into the concerns and ethos of Yom
Kippur. But what function might it have within the very different mood
of the three festival services? If the liturgy is not to become simply a per-
functory repetition of the same prayers on each of these occasions, then
perhaps we can expand the list of those we remember, appropriate to
the nature of the festival in question. Pesach might invoke those who

have striven for justice and liberation in Jewish life. Shavuot obviously lends itself to remembering those who have been our personal teachers in some aspect of our lives. Sukkot, the most universal of our festivals, might focus on those from the wider society who have been important in broadening our horizons. If we are not to appear "empty-handed" before God on those occasions, then as well as a charitable donation, we can bring an offering of lives that have enriched us.

Today we may find ourselves uncomfortable with religious rituals, so that precisely when we have need of them they are remote from us or unavailable. One of the saddest things, for example, is to witness family members of someone who has died struggling to read a transliteration of the *Kaddish*. Their hesitations and mistakes, sometimes in the presence of those of an older generation who know it by heart, can make such moments exquisitely painful—not just because of the clumsiness of the ritual performance, but because of what it says about the state of knowledge and experience in the Jewish world today. Perhaps that is another reason why the *Yizkor* service is the one that pulls us back to the synagogue. In that anonymous context we are saying *Kaddish* not only for our dead, but also for worlds and beliefs and knowledge that have died for us. The challenge remains to try to find ways of making our Jewish rituals, liturgies, and symbols speak once again to our experience, to our reality, and to our deepest needs.

෴

The Hippo of Recollection Stirring in the Muddy Waters of the Mind

Rabbi Charles H. Middleburgh, PhD

On Rosh Hashanah in 1987, my beloved father Chaim died, at the age of eighty-six. He died in Sussex, where he had lived and worked for more than sixty years, and because I was officiating at services in London, I was not with him as he breathed his last. Although I conducted services on Yom Kippur, a mere three days after his funeral, I asked a lay leader to conduct *Yizkor* in my stead, as it would have been impossible for me to control my grief.

Ever since, the *Yizkor* service has been the most powerful of all those that take place across the *Yamim Nora'im*, and it is invariably where I give the last sermon of the day. Marking my father's *yahrzeit* on Rosh Hashanah means that he is constantly in my mind through the Days of Awe, meaning that my personal investment in the service is total.

Editing the *Yizkor* service in *Machzor Ruach Chadashah* (the High Holy Day volume of the Liberal Jewish community of Great Britain)[1]

Rabbi Charles H. Middleburgh, PhD, is rabbi of the Cardiff Reform Synagogue and director of Jewish studies at Leo Baeck College in London, where he has taught since 1984; and coeditor with Rabbi Andrew Goldstein, PhD, of the Liberal Judaism *Machzor Ruach Chadashah*. He contributed to *Who by Fire, Who by Water*—Un'taneh Tokef, *All These Vows*—Kol Nidre, and *We Have Sinned: Sin and Confession in Judaism*—Ashamnu *and* Al Chet (all Jewish Lights).

was, therefore, much more than a liturgical exercise for me. For the very personal reason that I have described, it became supremely important that the cathartic potential of the service for both newly and long-term bereaved be fully realized.

Our good fortune was to be able to build on some powerful precursors in our two predecessor liturgies: volume 2 of *the Liberal Jewish Prayer Book* (LJPB of 1937)[2] and *Gate of Repentance* (*GOR*, its 1973 successor).[3] In fact, a significant constraint on major change was the love felt for the existing liturgy by many of our congregants, which we would have ignored at our peril.

Looking at the *Gate of Repentance* service, we were struck by the perfect balance between classical and modern/creative texts achieved by John Rayner and Chaim Stern, *zikhronam liv'rakhah*, but we were also surprised by how short the service was: a mere fourteen pages.

Deciding that we had room for more, we added the equivalent of three pages of more recent material, in a subsection titled "A Selection of Poems for Silent Meditation." The poems we chose are as follows:

- "Remember," probably the best-known poem by the nineteenth-century English poet Christina Rossetti[4]
- "After I Am Dead" by Chaim Nachman Bialik[5]
- "It Is Less Distant Now: A Yahrzeit Candle Lit at Home," by the peerless Harold M. Schulweis,[6] which becomes more meaningful with every passing year
- "My Father and Mother"[7] by an anonymous poet
- "I wanted a perfect ending"[8] by the late actress and comedienne Gilda Radner
- "On Healing"[9] by Marjorie Pizer

Each of these additions has the power to deepen and broaden the inherent catharsis in *Yizkor*; each possesses layers of meaning that congregants often struggle in vain to find in the classic liturgical formulations. Indeed, much of our deliberations were designed to evoke just those elements of human emotion that the traditional service lacks.

In addition, we looked at the prayer preceding *El Malei Rachamim*, written by John Rayner but inspired by the North American Reform Movement's *Union Prayer Book*,[10] the fourth paragraph of which makes a detailed reference to the Shoah, still at the forefront of most minds in

1973 when *Gate of Repentance* was published.[11] We decided to emend the prayer to make it include not just the sufferings inflicted by the Shoah but also "the suffering and persecution of our ancestors in countless lands and ages," thus indicating that although the Shoah was the worst act of mass murder our people had endured, it was nevertheless the apotheosis of a historic continuum stretching back into the most distant past.[12]

Where *Gate of Repentance* contained one *Yizkor* prayer, adapted from an original by the Reverend Herbert Richer in our daily and Shabbat prayer book *Service of the Heart*, we added a beautiful original by Rabbi Ron Aigen, in his *Machzor Chadeish Yameinu*,[13] recalling parents, spouses, and children, brothers, sisters, and friends "whose visible presence will never return to cheer, encourage or inspire us."[14] Unlike the standard *Yizkor* formula, *Yizkor Elohim*, this is not a prayer, from which we can distance ourselves if we choose, for it recognizes the truth that each and every one of us is bereaved and must come to terms with the meaning this has for our lives:

> All of us recall some beloved persons whose friendship, affection and devotion elicited the best in us, and whose visible presence will never return to cheer, encourage or inspire us. No longer can we express by deeds, which might do them good, our appreciation of all that they have done for us or meant to us. Only by thinking of their lives as part of Your eternal life, and of their love as part of Your infinite love, can we express our gratitude for the blessings that we enjoyed in our communion with them.[15]

What I have just said about the formulaic *Yizkor Elohim* is indicative of a more general problem I have with the key prayers in the traditional *Yizkor* service, which seem to me to suffer irredeemably from repetitiveness, verbosity, and theological irrelevance to the sort of beliefs that modern men and women hold today. The redundant remembrance prayers, for example, suggest that by our mechanistic act of giving *tz'dakah*, we ensure that our loved ones' souls can continue to enjoy patriarchal and matriarchal company (the idea of an eternity in the company of Rebecca or Jacob frankly horrifies me). *Av Harachamim* (which was prompted by the death meted out to Jews during the Crusades) may be interesting as a piece of history, but it bears no realistic scrutiny as a theologically coherent passage according to our twenty-first-century criteria, and its language is so irredeemably bloody as to be almost laughable, the last response any editor would wish it to provoke.

In addition, all this archaic verbiage seems to miss and even get in the way of the whole point of *Yizkor*, a dual purpose, actually. First, there is the need to facilitate mourning and moving on in life despite the absence of the loved one who has died. But equally, we find a secondary purpose that is less recognized, even though if anything, it is more important than the first.

That purpose is to act as a powerful reminder of how we will be remembered after we have gone; such a reminder cannot but act as a corrective to us throughout the year to come, a goad to get our act together and be worthy of good memories rather than bad.

It has long been my practice to preach my last Yom Kippur sermon during *Yizkor*, an idea I received from the late Rabbi Sidney Brichto,[16] who conducted High Holy Day services in my home congregation during the early 1970s. It is a final opportunity to explore the grand themes of the day as it inexorably draws to a close.

In my *Yizkor* sermon in 2007, the twentieth anniversary of my father's death, I shared with my congregation in Cardiff thoughts inspired by the anniversary, which were also reflections on the huge power of *Yizkor* in my own professional and personal life. Hopefully it sums up everything I have been trying to write:

> The Talmud says: *Rachamana liba ba'ei* ("God desires the heart"). What God wants even more than ritual and the mindless observance of minutiae is affection and a good heart; a pure soul matters much more than rites and sacraments, however important these may be in sustaining the love of our tradition and the continuity of our heritage. And if God desires the heart then, as our co-creators,[17] we must give our hearts similarly to the other parties in the triumvirate that gave us life.
>
> This time of the year, in our tradition, is one of beginnings, of fresh hope, fresh dreams, fresh opportunities.
>
> But at this service we also bring to mind endings, and with the endings of life we inevitably think of everything that we have lost through the absence of shining presences that gave light to our lives for many years. In the immediate aftermath of my father's death I thought about him

every day, and the thoughts caused me pain and grief. As the years went by I continued to think of him regularly, though the pain and grief came to be replaced with laughter, with understanding, and a real sense of communion with the man who, together with my mother, gave me life.

Today I think of him less often, but when I do really *think* of him, as opposed to gazing at his picture, smiling, and moving on to something else, I remember a real human being, not a concocted one built on fantasies, imagination, and loss; and because he is real I know exactly what he was, what he stood for, the values he embodied. I cannot *be* my father, I would not wish to be, but he remains alive in my heart through the honor I pay him by striving to be the man he brought me up to be.

I don't always succeed, but he gives me the impetus to try every day of my life.

And that, for me, is what *Yizkor* is all about.

ↂ

Re-membering
YIZKOR AND THE
DYNAMICS OF DEATH

Rabbi Jay Henry Moses

O ne of the reliable oddities of synagogue life is axiomatic among congregational rabbis: people show up for *Yizkor*. Like the passing of the seasons, four times a year, even relatively disaffected Jews drift in to recite prayers in memory of the deceased. This phenomenon is brought into particularly stark relief by the realization that for three of the four holidays on which *Yizkor* is recited, many synagogues are sparsely attended (Yom Kippur is the obvious exception). Even in shuls where the other three *Yizkor* days—Sh'mini Atzeret, the last day of Pesach, and Shavuot—draw respectable crowds, the presence of unfamiliar faces stands out. People come out of the woodwork for *Yizkor*—but why?

I'd like to suggest three reasons why *Yizkor* is compelling even for Jews who are not observant, not regular synagogue attendees, and/or not believers in a God who hears our prayers. In each case, the liturgy of the *Yizkor* service both generates and reinforces the underlying spiritual experience of the worshiper. These three reasons can be summed up with the terms *reliving, rehearsing,* and *reassuring.*

Rabbi Jay Henry Moses is director of the Wexner Heritage Program at The Wexner Foundation. Previously, he served for five years as associate rabbi at Temple Sholom of Chicago. Rabbi Moses has taught at Hebrew Union College–Jewish Institute of Religion, the Jewish Community Center in Manhattan and its Makom: Center for Mindfulness, and in many other adult education settings. He contributed to *We Have Sinned: Sin and Confession in Judaism*—Ashamnu *and* Al Chet (Jewish Lights).

Reliving

The most obvious function *Yizkor* serves is to evoke powerful memories. Reciting *Yizkor* reawakens emotions associated with our loved ones who have died. The prayer returns us to the moment when we learned of their death and to the intensity of the grief that followed. In short, we *relive* the loss and, with it, the rush of memories and emotions that the loss entailed.

Both the structure and the content of *Yizkor* reinforce this fundamental function of reliving. Structurally speaking, it is the only place in our liturgy where family members are mentioned individually. The traditional siddur lists as many as eight different versions of the prayer, each one with its own specific reference: not just immediate family members (mother and father, husband or wife, son and daughter), but also martyrs and family and friends in general.

Surely this last version, which accounts for anyone whose death we are mourning, should be sufficient for the ritual or legal purpose of fulfilling one's obligation as a mourner. But the siddur includes the versions for specific family members because we need to rehash the lives and deaths of our loved ones in a very personal way. When we ritually intone the words *avi mori* ("my father, my teacher") or *imi morati* ("my mother, my teacher"), we relive the countless powerful associations we have with the image of "mom" or "dad"—anything from attending synagogue together to tender moments of parental love and affection. It is this closeness and comfort, akin to the emotional experience of visiting a grave, that *Yizkor* evokes. For some, this public invocation of memory also raises feelings of guilt or pain, because of unresolved issues in connection with those being remembered. In either case, the opportunity for a communal and formal remembrance allows us to relive that person's life and death and to work through our own feelings and reactions to them.

Rehearsing

Reliving the loss of others leads to the second of *Yizkor*'s three functions: rehearsing our own eventual death. As much as *Yizkor* transports us to our past, it serves equally as a signpost to our own future and a reminder of our own mortality. When we surround ourselves with mourners and delve into the poetry of loss, remembrance, and vulnerability, the reality of our own eventual death is necessarily front and center. This is reinforced by the common custom in more traditional communities, where those who still have both parents living leave the sanctuary rather than be present while those who have lost parents say *Yizkor*. This mini-exodus leaves the worshiper feeling a part of a chorus of orphans.

The sense of *Yizkor* as a rehearsal for our own demise is contained in the collection of psalm verses with which the *Yizkor* service begins. The very first words are, "God, what are humans that You should acknowledge them, mortals that You should consider them? Humans are like a breath, their days like a passing shadow."

This passage, framed in the plural, establishes the image of humanity in general as infinitesimal in both time and significance. But the passage then turns inward, shifting to the first-person singular and bringing home the reality of death to each single worshiper: "My flesh and heart fail, but God is my heart's strength and my lot forever. Dirt returns to cover the earth as it was, and the spirit returns to God who gave it." Before we can even turn to reliving the memories and the loss of loved ones, we are reminded powerfully that death is a fate that awaits us too.

Whatever our life experience, our personal theological orientation, and our degree of comfort with Jewish ritual, we are guided by the liturgy to see *Yizkor* as the moment when all stand equal before the mystery of death. For most of us, the prospect of our own mortality evokes varying degrees of fear, confusion, and resignation. For some, there are also elements of fascination and even anticipation as we contemplate the inevitable. This access to a mix of deep emotions and psychospiritual realities is the second reason that *Yizkor* holds appeal even for those who never otherwise come to pray. It provides a ritualized moment to approach the great mystery of death from the safe distance of the pew, mediated through the comforting vessel of the written liturgical word.

Reassuring

We see, then, how worshipers enter the sanctuary burdened by feelings of loss, grief, and fear of the mystery of death. This awareness leads to the third compelling function that *Yizkor* serves in the life of a Jew. In the face of these overwhelming emotions, *Yizkor reassures* us of meaning in the mystery. We find comfort in the community that assembles to acknowledge and support one another in the sacred task of memory; likewise, the ritual's content addresses some of the deep issues that might disturb us. Here we look to the last two prayers in the *Yizkor* service: *El Malei Rachamim* ("God, full of compassion") and *Av Harachamim* ("Father of mercy"). The dominant imagery in both is of a world where even tragic deaths are put into a context of justice, grace, and ultimate meaning.

Both pieces draw their names and opening words from the comforting notion of God as the source of compassion and nurture (*rachamim*). In *El Malei Rachamim* (a response to the 1648 slaughter of Ukrainian Jewry), death brings "perfect repose under divine wings," and the soul of the deceased is "bound up in the bundle of life," their eternal paradise symbolized by invoking the image of the Garden of Eden. In *Av Harachamim* (a parallel response to the massacres of the medieval Crusades), we find similarly comforting notions of the rewards awaiting the righteous martyrs. Added to this is a plea for justice in the form of punishment and vengeance toward those who have slain the innocent among our people.

Taken together, these two prayers serve as a profound statement of reassurance in the face of the pain and confusion that so often accompanies a loss. Mourners come to *Yizkor*, then, to be reassured that death is not the end; that tragic or inexplicable deaths can be made more bearable if our theological context is broad and deep enough; and that the lives of our loved ones, and our own lives as well, have ultimate meaning beyond the reality that they will one day end. Simply put, we come to *Yizkor* to touch eternity, the ultimate reassurance of a realm beyond the binary mystery of human life and human death.

Re-membering

Contemporary biblical commentator Avivah Zornberg describes the patriarch Jacob as personifying the process of "re-membering the dismembered."[1] His life has been fragmented, a struggle to achieve wholeness in his identity and relationships. The Torah portrays this starkly when his sons confront him with Joseph's tunic, bloodied and torn apart—a physical manifestation of his fragmented or "dismembered" life. When he approaches his own death, Jacob will have to re-member the fragments of his life, weaving together his various journeys, failings, and lessons into a coherent whole that will allow him to die in peace.

Each of us who enters a synagogue to recite *Yizkor* is engaged in some combination of *re-membering*: bringing together the fragments of our own lives. We do so through *reliving, rehearsing,* and *reassuring,* dimensions of the *Yizkor*/memory experience that help us gather the disparate strands of our brush with the ultimate mystery and re-member them.

⊙⟶⟶⊙

Prayer for the Dead; Promise by the Living

Rabbi Aaron D. Panken, PhD

The prayers of the Yom Kippur *Yizkor* service all commence with precisely the same wording, *Yizkor Elohim* ("May God remember"). There then follow the particular parties we remember: beloved parents, then cherished spouses, and finally, the collective memory of sacred Jewish martyrs. Reading this formulation carefully, one notes that it shifts from a typical mourning stance in which *we* are doing the remembering, to a new stance in which we ask *God* to do the remembering on our behalf. Perhaps we believe that because God is eternal and omnipotent, divine remembrance will surpass any frail human recollection and our loved ones will be recalled perfectly and for all eternity.

And yet, there is something problematic in this. While imperfect, our memories are not impersonal. What made each departed person so unique and precious to us comprises, arguably, some of the most private and meaningful thoughts and aspirations of our lives. Why, then, do we ask God to do the remembering?

A solution may lie in the Torah, where the similar phrase *vayizkor Elohim* ("and God remembered") appears precisely four times: Genesis 8:1, 19:29, and 30:22; and Exodus 2:24. In each case, God's remembrance at a critical moment in history created ripples that changed the life of our people to this day. Whether or not the author of *Yizkor* consciously

---

Rabbi Aaron D. Panken, PhD, teaches Rabbinic and Second Temple literature at Hebrew Union College–Jewish Institute of Religion in New York. He is author of *The Rhetoric of Innovation* (University Press of America), and contributed to *Who by Fire, Who by Water*—Un'taneh Tokef, *All These Vows*—Kol Nidre, and *We Have Sinned: Sin and Confession in Judaism*—Ashamnu *and* Al Chet (all Jewish Lights).

had these precedents in mind, they surely form the background against which we can understand the liturgy as we know it.

Modern biblical commentator Nahum Sarna points out that "in the Bible, 'remembering,' particularly on the part of God, is not the retention or recollection of a mental image, but a focusing upon the object of memory that results in action."[1] All four occurrences of *vayizkor Elohim* do indeed focus on a particular party's challenging situation, followed by divine actions that assist that party in concrete ways.

The first instance, for example, Genesis 8:1, finds us in the middle of the story of Noah's ark. Noah, his family, and the manifold assembled animals are afloat and alone, buffeted by the turbid waters of a still-flooded earth after the wicked have perished in their watery graves. Here, God's remembrance ends the period of destruction and initiates the process of the waters' receding from the face of the earth: "God remembered Noah and all the beasts and the cattle that were with him in the ark, and God caused a wind to blow across the earth, and the waters subsided." Within a few verses, the ark comes to rest in the mountains of Ararat, allowing Noah and his charges to vacate their ship and resettle the earth. In this mythic tale, God's remembrance causes nothing less than the salvation of the entire ecosystem of the world's living creatures. Had God "forgotten," the world would have continued in its miserably liquid state, and all those in the ark would have perished. It is only through God's remembrance that the creatures of the world survive.

In Genesis 19:29, God destroys the cities of the Plain (Sodom and Gomorrah) because of the unrighteousness of their inhabitants. This time, God remembers Abraham and, for his sake, saves his nephew Lot from dying in the inferno. Here too, then, God remembers a righteous individual—this time, Abraham rather than Noah—but here the saving action is transferred from Abraham to Lot. Lot, it should be recalled, needs Abraham's intervention, both because it is Abraham who has an active covenant with the divine and because Lot has participated in seriously questionable behavior (see the rest of Genesis 19) that likely excludes him from the category of the truly righteous. But God's remembering of Abraham extends beyond the tzaddik himself to save even an undeserving member of his family from an awful sulfurous demise.

In a third example, the verses leading up to Genesis 30:22 find our matriarch Rachel feeling vulnerable and alone, losing badly in a competition of conception. All three of Jacob's other wives and concubines, Leah,

Bilhah, and Zilpah, have by now given birth to many children, while Rachel, his most beloved wife, is weighed down by childlessness. "Give me children," she pleads, "or I shall die" (Genesis 30:1). Again, God's remembrance initiates divine action: "Now God remembered Rachel; God heeded her and opened her womb" (Genesis 30:22). Immediately thereafter, Rachel gives birth to Joseph, the next link in the patriarchal chain that becomes the Jewish People. Through God's remembrance, Rachel becomes a mother not only of Joseph but also of the entire Jewish future.

God's final act of remembrance in the Torah appears in Exodus 2:24, after the people have left Canaan and gone down to Egypt. Suffering greatly there, they groan at the awful vicissitudes of slavery inflicted upon them by a merciless pharaoh. This time, God "remembers," but quite differently. In the other three cases, remembrance is focused on a single person with whom God has a relationship—Noah, Abraham, or Rachel—all of whom are alive at the moment of remembrance. God remembers them, that is, *in the present*—the way we might "remember" a person waiting to see us for an appointment. Here, however, it is not living persons alone who are remembered but all three patriarchs; and they are remembered *in the past* (for they have all died). "God remembered the covenant with Abraham and Isaac and Jacob" (Exodus 2:24). Further, when God's action takes place, it far transcends the individuals being remembered and their immediate families, for here God saves the entire people of Israel in an act that leads to Sinai, to the Promised Land, and eventually to our people's history all the way to today. Without this remembrance, the rest of Jewish history would not have happened.

God's remembrance, then, can encompass a single individual or a group, from the present or the past, and it can save the person remembered or other parties to whom the remembered party is related. Sarna's assessment is certainly on target: God's intense focus leads to decisive action at a critical transitional moment. With Noah, God sustains the world by causing the waters to recede. For Abraham, God saves Lot from the fate of the doomed Sodomites all around him. With Rachel, God provides offspring and continuation of the Jewish line. In Exodus, God saves all the Israelites. Thus, remembering becomes more than a simple mental act; it focuses divine attention on individuals and collectives who need deliverance from pain and destruction, thereby ensuring that Jewish history continues as God intends.

When we ask God to remember the souls of our departed at *Yizkor*, then, we request more than a mere mental act. We pray implicitly that by focusing on our loved ones' souls, God will take action on their behalf and save them from whatever pain they may be suffering, wherever they may be. At the same time, the implication is that this act of remembrance also constitutes a guarantee of Jewish continuity—well beyond just those we remember, and far beyond us as well. In remembering and in asking for God's remembrance, we request divine help in continuing our people's trajectory beyond ourselves, to achieve the ultimate aims of our people's history.

Words adapted from Leo Jung's writing on memorial prayers in 1926 may say it best:

> That is the meaning of the [memorial] words today when said for mother and father. Not a prayer for the dead, but a pledge from the living; not a superstitious phrase, but a person's motto of life. That is the meaning of *hazkarah* [remembrance]—that we continue where our parents ceased; that we do not allow the heritage of Israel to decay for want of ... the courage to bring sacrifices in a godless, thoughtless world.[2]

Yizkor is, in the end, not a prayer for the dead, but a promise by the living.

〇‱〇

When the Golden Shields Are Gone

Rabbi Jack Riemer

There are lots of famous people in the Bible. There are Abraham, Isaac, and Jacob, and Moses and Aaron, and Miriam, and Joshua, and David and Solomon, and Jeremiah, Isaiah, Amos, and Jonah, and many, many others.

And then there is Rehoboam, the son of King Solomon, not the most famous of our biblical heroes—indeed, hardly a hero at all, through most of his life—but my hero when it comes to thinking about *Yizkor*.

The non-heroic part of his history is his decision upon inheriting the throne to increase taxation to the point where his overburdened subjects in the north secede to found a separate northern kingdom (called Israel). With ten of the twelve tribes gone from the union, Rehoboam is left with only the southern kingdom (called Judah), comprising the lands of Judah and Benjamin. He is thus remembered as the king who split the Land of Israel into two separate realms, neither one of which proves sustainable.

But people do mature, and two chapters later, a chastened Rehoboam teaches us something profound. A crisis occurs when "Shishak, the king of Egypt, marched against Jerusalem and carried off the treasures of the House of Adonai, and the treasures that were in the royal palace.

Rabbi Jack Riemer, well-known author and speaker, has conducted many workshops and seminars to help people learn about the inspiring tradition of ethical wills and to prepare their own. As head of the National Rabbinic Network, a support system for rabbis across denominational lines, he gives sermon seminars to rabbis throughout the United States. He is editor of *The World of the High Holy Days* and *Wrestling with the Angel*, and coeditor of *So That Your Values Live On: Ethical Wills and How to Prepare Them* (Jewish Lights).

He carried off everything! He even carried off all the golden shields that Solomon had made" (1 Kings 14:25–26).

Egypt is infinitely stronger than Judah—especially now that the ten tribes have seceded—so there is no way for Judah to do anything other than stand helplessly by as the Egyptians pillage their holy city. Rehoboam's response, however, is as heroic a gesture as one can imagine. "King Rehoboam had bronze shields made [in place of the gold ones that he had lost], and he entrusted them to the officers of the guard who guarded the entrance to the palace" (1 Kings 14:27).

End of story—a story I think about every time the occasion arrives for saying *Yizkor*. Why was the manufacturer of bronze shields "heroic," and what do bronze shields have to do with *Yizkor*?

There comes a time for all of us when the golden shields that are the light of our lives, the golden shields that our parents represented, or the golden shields embodied by others whom we love—there comes a time, I say, when these are captured or destroyed. *Yizkor* reminds us of that time.

We once had a mother or a father whom we could turn to in every moment of distress, whom we knew would always protect us—and then we lost them. We may have had a life partner on whom we leaned, depended, turned to in every crisis—and then that partner was gone. We ourselves may have had a body that was strong and straight and power-ful—a body on which we could depend—and then that body gave out. Our back—which used to be so strong and straight—became bent over. Our health, which gave us so much pride and so much confidence, sud-denly weakened. And what do we do then?

What do we do when we lose our golden shields?

If we are wise, we do what King Rehoboam did. We make substitute shields, bronze ones, and we give these substitute shields the same dignity and honor that we gave the golden shields that we once had but lost.

I know people who have lost a life partner—and it was like nothing less than an amputation for them. They had no idea how to balance a checkbook or even how to write a check. They were completely lost, totally bewildered. And then, slowly, little by little, they recovered. Life was never quite the same again—golden shields are never fully replaced. But they made do with bronze shields, which they accorded the same dignity and respect they had given the golden shields that they no longer had.

I know people who have lost their health. A body that they once took for granted no longer functioned the way it used to. Now just getting up and sitting down were challenges. Now going for a walk was no longer a possibility. And yet, they managed to rebuild their lives around new realities. They use a walker to get around—not as well as before— but still, they do get around. They may move to a one-story house or install a machine that enables them to get up steps of the old one. It isn't as good, but it is something. It is a bronze shield, but they use it, and it suffices.

Franklin Delano Roosevelt was stricken with polio on the very threshold of his meteoric political career. He had every right and every reason to quit, to retire to his country estate at Hyde Park and sit life out from there. But he didn't. It was an era when most Americans would not have supported a president who seemed physically frail, so he worked out a deal with reporters never to photograph him on his crutches. And with those crutches, his own bronze shields, he went around the country, campaigning in every state. And he became the president of the United States four times!

Many years ago, I saw a performance of *Rumpelstilskin* put on by children who were what we politely call nowadays "physically challenged." They did the whole show—dancing, singing, acting, and all—in their wheelchairs! These were children from whom life had taken their golden shields. They had made bronze ones to take their place. And with those bronze shields they served their God supremely well.

At *Yizkor* time, we remember parents who at the end of their lives—and sometimes even before—had to live with bronze shields. Some of them finished out their lives after many years of living without the partners who had sustained them, or without their health, or without both. How many of us had parents who eventually had to surrender their driver's licenses—what a dreadful turning point that is! To give up a driver's license in our society is like giving up your legs, and yet, they did it, and continued to live, and maybe even managed to live well! How many of us had elderly parents whose bodies or minds gave out, who lived on medicines, life supports, and even institutionalized care instead of being the fully competent adults that they had hoped to be their whole lives through? But they did it. They carried on. They made do with bronze shields when their golden ones were taken away.

At *Yizkor* time as well, we may think of ourselves as aging, for we too are victims of mortality; we too will have golden shields taken from us eventually. Some of us are facing such a loss right now.

I think of one man who used to sit at the head of the table at all the community events. My brother used to say that the reason that they put him at the head of the table at every banquet was because they liked his handwriting—by which he meant the way he wrote checks. But now, his business has taken a turn for the worse, and he cannot write the checks he used to. He no longer sits at the head of the table. He occupies instead one of the tables in the back of the room.

But he still serves the causes he believes in. He goes to the office of the organization that he used to support financially and helps out personally, making phone calls, soliciting support, or just stuffing and addressing envelopes. He does whatever they need doing—and he does it cheerfully and with good spirit.

That man no longer has a golden shield with which to serve, but he can teach us all a lesson in how to serve with a bronze one. God bless this man for the good that he is doing and for the lesson that he teaches us all by his example.

For the truth is, at some time in our lives, we will all face the challenge of King Rehoboam. We will all lose the golden shields of our lives, the shields that made us proud and on which we depended so very much. And when that happens, we may grieve—how can you not grieve when you lose something so precious? But only for a while, let us hope, only long enough to get for ourselves bronze shields to take their place. And let us pick up these bronze shields and carry them bravely. And on these shields let us inscribe this motto: "We will serve our God with bronze as well as gold."

⟋⟋⟍⟍⟍⟋

A Soul-ar Eclipse

Rabbi Sandy Eisenberg Sasso

In 1993, at the age of forty-three, and only eight years into her marriage, Carol Ann Brush died tragically of a brain tumor. She left behind two children, aged five and two. She had been the wife of Douglas Hofstadter, professor of cognitive and computer science at Indiana University, and in 2007, Hofstadter wrote a brilliant and moving account of what it all meant: a book titled *I Am a Strange Loop*.

Hofstadter, already an outstanding scientific authority on cognition, taught me about memory in a way I had never thought possible. He suggests that when the life of one person touches another, the hopes and dreams of one continue in the other. So when people die, their hopes and dreams don't; they continue in the life of others to whom they were close. And this isn't just wishful thinking—it's true, not only in a religious or poetic sense, but also in a pragmatic and tangible way, because that is how the brain works. We absorb so much of our loved ones that when they die, they do not totally perish, because they, or at least significant parts of them, are still in us, in our brain. In this way, they live—in us. Their laughter and their joys, their hurts and their sorrows, their stories and their desires, their own personal sense of who they are and how they are in the world are not somehow trapped solely within them, doomed to vanish when they do. Our loved ones are not simply turned into dust and ashes; the parts that matter most are actually transportable to others.

Rabbi Sandy Eisenberg Sasso is rabbi emerita of Congregation Beth-El Zedeck in Indianapolis, where she has served for thirty-six years, and director of the Religion, Spirituality, and Arts Initiative at Butler University in partnership with Christian Theological Seminary. She is the author of award-winning children's books including *God's Paintbrush* and *Shema in the Mezuzah: Listening to Each Other*, winner of the National Jewish Book Award (both Jewish Lights). Her book for adults is *Midrash: Reading the Bible with Question Marks*. She contributed to *Who by Fire, Who by Water—Un'taneh Tokef* and *All These Vows—Kol Nidre* (both Jewish Lights).

What happens is what we might call an interweaving of souls—a mutual sharing of each other's goals and identity. We literally get into each other's heads. We are, each of us, in Hofstadter's language a "strange loop" constantly receiving feedback from the world outside us, making it a part of us and, in turn, affecting the world. But we harbor within us more than our own single loop. We know how our friends and loved ones see things, so that their loops intersect with ours. We are intertwined. Walt Whitman in "Song of Myself" wrote, "Do I contradict myself? Very well, I contradict myself. I am large, I contain multitudes." We all contain multitudes. We are inhabited to varying extents by other "I"s, other souls.

As Hofstadter expresses it, "Every normal adult human soul is housed in many brains at varying degrees of fidelity, and therefore every human consciousness or 'I' lives at once in a collection of different brains, to different extents."[1] In this way, we live inside other human beings, and other human beings live inside us. The books we read, the music we listen to, the art we see, the movies and sports we experience, everyone we meet (for good or for bad)—these all impact us by changing who we are, in small or big ways. And then there are a few people to whom we are very close, whose words and deeds, whose habits and narratives, occupy a large space inside us. They shape us not just minimally but fundamentally.

We are distinct individuals. We are created in the image of God, yet each of us is unique. So of course, you are you and I am I, living different lives, thinking different thoughts, and dreaming different dreams. But we also overlap. In some ways, I am I *because* you are you. I am changed by what you say to me, by how you embrace or shun me, by the way you move with me in the dance of life. When your life intersects with mine, I am transformed. Knowing you makes me a different person.

The political journalist and historian Theodore White once noted that when you press a block of pure gold against a block of steel, they exchange molecules with each other. "When people are pressed close, they act the same way," he observed. "Part of you enters them; part of them enters you.... Long after you forget the names and faces, the other times and place, they're still a part of you."[2]

Hofstadter compares this to a solar eclipse. When the moon crosses the sun, the full brightness of the sun disappears. But, nonetheless, the sun's glowing corona remains visible around the edges. And so it is, Hofstadter suggests, that when someone dies there is a "soul-ar" eclipse. Much is lost, but the glow of the soul remains.[3]

You cannot look directly at a solar eclipse. It can cause serious damage to the human eye. Similarly, the process of mourning teaches us that although we cleave to sweet reminiscences, our way of observing the glowing corona of the soul, we are cautioned to avoid a direct gaze. We are counseled also to forgive the ones we have loved and to forgive ourselves for the hurts we have inevitably inflicted on one another. These are means of loosening our grasp, lest by holding on too tightly, we damage our human spirit.

But that is not all. Just as we can use a mirror to reflect the light of the sun onto the sidewalk to view the solar eclipse, so we can use memory as our mirror to see the reflection of the souls of those we have lost.

I believe that when we say in our *Yizkor* prayers, "May God remember the soul of my beloved," we are doing just that. The prayers are mirrors through which we see more clearly the soft glow of our loved ones. We call forth the many ways they have changed us, not just how they have touched our hearts, but also how they have literally altered our brains, the very people we are.

Jewish folklore tells of an angel of losses called Yode'a.[4] That angel and his servants spend all their time looking for losses. They search with a light. That light is nothing more than a small candle flame. They look inside the places of unbroken darkness to find what has vanished, and they keep in memory all that has been lost.

That is what we do when we recite memorial prayers. At home before the Yom Kippur fast we kindle a small twenty-four-hour candle, whose light we carry with us in our mind's eye, to the synagogue, where more memorial lamps have already been lit. We wed those lights to the one we brought with us and then weave them all together with the *Yizkor* prayers we say, letting image and word illumine the unbroken darkness of the grave. Through that light of memory, we recall once again what we have lost. We recognize how deeply we carry our loved ones inside us, literally within our minds and our hearts. At that moment, we know that this is true. That is why the angel is given the name Yode'a, from the Hebrew word meaning "to know."

We are all servants of this angel of losses, who struggle in the places of deepest darkness, in the valley of shadows, to recover those losses and to rekindle within ourselves the glow of the souls of those who have died, for it becomes clear to us how we have been changed and what parts of ourselves are from our loved ones. We then know what we otherwise sometimes forget: that they are with us still. And we promise to live out the best that they have bequeathed to us.

That is how I understand the beautiful words of *El Malei Rachamim*:

> O God, full of compassion, eternal spirit of the universe, grant perfect rest under the wings of Your presence to our loved one who has entered eternity. Compassionate One, hide him/her in the secret embrace of your wings for all time. Bind his/her soul in the bond of eternal life.

Perhaps it is Yode'a, the angel of losses, guardian of memory, under whose wings our loved ones are hidden. They are carried in those secret places of our brains, inextricably bound up with us in the bond of life.

⌒⌘⌐

To Tear and to Sew

Rabbi David Stern

The mourners stand in the quiet circle before the funeral begins. We attach the black ribbons, then tear them. We speak words of benediction about God's just judgment—but the tearing rings louder than the words.

The custom of *k'ri'ah*, from the Hebrew root "to tear," is thousands of years old. In Genesis 37:34, Jacob tears his garment when he believes that Joseph has died. In 2 Samuel 1:11, David tears his clothes when he hears of the death of King Saul. And for generations since, it has been our people's custom to tear our garments upon hearing of the loss of a loved one. These days we may use a black ribbon instead of rending the garment itself—but we feel the tear all the same.

The symbolism speaks for itself: the tear in the ribbon represents our broken hearts and serves the added social function of identifying mourners to the community, so that if you saw someone walking down the street of your village with an intentionally torn garment, you would be alerted to your responsibility to offer comfort and support.

But for as long as it has been our people's custom to put a tear *into* the garment, it was never our custom to tear a piece *off*—the torn part of the garment always remained attached to the whole. And as we have stood in those quiet circles, we have learned to hold fast to both ends of the symbol, both dimensions of the ancient act. The tear is real: there is no gainsaying the rupture we feel in our lives when someone we love has died. But the "woven together" is real, too—their memory, their example, their influence, and their love remain threaded through the fabric of who we are.

Rabbi David Stern is senior rabbi of Temple Emanu-El in Dallas, Texas. He contributed to *Who by Fire, Who by Water*—Un'taneh Tokef and *All These Vows*—Kol Nidre (both Jewish Lights).

So the Talmud gives us passages about the reweaving of the mourner's garment, even prescribing which stitches to use. And the great Jewish tailoring wisdom of fifteen hundred years ago was this: the Talmud says you can use herringbone or cross-stitch, but you can't use the stitch of the skilled tailors of Alexandria, which was a stitch that makes the tear disappear altogether.[1] You're not allowed to sew up the fabric so completely or from the reverse side of the garment to make it look as if there were never a tear there—in this garment, in this ribbon, in this heart.

So we come to *Yizkor*, cross-stitched: torn and mending at once. Not to deny our losses, but to spend time in a sacred *Yizkor* hour, which allows us to feel them. And no less, to give thanks for all the ways that rupture finds repair. How the light of their lives still illumines our own. How time heals, if we work at it. How the attention of our friends and family heals, when we feel ready to let them in. How new life in new generations heals, and how some of those new lives even carry their names.

We are not the same as we were. But one stitch at a time, we do some mending. Because the loss is real, and the enduring gifts are real, and the desire to go on is real. Both the tear and the woven together are true—and to deny either one would be to live as less than we are.

Elie Wiesel wrote of his first trip back to his home village of Sighet, where almost no Jews were left:

> I met a Jew, one of the rare survivors, and we walked through the cemetery of Sighet. "To be a Jew," I asked, "what does it mean to you? Does it mean turning your heart into a cemetery?" "No," my companion said. "The heart of a man is a sanctuary ... To be a Jew is to fill the sanctuary with light, without betraying the cemetery."[2]

To fill the sanctuary with light, without betraying the cemetery. To be true to our losses, and no less, to be true to the gift of their lives. To know that the light of a new day does not betray them. That in time even the rough stitch feels good to the touch, because it has the texture of reality to it—of longing and sorrow and resilience and strength. Our tradition teaches that when the tear is first put into the garment, the mourner should be standing—out of respect for the deceased, and because standing is a demonstration of life even on a day of loss.

And I have come to believe that part of what stays woven together is our relationship with them. In fact, in a paradox that we can only begin to understand, sometimes the weave of that relationship becomes stronger now. Sometimes the wounds of living start to heal, right alongside the wounds of loss. The angry moments, the times when we felt diminished, the frustrations at misunderstanding: some we were able to heal when we walked here together—some find their resolution only now.

But what is certain is that memory involves choice. Just as two painters can stand at the edge of the same meadow and make utterly different artistic choices about where to draw our attention, we ourselves decide what to put on memory's canvas.

And in the same way that the artist who focuses on the bend in the willow tree is no more false or true than the artist who focuses on the woman's yellow sun hat, we decide what to capture in the fading light.

We decide which stories to keep telling and which can now rest. Not to repress truths, not to sew with invisible stitches, but to keep working the sacred fabric of loss and love. We decide whether it is worthwhile to continue fingering the jagged edge of pain, or whether we feel that we have learned all that we can learn, and it is time, even now, to do some mending. We decide how to paint peace in the relationships that endure—with both integrity and healing strokes.

Every mourner is a painter, and every mourner is a poet. One of the poet's favorite tools is synecdoche—using the part to stand for the whole. When the captain says, "All hands on deck," he doesn't just mean the hands—he means the whole sailor. When the teacher says, "All eyes on me," she doesn't just want the students' visual attention, she wants the students' complete attention.

So we are expert at the poetry of mourning. Because when we say we remember their eyes, we don't just mean their eyes—we mean the spirit that animated them, the joy that danced in them. And when we say we remember the sound of their footsteps in the hall, we don't just mean the rhythm of their gait—we mean the comfort of their presence, the strength in their companionship. And when we say we remember their seder table, we don't mean just the table—we mean every story and every great-aunt and every matzah ball. It's sacred synecdoche—the part for the whole—the visible, tangible dimensions of the souls that continue to bless our lives.

About a century and a half before Wiesel wrote of Sighet, William Wordsworth wrote these lines:

What though the radiance which was once so bright
Be now for ever taken from my sight,
Though nothing can bring back the hour
Of splendor in the grass, of glory in the flower;
We will grieve not, rather find
Strength in what remains behind.[3]

Yizkor: we are here to find strength in what remains behind. In their legacy, in the values by which they lived, in sunlight and storm, in the souls that somehow shine more brightly even as some of the physical details fade from sight. Strength: in the community that surrounds us, in the God who steadies our steps and guides our way.

Eit likro'a v'eit litpor, Ecclesiastes taught: "There is a time to tear and a time to sew" (Ecclesiastes 3:7). At *Yizkor,* we begin to find our healing way in the reality of it all—one tear at a time, one mending stitch at a time, one step at a time—toward a new year of peace and blessing, toward a new year of life.

☙

Remembering Our Past in Service to Our Future

Rabbi David A. Teutsch, PhD

E very once in a while when I glance down and see my hand, I get a jolt. It looks like my father's hand. And I remember the enveloping touch of that warm, dry hand—its gentle embrace of mine. Though a number of years have gone by since my father's passing, I suddenly feel his presence in my mind—sometimes when I least expect it. Usually that brings a smile to my lips. My relationship with my father has taught me that "love is strong as death" (Song of Songs 8:6). His is a beneficent presence bound up in my life because of the way that I remember him.

The death of a loved one brings disorientation, deep sadness, and a profound sense of loss. As the weeks and months following a death go by, these feelings fade, but they can return without warning, especially at holidays, when we remember how our loved ones once laughed and talked at festive meals and how it felt to sit next to them during worship.

Rabbi David A. Teutsch, PhD, is the Wiener Professor of Contemporary Jewish Civilization and director of the Center for Jewish Ethics at the Reconstructionist Rabbinical College, where he served as president for nearly a decade. He was editor in chief of the seven-volume *Kol Haneshamah* prayer book series. His book *A Guide to Jewish Practice: Everyday Living* (RRC Press) won the National Jewish Book Award for Contemporary Jewish Life and Practice. He is also author of *Spiritual Community: The Power to Restore Hope, Commitment and Joy* (Jewish Lights) and several other books. He contributed to *Who by Fire, Who by Water*—Un'taneh Tokef, *All These Vows*—Kol Nidre, and *We Have Sinned: Sin and Confession in Judaism*—Ashamnu *and* Al Chet (all Jewish Lights).

Holidays, then, are richly bittersweet because of the shadow presence of those no longer living.

For me these memories include my father's laughter at the seder table, my uncle's earnest explanations, the arguments about the matzah balls, my aunt's beatific smiles: the ordinary things of life. Those memories of seders more than forty years ago are with me still whenever I prepare for Pesach.

Judaism recognizes the recurrent pain of loss through the recitation of *Yizkor* on Yom Kippur and the last day of festivals: Pesach, Shavuot, and Sh'mini Atzeret at the conclusion of Sukkot. On holidays, we plunge into a sea of memories and then ease out of them as each holiday moves toward a conclusion.

When we write about someone who has died, Jews often place two Hebrew letters, a *zayin* and a *lamed*, after the deceased's name. These letters are an abbreviation for *zikhrono/ah liv'rakhah*, "may his/her memory be a blessing." How can a memory be a blessing? Clearly not all our memories do that or the wish would have no meaning. Memories are blessings when they bring warm feelings, reinforce virtues, or inspire positive action. Sharing such memories with others improves their lives and spreads the blessing.

In our more honest moments, we realize that life is fleeting and that we are by nature fragile and limited. Part of the meaning we see in our lives comes from what there is about us that will live on after we die. For some, that bequest lies in inventions, art, or writing, but for most of us, our legacy is the influence we have on others while we are alive and the memories that help shape their lives after we are gone. In that context, *zikhrono/ah liv'rakhah* contains the wish that the deceased's life will have meaning as a result of the memories we have of them. When a life remembered inspires good deeds, that is indeed a blessing. So are acts done specifically in their memories, acts such as participating in an AIDS walkathon, raising money for cancer research, planting trees in Israel, working to rebuild homes after a natural disaster, or funding a water purifier in Africa.

There are many ways that memories can be a blessing. Occasionally during *Yizkor* in my *minyan*, we take time to recall aloud qualities or anecdotes about the people we are remembering. Those stories prove inspiring, and sometimes they bring tears to the eyes of those who hear them; they are blessings that move and shape us.

Franz Rosenzweig eloquently portrays our lot as inescapably inhabiting the present. We bring the future into the present through anticipation and the past into the present as memory, but both past and future can be understood only from our vantage point in the present. Our present is impacted by our hopes and fears for the future. Both our future and our present are profoundly shaped by our memories of the past. The ideas, values, ideals, stories, and examples of those whom we have loved thus continue to pattern our present whenever we recall them; their memory *is* part of our present, making them genuinely part and parcel of *us*. This is particularly so when we consciously invoke their memory, as we do when we recite *Yizkor*.

My father, for example, modeled hard work, loyalty, concern for the Jewish community, love of family, care in judgment, thrift, and self-discipline. Those qualities helped make me what I am. When I recall my father at *Yizkor*, those qualities, which I try to emulate, are reinforced in me.

Memory is not history; it does not just reproduce the way things actually were. Rather, memory once lodged in the brain has a life of its own. Scientists have shown that the act of recalling a memory actually alters it. Bringing relatives and friends to mind makes us see them differently. If we remember them in a way that allows their memory to be a blessing, the aspects of them that were beloved, inspiring, and uplifting come newly to life for us. Each time we do that, the memories that uplift us further overshadow the parts of our relationships that were painful and difficult. Memory is not history. Our memories evolve each time we bring them to mind.

This plasticity of memory is especially important because all relationships inevitably involve at least some hurt or disappointment; some relationships are downright scarred by the intentional or unintentional pain that they have inflicted. The residue of hurtful relationships may always be with us, but in circumstances short of actual abuse, memory selects judiciously from the enormous array of data in our heads, helping us shape recollections that have positive power in our lives. Our aspiration that such memories should be a blessing can filter out the negative and emphasize the positive, thereby helping us heal with time.

Although the *effect* of the *Yizkor* service is to evoke memories of our loved ones, its liturgy does not ostensibly focus on doing so. The opening word of *Yizkor* asks that *God* remember, not that we do so. To understand what this might mean, it is helpful to consider the liturgical context. An early-morning prayer proclaims, "My God, the soul you gave me is pure" (*Elohai n'shamah shenatata bi t'horah hi*)—not just, "My soul was pure when You breathed it into me," but, in effect, "Despite all I have done to muddy myself by thought, word, and deed, my soul is *still* pure!" To rediscover that purity—and the divine within—I need only reach inside and reestablish contact with it. The belief that we can reconnect with our pure souls has important implications not only for the possibility of repentance (*t'shuvah*) but also for how we understand our lives more generally. We can cut off our contact from the divine within, but it is always there awaiting our return. The pure soul within us lives on unblemished.

In *Yizkor*, we ask that God remember the soul of our loved one and bind it up in the bundle of life along with the souls of the matriarchs and patriarchs. The notion that God may "bind the soul up in the bundle of life" reflects the belief that at our deaths, the pure soul departs from our bodies and rejoins all other souls that animate human beings. But what can it mean for God "to remember"? Jewish tradition teaches that we are to imitate God, a principle often called *imitatio dei*. The wish that *God* remember that pure soul is a lesson that *we* are to remember it. We remember, therefore, not only the good and bad that our parents did, not only what they taught and said, but the fact that despite all their failings and flaws, they had pure souls—the presence of divinity—within them. If we remember the purity of their souls and keep them bound with ours, then God remembers because we remember, and all of us who have ever lived are bound together with the divine. *El Malei Rachamim* repeats this lesson: across time and space our memories and actions bind our dead loved ones *bitzror hachayim*, "in the bundle of life."

So the traditional *Yizkor* prayer asks that the souls we remember may rest alongside those of our ancestors. But it predicates their ability to do so on our pledge of *tz'dakah* (literally, "justice," meaning, here, money given to charity) on their behalf. According to one traditional belief, *mitzvot* done in memory of the deceased accrue to the good deeds of that person, making it more likely that the deceased will arrive amidst the pure and holy souls. Those of us who do not take heaven so literally can understand that deeds done in the memory of others enhance our memories and bring goodness into the world. Pledging *tz'dakah* is part of the process of reshaping the memories of those we love.

Another aspect of giving *tz'dakah* is that it causes the simple inner glow of memory to impact others: it converts memory into action. Memory thus takes on world-redemptive power in Jewish tradition. Think, for example, about how Pesach recalls, "We were slaves to Pharaoh in Egypt" (*avadim hayinu l'faro b'mitzrayim*). What a tragic thing to remember! Yet Egyptian servitude is a critical part of Jewish self-understanding. We uplift and transform that memory by turning it into the commitment not to oppress the stranger, the widow, the orphan, or any other people who might be down on their luck or disadvantaged because of race, ethnicity, creed, gender, or class. The memory that we were slaves becomes a clarion call for social justice. Similarly, the act of remembering through reciting *Yizkor* takes on its intended meaning only if it results in action. Pledging *tz'dakah* or promising to do another *mitzvah* brings to fruition the hope that the memory will be a blessing.

Yizkor invokes not just the memories of those we have known but also those who have sacrificed their lives as martyrs (*al kiddush hashem*, "in sanctification of God's name"). *Kol Haneshamah*, the prayer book of the Reconstructionist Movement, specifies martyrs, victims of the Holocaust, and those who died defending the State of Israel. Unlike the traditional version of *Av Harachamim* (p. 136), *Kol Haneshamah* does not invoke revenge or punishment upon the perpetrators of those deaths. Instead, it inspires us to lead better lives so that their sacrifice may not turn out to have been in vain.

Both the loved ones whom we knew personally and those whom we remember only by reputation or by what they did (or, sometimes, were forced to do) are part of our legacy. We hold them in the bundle of life through memory, teaching, and deed. Memory of the past enriches our present and helps us shape our future with hope.

☙

"For I Pledge *Tz'dakah* on Her Behalf"

Rabbi Margaret Moers Wenig, DD

"In the rising of the sun ... we remember them."[1] What does it mean for us to remember? *Yizkor Elohim*—what are we asking God to "remember"?

Neurologists claim that "early influences can literally leave imprints on the brain that last a lifetime."[2] "Memories make us.... What we experience first filters what comes afterwards."[3] A child who was abused or neglected will ever be affected by that experience, as will a child who was well cared for and whose worth was affirmed. Even late-life experiences may change us forever, as this surviving lover testifies: "The break from now on is an inescapable part of who I am, perhaps the inescapable part. Hasn't it become my essential definition, my central fact: I loved a man who died."[4]

And yet remembering those who have affected us is not simply a process of opening a window and looking through it back in time. For "memory is not simply a videotape of experiences that can be replayed with accuracy."[5] We "cut and splice the magnetic tape on which our lives are recorded."[6] Yes, "memories make us," but ...

We make memories.... What we feel now can influence what we recall from the past. When we retrieve a memory from where it is stored in the brain, just as when we open a Word file, we automatically open it to "edit" and when we "save" the memory again and place it back into storage, we may well have modified it.[7]

Rabbi Margaret Moers Wenig, DD, teaches liturgy and homiletics at Hebrew Union College–Jewish Institute of Religion in New York and is rabbi emerita of Beth Am, The People's Temple. She contributed to *Who by Fire, Who by Water*—Un'taneh Tokef, *All These Vows*—Kol Nidre, and *We Have Sinned: Sin and Confession in Judaism*—Ashamnu *and* Al Chet (all Jewish Lights).

I thought my memories of my mother would never change. She was not warm, at least not after tragedy hardened her. Many years after her death, when I found myself tragically in her shoes, I saw my mother in a new light. I could not but forgive her for her emotional distance and her physical absence. And I recalled something I'd long forgotten: when my brother and I were young, my mother used to read to us at bedtime. Among the books she read was *Winnie the Pooh*. Now I sometimes listen to a recording of *Pooh* at night as if the loving part of my mother were once again reading her children to sleep.

We don't altogether choose our memories; they come to us, sometimes in our dreams. Sometimes they even haunt us. But they are malleable. Time and circumstances opened the files and edited my memories of my mother before saving them once again.

We imagine that God's memories of the deceased and of us will never change. We picture God the judge "opening the Book of Memories [*Sefer Hazikhronot*] and reading what we have inscribed therein with our own hand, with our own deeds. And yet we also plead, 'Wipe away and remove our sins from before Your eyes,'"[8] to which, we imagine, God replies, "I will remember your sins no more."

My mother inscribed her good and her bad deeds on my brain, affecting me for decades. But one Elul, in response to the plea "Wipe away and remove my sins from before your eyes"—a line that she was never able to utter during her lifetime—I replied, "I will remember your sins no more." And I was comforted.

My own experience is echoed in this Hasidic tale:

> In the night after the seven day mourning for Reb Abraham ... his wife had a dream. She saw a vast hall and in it thrones.... A door opened, and ... Abraham, her husband, entered. "Friends, my wife is angry with me because in my earthly life I lived apart from her. She is right and therefore I must obtain her forgiveness." His wife cried out: "With all my heart, I forgive you." And she awoke comforted.[9]

As much as the dead may need to obtain forgiveness from the living or the living may need to forgive the dead, so too, sometimes, the living need to ask forgiveness *of* the dead. According to Maimonides:

If you sin against another and he dies before you can repay him and ask his forgiveness, you bring ten Israelites to the dead person's grave as witnesses and say before them: I have sinned in such and such a way against so and so. If the deceased has heirs, you pay your debt to the heirs. If the deceased has no heirs, you pay your debt to the *bet din* and confess.[10]

Note that in Maimonides's teaching, pleas for forgiveness are accompanied by concrete deeds. Most traditional *Yizkor* formulas begin, "May God remember the soul of ... because I pledge *tz'dakah* on his/her behalf" (*Yizkor elohim et nishmat ... ba'avur she'ani noder/noderet tz'dakah ba'ado/ ba'adah*).[11]

This pledge is omitted from most liberal liturgies, out of discomfort with the notion that the verdict passed upon the dead can be improved by deeds that the living perform on the deceased's behalf. This objection, however, misses the nuanced brilliance of a crucial aspect of *Yizkor*: the ongoing relationship between the living and the dead and the changes that relationship may undergo.

When we plead for God to remember the soul of our loved one, we are not asking God simply to open the Book of Memories and read what has been inscribed there, but to take note of *something that hasn't yet happened, something that has yet to be inscribed*: some concrete act of ours that will change, if ever so slightly, our relationship with the deceased and thus the deceased's impact on the world.

It is as if we say, "Through this pledge and act of *tz'dakah* I hereby demonstrate my empathy for and forgiveness of .... Through this *tz'dakah*, I appeal to ... for the hurt I caused him. Through this *tz'dakah*, I hope, little by little, to externalize and thus also to internalize my lost one's love and, thereby, to feel her presence more and more and grieve her absence less and less. Through this *tz'dakah*, I hope to extend the reach of the good that ... did during his lifetime."

The Rabbis referred to the Day of Atonement as Yom Hakippurim— the plural—because, some say, it is a day of *kaparah* ("atonement") for both the living and the dead. *Yizkor* on Yom Kippur is, I believe, not about human frailty or the futility of human endeavors, as some *Yizkor* liturgies suggest; it is about the power of others to affect us, about our power to affect others, about the power of the dead and the living to continue to affect each other. *Yizkor* on Yom Kippur is not simply about remembering the dead, but about making memories, affecting *change* in our relationships with the dead, and thereby affecting change in ourselves and in our relationships with those who are still living.[12]

៚

A Time to Re-Member

Dr. Ron Wolfson

I love family reunions. On holidays and special life-cycle events like *brit milah* or *simchat bat*, bar/bat mitzvah, weddings and funerals, our family gathers from the far corners of the country to celebrate, catch up, or console one another as we share the next chapters in our life stories. The members of our clan make a concerted effort to be present for these gatherings, linking us together and reminding us of the times we have shared. It is a time for remembering.

"Remember" is an interesting word. In usual usage, it means "to keep in mind, to retain information." Sometimes the word means to "reward," as in "she was remembered in the will." Or even to convey greetings: "please remember me to him."

But there is another way to read the word: "re-member." A member is an individual in a group, like a member of the family. In this reading, "re-member" means reuniting the family, bringing together again those who are closest to us.

Dr. Ron Wolfson is Fingerhut Professor of Education at American Jewish University in Los Angeles, a cofounder of Synagogue 3000/Next Dor, and a member of Shevet: Jewish Family Education Exchange. He is author of *Relational Judaism: Using the Power of Relationships to Transform the Jewish Community*; *The Seven Questions You're Asked in Heaven: Reviewing and Renewing Your Life on Earth*; *God's To-Do List: 103 Ways to Be an Angel and Do God's Work on Earth*; the three volumes *Hanukkah, Passover,* and *Shabbat,* all family guides to spiritual celebrations; *The Spirituality of Welcoming: How to Transform Your Congregation into a Sacred Community; A Time to Mourn, a Time to Comfort: A Guide to Jewish Bereavement; Be Like God: God's To-Do List for Kids*; and, with Rabbi Lawrence A. Hoffman, *What You Will See Inside a Synagogue* (all Jewish Lights). He contributed to *Who by Fire, Who by Water*—Un'taneh Tokef, *All These Vows*—Kol Nidre, and *We Have Sinned: Sin and Confession in Judaism*—Ashamnu *and* Al Chet (all Jewish Lights).

I think of *Yizkor* as a time of "re-membering." It is that somewhat mystical experience of prayer in which each of us focuses on remembering our loved ones, the members of our families, who have died—our beloved mothers, fathers, wives, husbands, sisters, brothers, and children.

For me, as a child growing up in Omaha, Nebraska, *Yizkor* was that moment in the long Yom Kippur day when I was shooed out of the sanctuary, along with anyone else who had not experienced the loss of a loved one. This was endlessly fascinating to me. Clearly something important was happening during this private adult time in the service. The synagogue was packed to the rafters. The light bulbs illuminating each name on the memorial plaques were set ablaze, creating an aura of palpable holiness in the space. We kids retreated to the hallways, the basement, and, when the weather was good, outside, milling around for the half hour or so it took for the service to be completed.

I knew something spiritually significant was happening in there. From the alcove in the back of the sanctuary, I would sneak a peek at the proceedings: the cantor and rabbi, both dressed in white, leading the service with solemnity; the rabbi's words hushed and low; the cantor's sorrowful melodies punctuated with musical *geshries* and cries. Whatever the words meant, the impact was immediate. Many people were in tears, their sobs creating a steady hum that built to a crescendo as the entire congregation recited the Mourner's *Kaddish*. But what was being said? What was happening to move the people so profoundly?

I would not know the answer to this question for many, many years.

When I reached college, my beloved Zaydie, Louie Paperny, died. Like most people of their generation, my mother and father held the superstitious belief that children whose parents are still alive should not be present during *Yizkor*. But I wanted to remember my Zaydie, so I asked, "Is it okay for me to say *Yizkor* for my grandfather?" My mother asked the rabbi, who said it was not required by Jewish law, but was not forbidden either; technically speaking, anyway, a grandson could say *Kaddish* for a grandfather. And so, at age twenty-one I found myself staying in the sanctuary for the very first time, standing beside Mom and Dad during *Yizkor*.

I was not at all prepared for the experience. The liturgy was powerful and gut-wrenching. "What is man? What is man that You should be mindful of him?" "Though I walk through the valley of the shadow of death …" Then the individual readings for each loved one who had died—for a mother, a father, a husband, a wife, a brother, a sister, a child—with each person choosing the appropriate paragraph, and inserting the Hebrew or English name of the remembered into the prayer. It seemed to be the moment of personal grief renewed when the floodgates of tears opened. The rabbi intoned the names of those who had died in the past year. The supplementary booklet listed all those being remembered.

And, then, it struck me. The dead were not simply being remembered; they were being re-membered. Even in death, they were being brought back into the memory of their descendants. It was, in a way, a family reunion—the living inviting the dead back into their presence, back into their hearts, back into their memory.

This is the incredible power of *Yizkor*, the invitation to a spiritual reunification with our beloved family members. When we remember them, we "re-member" our families. As we read the words, our minds overflow with life review, with images of our loved ones—teaching us, feeding us, loving us. To this day, when I recite the Mourner's *Kaddish*, I close my eyes, reciting the words by heart, so my mind's eye can conjure up images of my mom, my dad, my in-laws, my uncles, aunts, cousins, and grandparents. I can see them in their prime: Zaydie Louie capturing me in his leg lock; Bubbie Ida lighting her Shabbes candles; Grandma Celia singing "Sailor Boy"; Mom teaching herself how to type Braille; Dad standing on the highest dive platform in the Peony Park swimming pool to show his boys how to be brave; Bubbie K. working the counter as Dippy Donuts' "Miss Sunshine"; Zadie K. relentlessly working out on a stationary bike at the age of one hundred; dear Uncle George enjoying the "Cajuzzi boobles" in the spa; cousins Bill and Paul Rosen fighting the terrible cancer that claimed them all too early in life. I even pause each *Yizkor* to whisper the prayer for our first baby, a daughter, born on May 6, 1974 ... who died thirteen hours later. Then, strict Jewish law prevented a funeral for a child not surviving thirty days; there was no *shivah*, no grieving. But there is remembering ... and even imagining how old she would be, how beautiful she would be, how much joy she would have brought into our lives, just as our children Michael, Havi, and Dave, and our grandchildren Ellie and Gabe have blessed us.

Yizkor is a time for remembering and re-membering, a spiritual reunification of those closest to us. In a way, it is a form of *m'chayei hametim*, of "bringing the dead to life" once more. *Zikhronam liv'rakhah—* may the memories of all our loved ones be forever a blessing.

Remembering Our Summers in the Autumns of Our Years

Rabbi Daniel G. Zemel

Yom Kippur. It is late in the afternoon and I get a sense that the sun is beginning to fade. The haunting chant of *Kol Nidre* from yesterday evening still seems to haunt the sanctuary. This morning's service is long over. We have confessed and atoned and pleaded for mercy. Torah has been read, twice. Jonah has been swallowed by the great fish and then set out for Nineveh. He has succeeded in the mission that he does not understand. *N'ilah* still feels far away—many pages in my *machzor* yet to turn. But *Yizkor* comes to refocus my attention. I am reawakened, called back to duty, called to be my truest self.

My truest self, not my usual self—for *Yizkor* comes to save us from our usual selves, the part of the self that is so fully modern that it cannot avoid the trap of undue skepticism brought on by our modern preference for history over memory, study over experience, analysis over being. Judaism, however, cherishes remembering, experiencing, and retelling— this is how we discover who we truly (if not usually) are.

Literary critic Hans Meyerhoff calls our situation "paradoxical":

> A situation has developed which is quite paradoxical in human terms: The barriers of the past have been pushed back as never before; our knowledge of the history of man and the universe has been enlarged on a scale and

---

Rabbi Daniel G. Zemel is the senior rabbi of Temple Micah in Washington, D.C. He contributed to *Who by Fire, Who by Water— Un'taneh Tokef, All These Vows—Kol Nidre*, and *We Have Sinned: Sin and Confession in Judaism—Ashamnu and Al Chet* (all Jewish Lights).

to a degree not dreamed of by previous generations. At the same time, the sense of identity and continuity with the past ... has ... steadily declined. Previous generations knew much less about the past than we do, but felt a much greater sense of identity and continuity with it.[1]

We need *Yizkor* because it connects us to personal memory in a way that history cannot grasp. Memory defines who we have been and creates who we will become. Through memory, that is, we revisit the loves, the passions, and the pivotal moments of our lives; and in doing so, we both discover and create ourselves. We relearn that we are what we remember. The attachments we have with the world around us arrive through memory. That which is forgotten loses its claim on us.

History gives us a museum to visit. Memory gives us a soul that animates and defines us.

In his poignant essay, "The Green Fields of the Mind," onetime president of Yale University and then Major League Baseball commissioner A. Bartlett Giamatti reflects on the power of baseball: "It breaks your heart. It is designed to break your heart."[2] He is writing about baseball, but isn't this the human experience as well? Giamatti continues, "Somehow, the summer seemed to slip by faster this time. Maybe it wasn't this summer, but all the summers that, in this my fortieth summer, slipped by so fast. There comes a time when every summer will have something of autumn about it."[3]

Yom Kippur has this "something of autumn" about it; it arrives in autumn and demands we consider the autumn of our lives. With *Yizkor*, this autumnal reflectivity reaches its climax.

Giamatti is on to something when he compares "this summer" to "all the summers," which pass by unequally. The summers of our youth lasted forever. As we age, they speed up: this summer, next summer, all summers—they elide together into memories of days that were not yet autumn. Memory thus merges with memory as days, summers, and years accumulate into sedimented personal pasts. With the passing of time, each *Yizkor* becomes more weighty than the last, because there is more to try to hold on to; more to consider; more to incorporate. Who can possibly remember it all? There is something in this *Yizkor* business that reveals our fragility, reminding us of the time piling up as we hurtle forward, quintessentially human and destined eventually to run out of time.

Someone passes me a booklet with the word *Yizkor* and the year printed on the cover. The pages within are a listing of names—just pages and pages of names. *Yizkor* asks God to remember all these names, and it leaves me a space to say the names of my own summers gone by.

I am reminded of Avishai Margalit, who relates the outline of a play about the Shoah by David Edgar—a story of children incarcerated in a train bound for a concentration camp: they are starving and eat the cardboard name tags around their necks. "It is clear," says Margalit, "that no trace of the children and no trace of their names will be left after they perish."[4] Without memories of who they were, the children will be murdered twice, first in body, then in name. A person's name is their memory—their *zecher*. *Zecher*, teaches Rabbi Lawrence A. Hoffman, has the sense of "pointing the way."[5] Without a *zecher*, they have lost that which points them out. Forget the names and they are more than dead: they are extinguished—blotted out.

This booklet in my hand is a burden—a responsibility. By this reckoning, it calls on me to save my own memories alongside the others already here. Remembering them all, I point the way to existence at least in name, in memory, and in some kind of life that is beyond the total amnesia of utter extinction.

Traditional *machzorim* don't officially include the Mourner's *Kaddish* in the *Yizkor* service. But Reform liturgies do, so my *Gates of Repentance* follows the traditional *El Malei Rachamim* with a *Kaddish*, which reinforces remembering the name. There may be no actual etymological connection between the Hebrew words for name (*shem*) and soul (*n'shamah*), but we remember by name, and *Yizkor* invokes memory of the soul. *El Malei* repeats this plea: "Bind the *n'shamah* with you—dear God!" The *n'shamah* (soul) with the *shem* (name) wrapped inside.

Kaddish follows immediately, asking God to magnify and make great God's own name in the world. All of *Yizkor* is a plea for God to remember. In our remembering, we are asking God to remember, and finally, we are in a sense also asking God to remember God. This is all we have. We who are dust are seeking to preserve ourselves in God's eternal memory.

Giamatti knows of what he writes when he says that "it breaks your heart":

It breaks my heart because it was meant to, because it was meant to foster in me again the illusion that there was something abiding, some pattern and some impulse that could come together to make a reality that would resist corrosion.... Of course there are those who learn ... and there are others who were born with the wisdom to know that nothing lasts. These are the truly tough among us, the ones who can live without illusion, or without even the hope of illusion. I am not that grown-up or up-to-date. I am a simpler creature, tied to more primitive patterns and cycles. I need to think something lasts forever.[6]

This is our *Yizkor* prayer. *Yizkor* tells its own tale. It weaves its own web. We step into a world of memory and in doing so we realize that we are our memories. That is who we are—each one of us. With each passing year, these memories become more precious, important, defining, and fleeting. They rush through us. There are so many—too many—but really never too many—never enough. We need to preserve them. The mere notion of losing them terrifies us beyond our ability to comprehend. We preserve the names in a book and, through *Yizkor*, connect them with the eternity that is God. We pray for God to remember. We pray for God to be great. What could be greater than the certainty of remembering forever?

All of this is what makes us human. This is *Yizkor*'s story. This is how we prepare to close the gates.

Appendix A

Full Text of Hashkavah, *the Sephardi Memorial Prayer, with Translation*

From *Seder T'fillot: Book of Prayer*, published by Union of Sephardic Congregations, 1983

Hashkavah according to the Ritual of Congregation Shearith Israel, the Spanish and Portuguese Synagogue in New York

[*Editor's note:* Sephardi experience and liturgy deserve recognition for their own distinctive spiritual contribution to Jewish life, and this volume, which covers the memorial customs, affords us the opportunity to provide it. The Sephardim, after all, have retained (among other things) their own distinctive ritual of *Hashkavah*, which has figured prominently not only among Sephardi Jews (see Bitton, pp. 19–21) but to some extent (in wording at least) among Ashkenazim as well, because reformers in Germany borrowed from it. The Hamburg community's 1819 prayer book integrated parts of the *Hashkavah* into a new version of the *Kaddish* (see Petuchowski, pp. 90–103), which eventually found its way, in part, into the *Union Prayer Book* of North American Jews as well. The actual custom of *Hashkavah*, however, remains distinctively Sephardi.

The version of *Hashkavah* reproduced here comes from the prayer book currently used by Congregation Shearith Israel of

New York, the oldest congregation in North America. It is titled *Book of Prayer According to the Custom of the Spanish and Portuguese Jews.*[1] The Hebrew title page, however, bears a somewhat different title: *Seder Hatefilot K'fi Minhag Has'fardim Ba'amerika Im Targum Angli*, which means "Book of Prayer according to the custom of the Sephardim in America, with an English translation"—not just "according to the custom of the Spanish and Portuguese Jews" in general, that is, but "according to the custom of the Sephardim in America." It is not just American, however, because it follows entirely the ritual of its predecessor in England, with the lengthy title *Seder T'filot; The Book of Prayer and Order of Service According to the Custom of the Spanish and Portuguese Jews, Edited and Revised by The Rev. The Haham* [chacham] *Moses Gaster, Ph.D., Chief Rabbi of the Spanish and Portuguese Jews' Congregations* (1901). The Gaster version credits the English translation as being "based principally on the work of the late Rev. D[avid] A[aron] De Sola, Minister of the Congregation, Bevis Marks, London." All of these rabbis were of such stature that they deserve brief biographies here.

Rabbi David Aaron De Sola (1796–1860)—the original translator—had served as *Haham* at Bevis Marks, the flagship Sephardi congregation in London. Jews in England had been expelled by Edward I in 1290; they had then smuggled themselves back in as conversos in the sixteenth century, but disappeared by 1609. By the 1650s, other Sephardi Jews found their way there, and from 1655 to 1660, Rabbi Manasseh ben Israel of Amsterdam pursued the cause of Jewish readmission to England, in negotiations with Lord Protector Oliver Cromwell. Only in 1698 were Jews officially recognized by an Act of Parliament, however, and Bevis Marks came into being just three years later.

De Sola's son, Abraham (1825–1882), emigrated to Canada to serve as rabbi of Shearith Israel, the Spanish and Portuguese Synagogue in Montreal, where he distinguished himself as a scholar and a polemicist against the developing Reform Movement in North America. President Ulysses

S. Grant invited him to come from Canada to deliver the invocation that opened the 1872 United States Congress.

Rabbi David de Sola Pool (1885–1970)—who authored the liturgy used here but drew on the translation of David Aaron De Sola in England—had left London for America in 1907 to accept Shearith Israel's call, and once here, he achieved national and even international stature. He served in a variety of capacities for the United States government (a member of Herbert Hoover's food conservation staff in 1917, for example), was an outstanding Zionist, and (as scholar and liturgist) wrote the signal study of the *Kaddish* in 1909.

Moses Gaster (1856–1939)—editor of the British prototype on which the Shearith Israel liturgy is based—was born in Romania, where he became an expert in Romanian literature. In 1885, the government expelled him for protesting its policies regarding Jews, after which he moved to England, taught Slavonic languages at Oxford, and (in 1887) served as *Haham* for British Sephardim until retiring in 1918. In 1917, Gaster hosted a meeting at his home at the request of cabinet member Herbert Samuel, where Zionist leaders and Sir Mark Sykes of the British Foreign Office hammered out the terms that would become the Balfour Declaration (the document establishing the Jewish right to a homeland).

New York's Congregation Shearith Israel was established in 1654 by the first Sephardi Jews to land here. They had fled Recife in Brazil, because the Portuguese had recently routed the Dutch and threatened the establishment of the Inquisition. Shearith Israel served as the only congregation in New York until 1825. Its first rabbinic leader (although not an ordained rabbi) was Gershom Mendes Seixas (1745–1816), an ardent American patriot who was named *chazzan* in 1768. He left for Philadelphia to escape British occupation during the Revolutionary War, helped found Congregation Mikveh Israel there, and returned to Shearith Israel in 1784. He was invited to President Washington's inauguration in 1789 and served as trustee of the Humane Society and Columbia University. Rabbi Jacques Judah Lyons served from 1839 to 1877 and (among other things) collaborated with Abraham De Sola in Montreal in establishing a fifty-year Hebrew calendar. Henry Pereira Mendes, who followed and who served the congregation from 1877 until his death is 1937, joined Sabato Morais (1823–1897, and from 1851 until his death, the *chazzan* of Philadelphia's Mikveh Israel) in cofounding The Jewish Theological Seminary. David De Sola Pool came thereafter.

The text supplied here exactly follows the English of its source except for minor punctuation marks that vary today in style from what the editor originally supplied. Also, indentification of the verses cited has been added here.]

Memorial Prayer (*Hashkavah*)

When the memorial prayer is recited in memory of a distinguished rabbi it is introduced by these and the following verses:

"Whence shall wisdom be found, and where is the abode of understanding [Job 28:12]? Happy is the man who has found wisdom, the man who has obtained understanding [Proverbs 3:13]."

וְהַחָכְמָה מֵאַיִן תִּמָּצֵא. וְאֵי זֶה מְקוֹם בִּינָה: אַשְׁרֵי אָדָם מָצָא חָכְמָה. וְאָדָם יָפִיק תְּבוּנָה:

The following verses are recited introducing the prayer in memory of a man of eminence:

"How great is Thy goodness Thou hast reserved for those who revere Thee, Which Thou hast wrought for those who trust in Thee, in the presence of men [Psalm 31:20]. How precious is Thy loving-kindness, O God! The children of men take trustful refuge in the shadow of Thy wings [Psalm 36:8]. They shall drink of the rich joy of Thy dwelling place, Thou wilt cause them to quaff of the stream of Thy bliss [Psalm 36:9]."

מָה רַב־טוּבְךָ אֲשֶׁר־ צָפַנְתָּ לִּירֵאֶיךָ. פָּעַלְתָּ לַחוֹסִים בָּךְ נֶגֶד בְּנֵי אָדָם: מַה־יָּקָר חַסְדְּךָ אֱלֹהִים. וּבְנֵי אָדָם בְּצֵל כְּנָפֶיךָ יֶחֱסָיוּן: יִרְוְיֻן מִדֶּשֶׁן בֵּיתֶךָ. וְנַחַל עֲדָנֶיךָ תַשְׁקֵם:

For a Man

"Better is a good name than precious ointment and the day of death than the date of birth [Ecclesiastes 7:1]. The end of the matter after all has been heard—revere God and keep his commandments, for this is the whole duty of man [Ecclesiastes 12:13]. May the pious be joyful in glory, and rejoice in their repose [Psalm 149:5]."

May the destined portion for the soul of ... be true repose under the wings of the divine presence in the celestial realm, the sphere of the holy and pure, shining resplendent as the luminous firmament. May he know redemption and compassionate grace from Him who is enthroned on high, and happy participation in the life of the world to come. May the spirit of the Lord grant rest in the happiness of the Beyond to him who has departed from this world according to the will of God, Lord of heaven and earth.

May the supreme King of kings in His mercy show him love and compassion. May peace attend him and his repose be peaceful, as it is written, "They shall enter into peace; they who walk in their uprightness shall have repose in their resting places [Isaiah 57:2]." May he and all his people of Israel slumbering in the dust be included in mercy and forgiveness. May this be the divine will, and let us say, Amen.

טוֹב שֵׁם מִשֶּׁמֶן טוֹב. וְיוֹם הַמָּוֶת מִיּוֹם הִוָּלְדוֹ: סוֹף דָּבָר הַכֹּל נִשְׁמָע. אֶת־הָאֱלֹהִים יְרָא, וְאֶת מִצְוֹתָיו שְׁמוֹר. כִּי זֶה כָּל־הָאָדָם: יַעְלְזוּ חֲסִידִים בְּכָבוֹד. יְרַנְּנוּ עַל־מִשְׁכְּבוֹתָם: מְנוּחָה נְכוֹנָה בִּישִׁיבָה עֶלְיוֹנָה. תַּחַת כַּנְפֵי הַשְּׁכִינָה. בְּמַעֲלַת קְדוֹשִׁים וּטְהוֹרִים. כְּזֹהַר הָרָקִיעַ מְאִירִים וּמַזְהִירִים. וְחִלּוּץ עֲצָמִים וְכַפָּרַת אֲשָׁמִים. וְהַרְחָקַת פֶּשַׁע וְהַקְרָבַת יֶשַׁע. וְחֶמְלָה וַחֲנִינָה מִלִּפְנֵי שׁוֹכֵן מְעוֹנָה. וְחֻלָּקָא טָבָא לְחַיֵּי הָעוֹלָם הַבָּא. שָׁם תְּהֵא מְנָת וּמְחַצַּת וִישִׁיבַת נֶפֶשׁ הַשֵּׁם הַטּוֹב רוּחַ יְיָ _____

תְּנִיחֶנּוּ בְגַן עֵדֶן. דְּאִתְפְּטַר מִן עָלְמָא הָדֵן. כִּרְעוּת אֱלָהָא מָרֵא שְׁמַיָּא וְאַרְעָא: הַמֶּלֶךְ בְּרַחֲמָיו יָחוֹס וְיַחְמוֹל עָלָיו. וְיִלְוֶה אֵלָיו הַשָּׁלוֹם. וְעַל מִשְׁכָּבוֹ יִהְיֶה שָׁלוֹם. כְּדִכְתִיב. יָבוֹא שָׁלוֹם. יָנוּחוּ עַל־מִשְׁכְּבוֹתָם. הֹלֵךְ נְכֹחוֹ: הוּא וְכָל־שֹׁכְבֵי עַמּוֹ יִשְׂרָאֵל בִּכְלַל הָרַחֲמִים וְהַסְּלִיחוֹת. וְכֵן יְהִי רָצוֹן. וְנֹאמַר אָמֵן:

For a Woman

"A virtuous woman who so finds—Far above corals is her worth [Proverbs 31:10]. Give her of the fruit of her hands, and let her own works praise her in the gates [Proverbs 31:31]."

By the word of the most merciful One whose attribute is mercy were created both this world and the future world wherein He treasures the souls of the true and pious who do His will. May He through His glory and His word of power ordain that the memory of His good and honored daughter ... come into His presence. May the spirit of the Lord grant rest in the happiness of the Beyond to her who has departed from this world according to the will of God, Lord of heaven and earth.

May the supreme King of kings in His mercy show her love and compassion. May peace attend her and her repose be peaceful, as it is written, "They shall enter into peace; they who walk in their uprightness shall have repose in their resting places [Isaiah 57:2]." May she and all daughters of Israel slumbering with her in the dust be included in mercy and forgiveness. May this be the divine will, and let us say, Amen.

אֵשֶׁת חַיִל מִי יִמְצָא. וְרָחוֹק
מִפְּנִינִים מִכְרָהּ:
תְּנוּ־לָהּ מִפְּרִי יָדֶיהָ. וִיהַלְלוּהָ
בַשְּׁעָרִים מַעֲשֶׂיהָ:
רַחֲמָנָא דְרַחֲמָנוּתָא דִּלֵהּ הִיא.
וּבְמֵימְרֵהּ אִתְבְּרִיאוּ עָלְמַיָּא.
עָלְמָא הָדֵן וְעָלְמָא דְאָתֵי.
וּגְנַז בֵּהּ צִדְקָנְיוֹת וְחַסְדָּנְיוֹת
דְעָבְדָן רְעוּתֵהּ. וּבְמֵימְרֵהּ
וּבִיקָרֵהּ וּבִתְקָפֵּהּ יֵאמַר
לְמֵעַל קָדָמוֹהִי. דְּכְרַן הָאִשָּׁה
הַכְּבוּדָה וְהַצְּנוּעָה וְהַנִּכְבֶּדֶת.
מָרַת _____

רוּחַ יְיָ תְּנִיחֶנָּה בְּגַן עֵדֶן.
דְּאִתְפְּטָרַת מִן עָלְמָא הָדֵן.
כִּרְעוּת אֱלָהָא מָרֵא שְׁמַיָּא
וְאַרְעָא: הַמֶּלֶךְ בְּרַחֲמָיו יָחוֹס
וְיַחֲמוֹל עָלֶיהָ. וִילַוֶּה אֵלֶיהָ
הַשָּׁלוֹם. וְעַל מִשְׁכָּבָהּ יִהְיֶה
שָׁלוֹם. כְּדִכְתִיב. יָבוֹא שָׁלוֹם.
יָנוּחוּ עַל־מִשְׁכְּבוֹתָם. הֹלֵךְ
נְכֹחוֹ: הִיא וְכָל־בְּנוֹת יִשְׂרָאֵל
הַשּׁוֹכְבוֹת עִמָּהּ. בִּכְלַל
הָרַחֲמִים וְהַסְּלִיחוֹת, וְכֵן יְהִי
רָצוֹן. וְנֹאמַר אָמֵן:

Appendix B

El Malei Rachamim
A Chronicle from the Chmielnicki Pogroms

Translation and Commentary by Dr. Joel M. Hoffman

[Editor's note: The following introduction to *El Malei Rachamim* comes from *Amudei Ha'avodah*, an early and classic study of synagogue poets (*pay'tanim*) and poetry (*piyyutim*) compiled between 1857 and 1862 by Eliezer Landshuth (1817–1887).[1] Its full title, *Amudei Ha'avodah* (*Onomasticon Auctorum Hymnorum Hebraeorum*), suggests the author's exceptional regard for the scientific study of Jewish sources that was just in its early stages in his day. Although relatively unrecognized by posterity, Landshuth was, in his time, a scholar of some consequence, with a special interest in this fledgling field of tracing Jewish prayer to its origins.

Landshuth provides an early version of *El Malei Rachamim*, along with the preamble translated here— a shorthand account of the Chmielnicki pogroms of 1648–49 (see Introduction, pp. 1–16)—without, however, identifying where he found either. The primary source for the Chmielnicki period is *Yeven M'tzulah*, by Nathan of Hanover, an eyewitness to the devastation, but

236

Landshuth's account is not directly drawn from it, and he labels it as the form of prayer used to commemorate a relatively late stage in the massacres that had begun in 1648–49 but that continued sporadically for several years thereafter. As we saw in the introduction (pp. 1–16), Nathan refers to the use of *El Malei* in connection with the slaughter of Shavuot, 1648. This version, and the introduction to it, come from 1656.

Accounts of Jewish martyrdom were often intended not solely as history, in the modern sense of the term, but as liturgical chronicles, from which readings might be drawn to accompany the communal recitation of memorial prayers. The Landshuth introduction was probably composed as such a document, a preamble to *El Malei Rachamim* that would have been recited for liturgical ends.[2]]

The Version of *El Malei Rachamim* for the Decrees of 1648 for the Holy Ones Murdered in 1656 in Warsaw, Złotów, Lobzenica, Rogozno, Łeczyca, Pakoéć, Inowroclaw, and Poznan

[1] God, full of compassion, dwelling on high: protected by divine wings, among the holy and blameless who shine with the radiance of the sky, grant perfect repose to mighty heroes who listen to the creator of mountains, who by their study and their good deeds used to light up the earth and its inhabitants.

אל מלא רחמים שוכן [1]
במרומים, המציא מנוחה
נכונה, בסתר כנפי השכינה,
במעלות קדושים וטהורים,
כזוהר הרקיע מזהירים,
גבורי כח לשמוע בקול
יוצר הרים, בתורתם
ובמעשיהם הטובים היו
מאירים לארץ ולדרים.

[1] *God, full of compassion*: This long prayer, which introduces *El Malei Rachamim*, is at times extraordinarily poetic, introducing nuances by alluding to the Bible and commentary on it, but doing so obliquely. It differs from other texts that tend to quote the Bible and commentary directly, word for word, in that it maintains the biblical themes but plays with the words. A similar process in English, referring, say, to Shakespeare's *Romeo and Juliet*, might reference the famous line "'Tis the east, and Juliet is the sun," but instead of citing it directly, it might prefer "with Juliet in east," the point of which would be to highlight impossible love. Alternatively, instead of "A rose by any other name would smell as sweet," it might say simply, "Sweet-smelling roses," with the intent of emphasizing the immateriality of names. Readers would be assumed to have such thorough-going familiarity with the sources that they would recognize the allusions. That is rarely the case today, however, so we have tried to spell out these allusions in the notes. At times, the Hebrew is also at odds with standard linguistic usage, to the point of appearing ungrammatical. In these cases, we have nevertheless translated it into standard English.

²The Year of Creation 5408 was a time to gather in the exiled of the dispersed Israel. According to the books and authors who know the secrets of the Torah, we had hoped for peace without end, but the hand of God has left us, and all its glory has been taken from us. ³Little Poland, Lithuania, Russia and the Ukraine, and the surrounding area, Volhynia, and Podolia, all of them quiet and easygoing settlements. ⁴God has tossed aside my warriors and our pleasant villages, from on high sending fire deep into our bones. ⁵Yeshivah heads, parents, and teachers have been killed, their blood spilled like rivers of cascading water.

²שנת חמשת אלפים וארבע מאות ושמונה ליצירה, היתה עת לקבץ נדחי ישראל שה פזורה, מפי סופרים וספרים יודעי רזי התורה, קוינו לשלום ואין קץ ויצאה בנו יד יי ונלקח כל הדרה. ³ פולין קטן, וליטא ורוסיא ואקריינא, וגליל, וואלין, ופאדאליא, כולם ישבו שקט ושאננה סלה ⁴ כל אבירי ומחמדינו ממרום שלח אש בעצמותינו וירדנה, ⁵נהרגו ראשי ישיבות והורים ומורים נשפך דמם כנחלי

---

³*Little Poland*: Part of Poland, consisting very roughly of the southeast quarter of today's Poland. It contains Cracow, Sandomierz, and Lublin.

⁴*God*: Hebrew, "he." The passage quotes Lamentations 1:15, "Adonai has tossed aside all my warriors around me."

⁴*Pleasant villages*: Hebrew, just "pleasant," probably quoting Isaiah 64:10, "Our beautiful and holy house, where our ancestors praised You, has been burned in fire, and our pleasant [places] destroyed."

⁴*From on high ... bones*: Essentially quoting Lamentations 1:13.

⁵*Rivers of cascading water*: From Micah 1:4, "The mountains will melt under Him and the valleys burst open, like wax before fire, like water cascading down."

⁶They drew near with their heads and cuttings and suet, for sacrifice, a fire for Adonai, the creator who creates all creatures. ⁷Benefactors, cantors, and other respectable people were killed by brazen non-Jews.

מים המוגרים, ⁶ קרבו עצמן הראש והנתחים והפדרים, לקרבן אשה ליי יוצר וצר צורים, ⁷ פרנסים וחזנים ושאר אנשים הגונים, נהרגו על ידי גוי עז פנים.

⁶*They drew near*: From *Numbers Rabbah* 1:12, midrashic commentary on Numbers 1:49. The context is the prohibition in Numbers against counting the Levites. The midrash here (quoting Numbers 3:12) explains that the Levites belong to God, because God draws near to anyone who draws near to God. So our text here indirectly compares the yeshivah heads, parents, and teachers to the Levites.

⁶*Heads and cuttings and suet*: Both the recipe for the burnt offering in Leviticus 1:8 and the way Moses prepared the sacrifice (in Leviticus 8:20) with which he ordained the Levites.

⁶*For sacrifice:* The letters *k.r.b* in Hebrew make up the verb "to draw near" and also the verb "to sacrifice." What started as the Levites "drawing near" to God—we know it's the Levites because of the reference to *Numbers Rabbah*—ends up with the Levites becoming their own sacrifice. The shift in Hebrew is subtle. We have to spell things out more starkly in translation.

⁶*Creator who creates all creatures*: Our English reflects the repetition in the Hebrew. The phrase is based on a line from a Tish'a B'av poetic lament (technically called a *kinah*) about the ten sages tortured by Emperor Hadrian following the Bar Kokhba revolt in the year 135. An embedded acrostic in the poem identifies the author as Meir ben Rabbi Yechiel.

⁸And fathers and mothers and small, tender children were shaken in the streets, and trampled like twigs and pebbles. ⁹Young men and women and grooms and brides, tied in love like cords: their bodies trampled and squeezed in wine presses. ¹⁰Those worth their weight in gold, those brought up in luxury, embrace refuse.

⁸ואבות ואמהות וילדים רכים וקטנים נתפלשו בחוצת ונדרכו כעצים ואבנים. ⁹בחורים ובתולות וחתנים וכלות המקושרים באהבה כעבותות, נדרכו גופם ונרמסו בגתות, ¹⁰המסולאים בפז והאמונים עלי תולע חבקו אשפתות.

⁸*In the streets*: Hebrew, the rare word *b'chutzot*, deliberately written *chaser* (without the penultimate *vav*) as in 2 Samuel 1:20, where the context is David mourning for Saul and Jonathan. The previous line, 2 Samuel 1:19, ends with the famous "How the mighty have fallen."
⁹*Grooms and brides*: We follow the Hebrew word order here, to mirror "men and women," immediately above. "Groom and bride" is the usual phrase in Hebrew, even though in English we usually prefer "bride and groom."
⁹*Tied in love like cords*: A rephrasing of Hosea 11:4, where God leads humans in "cords of love," often translated "bands of love."
⁹*Squeezed*: Better would be "trampled," but we've already used that English word for a different Hebrew one.
¹⁰*Worth their weight in gold*: A cliché now, the text cites Lamentations 4:2, where the context is the punishment of Israel.
¹⁰*Luxury*: Literally, "scarlet." Like "silver" and "platinum" in English, the Hebrew "scarlet" was part of the group of precious items to which "gold"—in both languages—belongs. So the Hebrew has "gold" and "something akin to gold," where our translation does not. "Brought up with a silver spoon" is a tempting translation here. The line (including "embrace refuse") cites Lamentations 4:5.

¹¹They gave their lives to sanctify the one great name, grantor of life and death. ¹²Teachers and students and authors, experts in the minutia of text: these are the ones whom the cruel killed in bitter beds; these are the ones whom the living buried in graves; these are the ones who were drowned in cisterns and in mighty water. ¹³Who can count the dead in their hundreds and their thousands, the binding of their souls in the bundle of life, and like holy creatures and seraphim, neither my tongue nor lips can count them. ¹⁴Quickly avenge them, as it is written, "I will purify their blood that I have not purified."

11 מסרו נפשם על קדושת השם האדיר והמיוחד מחיה וממותת 12 מלמדים ותלמידים וסופרים ספרים, דורשי רשומות וגזירות שוות קלים וחמורים, מהם המיתו אכזרים במיתות תמרורים מהם קברו חיים בקברים, מהם הטביעו בבורת חצובים ובמים אדירים. 13 מי יוכל לספר הרוגים למאות ולאלפים, תצרור נפשם בצרור החיים וכחיות הקודש ושרפים, לא יוכל לספר אותן לשוני ושפתי. 14 ותנקום נקמתם מהרה ככתוב: ונקתי דמם

¹¹*One great name*: The Hebrew for "one" here is *m'yuchad*, a kabbalistic term.

¹²*Authors*: Literally, "authors of books."

¹²*Experts in the minutia of text*: The Hebrew has several technical terms that defy translation. We summarize them with "minutia."

¹²*Cisterns*: The Hebrew is, "hewn cisterns," a phrase that appears in Deuteronomy 6:11 as part of "hewn cisterns that you did not hew," in the context of the more general point that God created the Land of Israel and the Israelites should be careful not to forget the source of their bounty.

¹⁴*Avenge*: Or "seek vengeance."

¹⁴*Purify ... purified*: From Joel 4:21. An alternative translation tradition reads, "I will avenge their blood that I have not avenged."

¹⁵A little time and distance, as we've kept quiet, until the year 5416 in Great Poland: we almost perished, with various decrees against us. ¹⁶Lamentation and weeping, crying and wailing, were known in every district and region, and those renowned in Israel for Torah and knowledge were killed.

לֹא נִקֵּיתִי. ¹⁵ מְעַט זְמַן וּרְוָוחָה וְהַשְׁקֵט שְׁקַטְנוּ, עַד שְׁנַת תט"ז לָאֶלֶף הַשִּׁשִּׁי בְּפוֹלִין גָּדוֹל כִּמְעַט אֲבַדְנוּ, הָיוּ עָלֵינוּ גְזֵרוֹת כָּהֵנָּה וְכָהֵנָּה. ¹⁶ נְהִי בְּכִי קִינָה וִילָלָה, גָּדְלָה בְּכָל פֶּלֶךְ וּקְהִלָּה, וְנֶהֶרְגוּ גְּדוֹלֵי יִשְׂרָאֵל בַּתּוֹרָה וּגְדוּלָה.

¹⁵*Distance*: Or "space," but we want to avoid the English expression "time and space," which is not what the Hebrew means.

¹⁵*5416*: Hebrew, "416 in the sixth millennium" (because the usual way of reckoning years in Hebrew excludes the thousands—on the probably reasonable assumption that most people know which millennium it is). The sixth millennium is the 5000s, just as this book was printed in the twenty-first century, that is, the 2000s.

¹⁵*Great Poland*: Its main city was Poznan; as opposed to Little Poland, centered in Cracow.

¹⁵*Lamentation and weeping*: From Jeremiah 31:15, in the context of exile: "A voice is heard on high: lamentation and bitter weeping. Rachel is weeping for her children."

¹⁶*Crying*: An uncommon word in Hebrew.

¹⁶*Wailing*: A rare Hebrew word, from Zephaniah 1:10, in the context of judgment on Judah.

¹⁶*Were known*: Literally, "grew," from the root *g.d.l*, setting the stage for two more words from the same root immediately below, which we translate "renowned" and "knowledge."

¹⁶*Renowned in Israel for Torah and knowledge*: Literally, "great [people] of Israel, in Torah and greatness," repeating the Hebrew root *g.d.l*, from immediately above. Because the "great ones of Israel" are commonly understood to be scholars, we use "knowledge" in place of "greatness,"

¹⁷And we were seized by shaking and anguish, every head sick and every heart faint. ¹⁸For the great rabbi from the holy congregation of Warsaw, beloved in Israel, our teacher and rabbi, Rabbi Efraim, and for the great and righteous rabbi, head of the rabbinic council from the holy congregation of Złotów, descended from the Levites: they were caught in a fishing net and surrounded and their blood was spilled like deer and gazelles. ¹⁹The messengers of peace cry bitterly on high for the great rabbi our teacher and rabbi, Rabbi Zelig, head of the rabbinic council of the holy congregation of Lobzenica, whose head was axed off.

ואחזתנו בנו רעדה וחלחלה¹⁷
כל ראש לחלי וכל לבבות
דווים. ¹⁸ על הרב הגדול
דק"ק וורעשנא חמדת
ישראל מהר"ר אפרים,
ועל הרב הגדול החסיד אב"ד
דק"ק זלאטווי מזרע הלוים,
פרשו עליהם מכמורת וסבבו
אותם ונשפך דמם כאלים
יצבוים. ¹⁹ מלאכי שלום מר
יבכיון במרומים, על הרב
הגדול מוהר"ר זעליג אב"ד
דק"ק לובזעניץ שנטלו ראשו

making possible the progression from "were known" to "renown" and "knowledge," capturing the flavor of the Hebrew.

¹⁷*Seized by shaking*: Perhaps in reference to Isaiah 33:14, where Isaiah prophesies deliverance.

¹⁷*And anguish*: An oblique reference to Isaiah 21:3, where the context is the oracles about Babylon, Edom, and Arabia.

¹⁷*Every head sick and every heart faint*: Quoting Isaiah 1:5, on Judah's wickedness.

¹⁸*Head of the rabbinic council*: A technical term in Hebrew.

¹⁸*Caught in a fishing net*: Literally, "a fishing net was cast," after Isaiah 19:8, in the context of an oracle about Egypt.

¹⁹*The messengers of peace cry bitterly*: Quoting Isaiah 33:7, in the context of Isaiah's prophecy of deliverance.

²⁰He will be called holy for the binding of Isaac on one of the mounts, for the great rabbi of the holy congregation of Rogozno, who was killed and who sanctified the one name of the mightiest of the mighty. ²¹For the slain of Łeczyca and Pakoéć and Inowroclaw let laments be lamented and eulogies recited, and for the rest of the communities and blameless, upright individuals I will eulogize bitterly and my soul will cry in secret, for the woe and suffering and pain on account of our wounds. ²²For the holy and the pure: the great, righteous and holy rabbi, our teacher and rabbi, Rabbi Aryeh Yehudah Ya'akov and our teacher

20. קָדוֹשׁ יֵאָמֶר בְּקָרְדֻּמִים לוֹ עַל עֲקֵדַת יִצְחָק עַל אֶחָד הֶהָרִים, עַל הָרַב הַגָּדוֹל דק"ק רַאגָאזְנִי שֶׁהֲמִיתוּ אוֹתוֹ וְקִידֵשׁ שֵׁם הַמְּיוּחָד אַדִּיר בָּאַדִּירִים, 21 עַל הֲרוּגֵי לוּנְטְשִׁיץ וּפְקִישׁ וּלְעֶסְלָא יְקוֹנֵן הַמְּקוֹנֵן וְיַסְפִּיד הַסְפוּדִים, וְעַל שְׁאָר קְהִלּוֹת וִיחִידִים תְּמִימִים וִישָׁרִים, אֶסְפֹּד מַר וְתִבְכֶּה נַפְשִׁי בְּמִסְתָּרִים, כִּי הָיְתָה אוֹי וַאֲבוֹי וָשׁוֹד עַל שְׁבָרִים. 22 וְעַל הַקְּדוֹשִׁים וּטְהוֹרִים

²⁰*He will be called holy*: From Isaiah 4:3, in the context of future glory for the people of Zion.

²¹*Eulogies recited*: Hebrew, the more poetic "eulogies eulogized," but in English it's the people, not the eulogies, that are eulogized.

²¹*In secret*: Hebrew, *bamistorim*, perhaps a reference to Psalm 64:5, part of a prayer for protection in which enemies shoot at the blameless from *bamistorim*, "from in hiding places."

²¹*Woe ... wounds*: After Jeremiah 10:19 ("woe is me on account of my wound"), in the context of Jeremiah's prophecy of coming exile. The intermediate words ("suffering" and "pain" in our translation) are rough synonyms for "woe." The second one, *avo'i*, sounds similar to the first, creating the common (modern) Hebrew phrase, *oy va'avoi*—"Oh no!"— and forming a wordplay we cannot mimic in English. The third word, *shod*, is not commonly found with the first two, but often does form a pair with the singular "wound," as in, for example, Isaiah 60:18, where that prophet promises an eventual end to "pain and wound" (or, as in JPS's nice poetic translation, "wrack and ruin").

and rabbi, Rabbi Joseph Darshan from
the holy congregation of Poznan, the
light of whose teachings would light
the land and its inhabitants. [23]And
caught up with the righteous was a
righteous and holy man, a man who
feared God, pure in his deeds,
honored and holy, our teacher and
rabbi, the Rabbi Abraham Ya'akov
and his friend Rabbi Pinchas Yitzchak,
the great benefactor from the holy
community of Poznan, where they
suffered harsh, bitter torture on the
holy, awesome Day of Atonement,
and they sanctified the one name,
mighty among the most mighty; may
their blood be considered the blood
of bulls, and the pangs that cleanse
their limbs like sacrifices and suet.

הרב הגדול והחסיד וקדוש
מהור"ר אריה יהודא יעקב
במוהר"ר יוסף דרשן דק"ק
פוזנן אשר אור תורתו
היה מאיר לארץ ולדרם.
[23] ונטפל עם הטהור טהור
גברא קדשה איש ירא
אלהים ותמים במעשיו ה"ה
הקדוש מוהר"ר אברהם
יעקב בהההבר ר' פינחס יצחק
שתדלן הגדול דק"ק פוזנן
שסבלו ענוים קשים ומרים,
ביום הקדוש ונורא יום
הכפורים וקדשו שם המיוחד
אדיר באדירים, תחשב דמם
כדם פרים, ויסורין הממרקין
אבריהם כאמורים ופדרים.

[23]*Torture*: The word for "torture" here is a noun from the root that
forms the verb "to afflict" or (as in JPS) "practice self-denial." That verb
is used in Leviticus 16:31 in the original description of Yom Kippur.
Our text here thus sets the stage for what immediately follows.
[23]*Blood of bulls*: After Leviticus 16:27, where the blood of bulls will be
brought in atonement on the Day of Atonement.
[23]*Pangs that cleanse*: From the Babylonian Talmud, Berakhot 5a, where pangs
cleanse a person's afflictions. (The discussion there explains that this cleansing
is like what salt does to meat, "sweetening" it and rendering it more fit.)
[23]*Like sacrifices and suet*: From the *Zohar* to *Parashat Tzav* 28a. Thanks
to Dr. Sharon Koren, who notes the *Zohar*'s general use of sacrificial
terms here to refer obliquely to martyrdom.

²⁴For this, too, my heart trembles and my stomach groans greatly, for the decrees on the rest of the lands of Germany, France, and Spain, where there was Torah and greatness like the inhabitants of Jerusalem.

²⁵God's hand was upon them, decree after decree, doubly and triply: great rabbis of Torah and repute, scholars of the land, from all manner of communities, houses of study and houses of meeting, masters of law and masters of tradition, authors of books beyond measure and compare.

²⁴ גם לזאת יחרד לבי ומעי הומים בהומין, על גזירות שאר ארצות אשכנז וצרפת ואספמיא. שם היתה תורה וגדולה כיושבי ירושלים.

²⁵ ויד יי היתה בם גזירה אחר גזירה. בכפלי כפלים רבנים גדולים לתורה ולתעודה. גאוני ארץ מקהילי קהילת לבתי מדרשות בית וו_עדה. בעלי פוסקים ובעלי קבלה. מחברי ספרים בלי שיעור

²⁴*For this, too, my heart trembles*: From Job 37:1, in the context of Job's companion Elihu's proclamation of God's majesty.

²⁴*Stomach groans*: After Jeremiah 31:20, in the context of God's love for the dear Ephraim (who stands symbolically for the people Israel), and God's promise to remember him and have mercy on him. The Hebrew for "stomach" is the more general "innards" and is used to represent the seat of emotion, so we choose "stomach" here in English.

²⁴*Greatly*: Literally, "groans and groans," using first a Hebrew form, then an Aramaic one. This repetition serves as emphasis and also as foreshadowing of the next line.

²⁵*God's hand was upon them*: From Deuteronomy 2:15, in the context of God rooting out a generation of warriors from the people Israel while they wandered in the desert. Additionally, in Deuteronomy 2:15, God's hand came to *hamem* them—from the root *h.m.m*—an onomatopoetic root that literally means "to make noise." We just saw a similar onomatopoetic root, *h.m.h*, doubled in the previous line.

²⁵*Doubly and triply*: Hebrew: "Doubly double," or "multiply multiple." "Double" or "doubly" is a common Hebrew word, perhaps used here in

²⁶Beyond belief even if told in riddles, what can we say and what can we report on the houses of worship, the smaller assemblies, and the houses of study. ²⁷Everything there, small and great, vibrate and tremble. ²⁸Look, Adonai, and see, other nations have come to the temple and defiled every pure thing like menstrual impurity.

ומדה. ²⁶ לא יאומן כי יסופר בחידה, מה נאמר ומה נדבר על בתי כנסיות מעט מקדשות ובתי מדרשות. ²⁷ שם הכל קטנים וגדולים רווחשות ורעשות. ²⁸ ראה יי והביטה כי באו גוים מקדשה וטמאו כל טהרה

reference to Isaiah 40:2, in the context of God's comforting Jerusalem, which has received "from the hand of God double" what "all her sins" warrant.
²⁵*Scholars*: Hebrew, *ga'on*, a technical term for one kind of scholar (and also the modern Hebrew word for "genius").
²⁶*Beyond belief even if told*: A common Hebrew idiom, originating in Habakkuk 1:5, in the context of God's rousing the Chaldeans, who in violence march across the earth wreaking havoc.
²⁶*In riddles*: Perhaps continuing the theme of Habakkuk, from verse 2:6, in the context of Israel's vindication.
²⁶*What can we say and what can we report*: After Genesis 44:16, in the context of Judah wondering how he and his brothers can clear their name before Joseph.
²⁷*Small and great*: After Jeremiah 16:6, where the "great and small" all die in the land, not to be buried.
²⁷*Vibrate*: Perhaps a reference to the Jerusalem Talmud (Berakhot 13a, Mo'ed Katan 18b, and Shekalim 11a), where citing a teaching in the name of its author causes the author's lips to vibrate in the grave.
²⁸*Look, Adonai, and see*: Quoting Lamentations 2:20.
²⁸*Other nations have come*: Quoting Psalm 79:1, where "other nations have come into [God's] inheritance, defiled the holy Temple, and laid Jerusalem in ruins."
²⁸*Menstrual impurity*: A biblical concept. The text here may specifically reference Ezekiel (22:10 and again 36:17), in the context of Jerusalem's impurity.

²⁹Save us, for our children have come to the point of birth, but there is no strength to give them birth. ³⁰If we suffer the humility of your children in silence, what will You do about your holy Torah, more precious than rubies and sweeter than honey? ³¹How many Torah scrolls and other books have been cut up with the merchant's knife? ³²The parchment is burning, but the letters are flourishing in the air. ³³After all this, will You restrain Yourself and keep quiet?

כטמאת הנדה ²⁹ הושיעה יי כי באו בנים עד משבר וכח אין ללידה. ³⁰ אם עלבון בניך נשתוק בשתיקה, מה תעשה לתורתיך הקדושה והיקרה מפנינים ומדבש מתוקה. ³¹ כמה ספרי תורה וספרים קרעו בתער השכיר. ³² גווילם נשרפים ואותיות פורחים לאווירם. ³³ העל אלה תתאפק ותחשה.

²⁹*Save us*: Hebrew, just "save." Hebrew doesn't require an object (like "us") when it's clear from context.

²⁹*For our children ... birth*: Quoting Isaiah 37:3. The original Hebrew is considerably more poetic than our English translation. (And we add "our" here, not in Isaiah, because the context of this prayer demands it.)

³⁰*Humility of your children in silence*: After the Midrash (*Mekhilta D'rabbi Yishmael*) to Exodus 15:11, where "who is like You among the gods [*elim*, spelled *alym*]" is creatively reread as "who is like You among the silent [*ilmim*, spelled *almym*]," that is, according to the Midrash, "You who hear about the humility of your children and keep silent."

³¹*Cut up with the merchant's knife*: After Jeremiah 36:23, where King Jehoiakim cuts up a Torah scroll bit by bit with a scribe's knife and throws the pieces into a fire.

³²*The parchment ... air*: Quoting the Talmud (Avodah Zarah 18a), where Rabbi Chanina ben Teradion, sentenced to death by the Romans and burnt alive wrapped in a Torah scroll, tells his students that even though the parchment is burning, the letters are flourishing in the air.

³³*Restrain Yourself and keep quiet*: After Isaiah 64:11, where the prophet asks Adonai that same question, in the aftermath of "our holy and glorious house" (Isaiah 64:10, quoted above in line 4) having been burned to the ground.

³⁴How long until You avenge the people of Israel and your holy Torah? ³⁵After all this, will You restrain Yourself, exalted, most triumphant. ³⁶Why are You like a confused man, like a warrior who cannot save? ³⁷You who comfort the Tishbi who brings word and brings tidings, send us the son of David, humbled and riding on a donkey, to return the hearts of parents to children, and the hearts of children to parents, and to awaken the souls of your people Israel from their graves. ³⁸Then they will see our happiness, and we their happiness, quickly, in our day. And let us say: Amen.

³⁴ עַד מָתַי לֹא תִּנְקוֹם נִקְמַת עַמְּךָ יִשְׂרָאֵל וְנִקְמַת תּוֹרָתֶיךָ הַקְּדוֹשָׁה. ³⁵ הַעַל אֵלֶּה תִּתְאַפַּק רָם גֵּאֶה גֵּאָה. ³⁶ לָמָּה תִהְיֶה כְּאִישׁ נִדְהָם כְּגִבּוֹר לֹא יוּכַל לְהוֹשִׁיעַ. ³⁷ מְנַחֵם תִּשְׁבִּי מְבַשֵּׂר וְאוֹמֵר תִּשְׁלַח לָנוּ בֶּן דָּוִד עָנִי וְרוֹכֵב עַל הַחֲמוֹר, לְהָשִׁיב לֵב אָבוֹת עַל בָּנִים, וְלֵב בָּנִים עַל אֲבוֹתָם, וּלְעוֹרֵר נַפְשׁוֹת עַמְּךָ יִשְׂרָאֵל מִקְּבוּרָתָם. ³⁸ וְהֵם יִרְאוּ בְשִׂמְחָתֵינוּ וַאֲנַחְנוּ בְשִׂמְחָתָם בִּמְהֵרָה בְּיָמֵינוּ וְנֹאמַר אָמֵן.

³⁴*Avenge the people of Israel*: After Numbers 31:2, where God tells Moses to avenge the children of Israel in the face of the Midianites.

³⁵*Most triumphant*: Returning to Exodus (see "Humility of your children in silence," above), where God triumphs: "I will sing to Adonai, who has triumphed, hurling houses and riders into the sea" (15:1).

³⁶*Why are You ... who cannot save*: Quoting Jeremiah 14:9, where the line continues, "You are in our midst, Adonai. We carry your name. Do not forsake us!"

³⁷*The Tishbi*: That is, Elijah the prophet.

³⁷*The son of David*: Again, Elijah the prophet.

³⁷*Humbled and riding on a donkey*: Quoting Zechariah 9:9, and yet again in reference to Elijah the prophet.

³⁷*Hearts of parents to children ... children to parents*: Quoting Malachi 3:24, in reference to Elijah the prophet, who will be sent before the great and awesome day of God.

Appendix C

El Malei Rachamim
Music of 1888

Composition by Eduard Birnbaum

[Editor's Note: Wilhelm I, better known to English readers as William I, became king of Prussia in 1861 and ruled throughout the period of German unification, which was completed in 1871. He served, therefore, as both king of Prussia and emperor, or kaiser, of Germany, until his death in 1888. Among the tributes to him was this composition by the noted cantor and musicologist Eduard Birnbaum (1855–1920).]

Birnbaum was born in Cracow and spent three years under the tutelage of Solomon Sulzer, the pioneering composer and modern cantor in Vienna. He eventually found his way to Königsberg, where he served as cantor, composed music on his own, and assembled the now-famous Birnbaum music collection housed at Hebrew Union College in Cincinnati. The following pages replicate the manuscript of Birnbaum's 1888 composition.

The Hebrew and German are not quite identical. They both integrate an extended reference to King Wilhelm into the standard lyrics of *El Malei Rachamim*, but provide slight differences in the prayer's wording. The translation from the Hebrew (see Figure A, p. 254) reads as follows:

> God, full of compassion, dwelling on high: Under the shadow of God, who dwells in heaven, grant perfect repose

among the holy and blameless who shine with the radiance of the sky, to the soul of our lord, the king and kaiser, Wilhelm I, chosen by God to stand and serve in God's name. He dedicated all of his days to his people and land. May he have ascended on high on account of the prayer and supplication in memory of his soul. Therefore, may the master of mercy protect him under his protective wings forever, and bind his soul in the bundle of life. God is his inheritance. May his rest be in the Garden of Eden, and may he rest on his bed in peace. And let us say: Amen.

As mentioned above, the German introduces its own peculiar wording in spots. More than just the wording, however, the German carries its own distinctive tone, so even when the German words do parallel the Hebrew, our usual English will not do. Dr. Annette M. Boeckler, one of our regular contributors in this series (see Boeckler, above, pp. 113–126) has graciously translated the German so as to capture that nuance. She notes, for example, the following:

> The German does not intend to give a verbal translation. Its opening words are "All-loving father" (*Allliebender Vater*), a far cry from, simply, "God, full of compassion," as we have it in the Hebrew. Wilhelm was regarded as "father" of the German people, a very typical portrayal of the kaiser. The prayer thus juxtaposes the image of God as Father to the parallel image of Wilhelm as father, but puts the divine Father above the merely earthly one.
>
> Similarly, The second line in German reads, "grand blissful rest," thus adding the notion of "blissful," which occurs nowhere in the Hebrew.
>
> Finally, the third line introduces the German *vorsehung*, meaning "provision," something foreseen and provided by God. This is typical kaiser-language, in that the kaiser was regarded as God-given. The Hebrew has no parallel term.

The accompanying translation from the German (see Figure A, p. 254) reads:

O Loving Father in heaven's heights
Grant blissful peace
In your providence's shelter,
In the circles of the saints and pure,
shining bright in heavenly light,
To our glorified emperor and king,
Wilhelm I,
Who dedicated his whole life
To elevated rulership,
Called upon by You
For happiness and greatness of the fatherland.
In your heights he dwells!
Hear, O God, our prayer and supplication
For the rest of his soul.
O Most Merciful,
Shelter him in your loving protection,
May eternal life be his share,
Let him dwell in Eden,
Let him rest in peace.
Amen.

Synagogal-Liturgischer Trauergesang

auf weiland

Seine Majestät den Kaiser und König Wilhelm I.

Allliebender Vater in Himmelshöhen!
Bereite selige Ruhe
Im Schutze Deiner Vorsehung,
Im Kreise der Heiligen und Reinen,
Die in himmlischer Klarheit leuchten,
Unserem verklärten Kaiser und Könige

Wilhelm I.

Der Sein ganzes Leben geweiht
Dem hohen Herrscheramte,
Zu dem Du Ihn berufen,
Dem Glücke und der Größe des Vaterlandes.
Er weilt in deinen Höhen!
Erhöre, o Gott, unser Gebet und Flehen
Für die Ruhe Seiner Seele.
O, Allerbarmer,
Birg Ihn in Deinem liebenden Schutze,
Ewiges Leben sei Sein Anteil,
Laß Ihn im Eden weilen,
Laß Ihn in Frieden ruhen.
Amen.

אֵל מָלֵא רַחֲמִים ׃ שׁוֹכֵן מְרוֹמִים ׃
הַמְצִיא מְנוּחָה נְכוֹנָה ׃
בְּצֵל אֵל שׁוֹכֵן מְעוֹנָה ׃
בְּמַעֲלוֹת קְדוֹשִׁים וּטְהוֹרִים ׃
כְּזֹהַר הָרָקִיעַ מַזְהִירִים ׃
אֶת־נִשְׁמַת אֲדוֹנֵנוּ הַמֶּלֶךְ וְהַקֵיסֶר

ווילהעלם הָרִאשׁוֹן

אֲשֶׁר בָּחַר בּוֹ יְיָ ׃
לַעֲמֹד לְשָׁרֵת בְּשֵׁם יְיָ ׃
וְהִתְנַדֵּב כָּל־יָמָיו ׃
בְּעַד עַמוֹ וְאַרְצוֹ ׃
שֶׁעָלָה לַמָּרוֹם ׃
בַּעֲבוּר הַתְּפִלָּה וְהַתְּחִנָּה ׃
בְּעַד הַזְכָּרַת נִשְׁמָתוֹ ׃
לָכֵן בְּעַל הָרַחֲמִים ׃
יַסְתִּירֵהוּ בְּכֶתֶר כְּנָפָיו לְעוֹלָמִים ׃
וְיִצְרֹר בִּצְרוֹר הַחַיִּים אֶת־נִשְׁמָתוֹ ׃
יְיָ הוּא נַחֲלָתוֹ ׃ בְּגַן־עֵדֶן תְּהֵא מְנוּחָתוֹ ׃
וְיָנוּחַ עַל מִשְׁכָּבוֹ בְּשָׁלוֹם ׃
וְנֹאמַר אָמֵן ׃

Figure A

El Malei Rachamim:
Synagogue-Liturgical Requiem
Upon the Death of His Majesty
the Kaiser and King
Wilhelm I
For Choir and Organ
Composed by Eduard Birnbaum
Königsberg in Prussia, 1888

Notes

Introduction: *Yizkor* and Memorial in Jewish Tradition, by Rabbi Lawrence A. Hoffman, PhD

1. Technically, it does not qualify as a service, because the word is properly used only for sets of prayers in which there is an *Amidah*. But by now, the term is widely used nonetheless.
2. Solomon B. Freehof, "*Hazkarath Neshamoth*," *Hebrew Union College Annual* 36 (1965): 179–89. We are grateful to Hebrew Union College for granting us the right to reproduce Freehof's essay.
3. Jakob J. Petuchowski, *Prayerbook Reform in Europe* (New York: World Union for Progressive Judaism, 1968), chap. 10, "*Kaddish* and Memorial Services." We are grateful to the World Union for Progressive Judaism for granting us the right to reproduce this chapter.
4. Eric L. Friedland, *Were Our Mouths Filled with Song* (Cincinnati: Hebrew Union College Press, 1977), chap. 10, "The Yom Kippur *Yizkor* Service in the American *Machzor*," 146–84.
5. Translation mine. For a standard English version of Nathan's account, see Abraham J. Mesch, trans., *Abyss of Despair (Yeven Metsulah)*, by Nathan of Hanover (New York: Bloch Publishing, 1950). The reference to *El Malei Rachamim* is on p. 45.

Remembering the Dead: By Us and by God, by Rabbi Lawrence A. Hoffman, PhD

1. For eminently readable background, see Eric R. Kandel, *In Search of Memory* (New York: W. W. Norton, 2006).
2. Augustine of Hippo, *Confessions* 11:14, section 17.
3. My source for what follows is *Seder Rav Amram*, from which I have extracted every instance in which the root *z.kh.r* appears. References are to the standard E. D. Goldschmidt edition and are listed by number corresponding to the sections there, with a preliminary A or B to designate the two halves into which the book is divided.
4. B6 (the *Magen Avot*).
5. The usual formation for *Kiddush al hakos* (*Kiddush* over a glass of wine, inaugurating the eve of Shabbat or holidays); B12.

6. Cf., e.g., Berakhot 2b, citing Nehemiah; 4:15 and Shabbat 20a, citing Ezekiel 15:4.
7. A97, from the liturgy of *Kri'at Hatorah*.
8. A65, from the *Tachanun*.
9. A frequent request in *Seder Rav Amram*, e.g., A97: *Z'khor rachamekha asher me'olam hemah*.
10. *Zokhrenu vo l'tovah ufokdenu vo livrakhah*.
11. Rosh Hashanah 32b. Amram too juxtaposes "visit" and "remember" in the introduction to the *Zikhronot*: "You remember the creation of the world, and visit all creatures from of old" (B114). Cf. Rosh Hashanah 11a, which juxtaposes "God remembered Rachel" (Genesis 30:22) and "God remembered her [Hannah]" (1 Samuel 1:19) with "Adonai had visited Hannah" (1 Samuel 2:21) and "Adonai visited Sarah" (Genesis 21:1)—and all four of these with *zikhron t'ru'ah* (Leviticus 23:24) to conclude that the New Year is a time when the foremothers generally were "visited" = "remembered" with successful conceptions.

Memorializing the Shoah, by Rabbi Dalia Marx, PhD

1. See Gabrielle M. Spiegel, "Memory and History: Liturgical Time and Historical Time," *History and Theory* 41, no. 2 (2002): 149–62.
2. For a comprehensive account of the rituals of commemoration in the Ashkenazi world, see Ivan Marcus, *The Jewish Life Cycle: Rites of Passage* (Seattle: University of Washington Press, 2004), 227–44.
3. Leon Wieseltier, *Kaddish* (New York: Knopf, 1998), 81.
4. Marcus, *Jewish Life Cycle*, 229.
5. According to the Polish-Lithuanian tradition, it is recited every Shabbat except for Shabbatot that coincide with a festival, Rosh Chodesh, and so on. In German tradition, it is recited only twice a year, on the Shabbat before Shavuot, when the pogroms took place, and on the Shabbat before Tisha B'av, which is sometimes referred to as the "Black Shabbat."
6. See bibliography in Dalia Marx, "From the Rhine Valley to Jezreel Valley: Innovative Versions of the Mourner *Kaddish* in the Kibbutz Movement" (forthcoming).
7. Solomon B. Freehof, "*Hazkarath Neshamoth*," *Hebrew Union College Annual* 36 (1965): 179–89 (reproduced in this book, pp. 77–89).
8. Gabriel Sivan, "The Hymns of the Isles," *Judaism* 39 (1990): 328–29. It should also be noted that the daily recitation of *Alenu*, a prayer that originally appeared in High Holy Day liturgy, began then, as it is documented in Rabbi Efrayim of Bonn's *Book of Remembrance* that the martyrs sang it when the flames burned; see Abraham Meir Habermann, *Sefer Hag'zerot Ashkenaz V'tsarfat* (Jerusalem: Tarshish, 1945), 124–26.
9. The twentieth of Sivan was suggested as a commemoration day for specifically Hungarian Jews murdered in the Holocaust. See Judith T. Baumel, *Kol Bikhiot: The Holocaust and Prayer* (Jerusalem: Bar-Ilan, 1992), 150.

10. Cited from *Hazmanah L'piyyut* website (www.piyut.org.il/textual/696.html). Every effort has been made to trace and acknowledge the copyright holders for the material included in this chapter. I apologize for any errors or omissions that may remain and ask that any omissions be brought to my attention so that they may be corrected in future editions. I thank Dr. Joel M. Hoffman for translating most of the Hebrew texts, a task that in some cases was especially demanding.

11. Cited from *Hazmanah L'piyyut* website (www.piyut.org.il/textual/329.html). Translation Tzvi Hersh Weinreb, *Mesorat Harav Kinot* (Jerusalem: Koren, 2010), 628–32.

12. I deliberately translate *akha'i* as "brothers," not the gender-neutral "siblings," to retain in English the more emotionally charged term.

13. Haim Sabato, *Bo'i Haru'ach* (Tel-Aviv: Aliyat Hagag, 2008), 79–80.

14. See www.modzits.org.

15. These hymns are usually welcomed in Hasidic circles, while rejected in Lithuanian (Mitnagdic) ones. See Judith Tydor Baumel, "In Perfect Faith: Jewish Religious Commemoration of the Holocaust," *Studies in Religion* 30, no. 1 (2001): 14–15.

16. The aggadic stipulation "In the month of Nisan they were delivered, and in the month of Nisan they will be eventually delivered" (Talmud, Rosh Hashanah 10b) became prominent in medieval Europe because of the frequent persecution of Jews around the Christian Easter and, therefore, Passover.

17. Abe Katz, www.beureihatefila.com (vol. 7, no. 28).

18. Ibid. See also Hasia Diner, *We Remember with Reverence and Love: American Jews and the Myth of Silence after the Holocaust, 1945–1962* (New York: New York University Press, 2009), 18–20.

19. Katz is referring here to Menachem M. Kasher's Haggadah. Before the recitation of the passage "Pour Out Your Wrath," Kasher instructs to add a prayer acknowledging both the Holocaust and the establishment of the State of Israel, saying, "We members of the most unfortunate generation in all the years of Israel's exile, with our own eyes we beheld the annihilation of one third of our people.... By saying the complete Great *Hallel* ... we give thanks to God, and pray that we be enabled to behold all His children speedily and happily gathered in our own days within the boundaries of the Land of Israel" (Menachem M. Kasher, ed., *Israel Passover Haggadah* [New York: Shengold, 1975], 192–93).

20. This translation, taken from the Reform Haggadah, is a somewhat softer translation than the harsher Hebrew text.

21. Herbert Bronstein, ed., *A Passover Haggadah* (New York: Central Conference of American Rabbis, 1974), 45–48.

22. Irving Greenberg, *The Jewish Way: Living the Holidays* (New York: Touchstone, 1993), 421–23.

23. Composed by Hirsh Glick (1922–1944), in memory of the partisans of the Warsaw Ghetto Uprising. He was killed during combat against the Germans in Estonia. It became one of the most popular songs relating to the Holocaust,

partly because it emphasizes Jewish heroism instead of suffering. A Hebrew version, by Avraham Shlonski, of the Yiddish song became a standard in most commemoration ceremonies for the Holocaust both in Israel and in the diaspora.

24. It stresses especially the Jews in Czechoslovakia, which had just recently been annexed by Nazi Germany.

25. This Haggadah is found in the National Library in Jerusalem.

26. See interview (in Hebrew) with Matti Shmuelov, published in Bet Avi-Chai's website in April 14, 2011, under the title "The Sixth Scroll."

27. The citation from the scroll of Lamentations 1:16 is embedded in a powerful midrash, regarding the martyrdom of a certain woman's seven sons, who were killed by the Roman Caesar. The midrash ends with the words "And the Holy Spirit screams, saying: 'For these do I weep'" (*Lamentations Rabbah* 1:50).

28. The story of the characters in this part appeared in the previous chapters.

29. Greenberg, *The Jewish Way*, 344–63.

30. Jules Harlow, ed., *Mahzor for Rosh Hashanah and Yom Kippur* (New York: Rabbinical Assembly, 1972), 558–68; Jules Harlow, ed., *Siddur Sim Shalom* (New York: Rabbinical Assembly, 1985), 812–42; Elyse Goldstein, ed., *Mishkan T'filah: A Reform Siddur* (New York: CCAR Press, 2007), 533.

31. Haberman, *Sefer Hag'zerot*, 11 (translated from Hebrew).

32. Lawrence A. Hoffman, *Beyond the Text* (Bloomington: Indiana University Press, 1987), 85–86.

33. See, e.g., Emil L. Fackenheim, *From Bergen-Belsen to Jerusalem: Contemporary Implications of the Holocaust* (Jerusalem: Hebrew University), 1975.

34. See Baumel, "In Perfect Faith."

35. Rabbi Joseph B. Soloveitchik, *The Lord Is Righteous in All His Ways* (New York: Toras-HoRav, 2006), 291.

36. Educators report regrettable responses of non-Ashkenazi children referring to the Holocaust Memorial Day as "the Ashkenazi holiday."

37. This lack is reflected in the liturgies through language (Yiddish and not Ladino, for example), place-names, and experiences.

38. For an initial definition of civil religion in Israel, see Yarden Ophir, "The Sanctity of Mount Herzl and Independence Day in Israel's Civil Religion," in *Sanctity of Time and Space*, eds. A. Houtman, M. J. H. M. Poorthuis, and J. Schwartz (Leiden: Brill, 1998), 317–48.

39. I thank Rabbi Lawrence A. Hoffman, the editor of this volume, for his insights and help. I thank Rabbi Shelton Donnell, Mr. Abe Katz for his abundant help, and Dr. Avraham Fraenel for his comments. I also discussed the matter thoroughly with colleagues at MaRaM (The Israel Council of Progressive Rabbis) and wish to thank Rabbis David Ariel-Joel, Meir Azari, Nir Barkin, Ariella Graetz-Bartuv, Benjie Gruber, Naamah Kelman, Yehoram Mazor, Uri Regev, and Moshe Silberschein; and students Jordan Raber, Ayala Samuels, Tati Schagas, Tamara Shifrin, and Nico Sokolowsky. I also thank Ms. Ellen Shoham for her help.

Sites and Subjects: Memory in Israeli Culture, by Dr. Wendy Zierler

1. Pierre Nora, "Between History and Memory: *Les Lieux de Mémoire,*" *Representations* 26 (Spring 19891): 7.
2. Ibid., 8.
3. Yehuda Amichai, *Shirei Yerushalayim* (Tel Aviv: Schocken, 1987), 108.
4. For a history of Zionist *Yizkor* texts and the dispute that arose between religious and secular constituencies, see www.izkor.gov.il/Page.aspx?pid=32.
5. See www.izkor.gov.il/Page.aspx?pid=32.
6. A Hebrew version of this text can be found at www.mkm-haifa.co.il/schools/ofarim/hagim/memory/yomatzmaut.htm. Translation mine.
7. For the original Hebrew text, see www.mazornet.com/holidays/YomHaatzmaut/BabElWad.htm. Translation mine.
8. For the full Hebrew text of Amichai's poem, included on a memorial site for the poet, see www.hofesh.org.il/archive/00/amichai.html.
9. Aviv Geffen, "Ani holekh livkot lekha," http://shironet.mako.co.il/artist?type=lyrics&lang=1&prfid=34&wrkid=1866. Translations mine.

Would Jeremiah Have Recited *Yizkor? Yizkor* and the Bible, by Dr. Marc Zvi Brettler

1. For a somewhat different presentation, which assumes that the Bible has a slightly greater sense of a differentiated afterworld, see Jon D. Levenson, *Resurrection and the Restoration of Israel: The Ultimate Victory of the God of Life* (New Haven: Yale University Press, 2006). All translations from the Bible follow the NJPS *Tanakh*, with "the LORD" reflected by "Adonai."
2. James B. Pritchard, ed., *Ancient Near Eastern Texts Relating to the Old Testament* (Princeton, NJ: Princeton University Press, 1969), 307.

Hazkarat N'shamot ("Memorial of Souls"): How It All Began, by Rabbi Solomon B. Freehof, PhD *(z"l)*

1. Siegmund Salfeld, *Das Martyrologium des Nürnberger Memorbuches* (1898), 81.
2. Adolph Gerloczi, *Jüdische Litteraturblatt*, XXVII, 90.
3. See, e.g., Salfeld, *Martyrologium*, 175–77 n10, where this prayer follows the list of those martyred in Worms in 1349.
4. Salfeld, *Martyrologium*: xiii, 85.
5. Ibid., 86.
6. Ibid., 87, where the list has hundreds of names.
7. Ibid., vii, 87.
8. Ibid., 85.
9. Gagin [Shem Tov Gaguin, nineteenth to twentieth century, England], *Keter Shem Tov*, 1: 671.
10. Text adapted from Solomon B. Freehof, "*Hazkarath Neshamoth*," *Hebrew Union College Annual* 36 (1965): 179–89.

Kaddish and Memorial Services,
by Rabbi Jakob J. Petuchowski, PhD *(z"l)*

1. Cf. David de Sola Pool, *The Old Jewish-Aramaic Prayer, the Kaddish* (Leipzig: Rudolf Haupt, 1909).

2. Ismar Elbogen, *Der jüdische Gottesdienst in seiner geschichtlichen Entwicklung* (Hildesheim: Georg Olms, 1962), 95ff.

3. Cf. Philip Birnbaum, *High Holyday Prayer Book* (New York: Hebrew Publishing Co., 1949), 737–39.

4. Ibid., 137.

5. *Ordnung der öffentlichen Andacht* (Hamburg, 1819), 22–25.

6. M. Sanhedrin 10:1, quoting Isaiah 60:21.

7. Berakhot 17a, quoting Ecclesiastes 7:1 with minor derivations from the Talmudic wording.

8. M. Avot 2:16, with minor omissions and changes.

9. For the text, see *The Order of Prayer and Order of Service according to the Custom of the Spanish and Portuguese Jews*, ed. Moses Gaster (New York: Oxford University Press, 1949), 1:200–203, 205–6.

10. Birnbaum, *High Holyday Prayer Book*, 737.

11. Ibid., 45–47.

12. *Gebetbuch für israelitischen Gemeinde in Aachen* (Aachen, 1853), 199f.

13. *Israelitisches Gebet—und Andachtsbuch*, ed. Maier (Stuttgart, 1848), 29–31.

14. *Israelitisches Gebetbuch*, ed. Geiger (Breslau, 1854), 233ff.

15. *Gebetbuch, etc.*, ed. Stein (Frankfort am Main, 1860), 52–54.

16. *Israelitisches Gebetbuch* (Hamburg, 1868), 44–47.

17. *Israelitisches Gebetbuch*, ed. Geiger (Berlin, 1870), 69f.

18. *Gebetbuch für die neue Synagoge in Berlin* (Berlin, 1881), 1:275.

19. Ibid., 101.

20. *Gebetbuch für israelitische Gemeinden*, ed. Stein (Mannheim, 1882), 39.

21. *Israelitisches Gebetbuch*, ed. Vogelstein (Westphalia, 1894), 1:106–9.

22. *Israelitisches Gebetbuch*, ed. Seligmann (Frankfurt am Main, 1910), 1:350–53.

23. Cf. A. Hyman, *Otsar Divrei Chakhamim Ufitgameihem*, 3rd printing (Tel Aviv: Dvir, 1955), 179–89.

24. Solomon B. Freehof, "Hazkarath Neshamoth," *Hebrew Union College Annual* 36 (1965): 179–89 (reprinted in this volume, pp. 77–89).

25. See pp. 129–137 in this volume.

26. Joseph H. Hertz, ed., *The Authorized Daily Prayer Book*, rev. ed. (New York: Bloch, 1948), 1107.

27. Max Joseph, "Haskarat Neschamot," in *Jüdisches Lexikon*, 2:1450–52.

28. *Ordnung der öffentlichen Andacht, etc.* (Hamburg: 1819), 279–288.

29. A. Wiener, *Der öffentliche Gottesdienst, ein Wort zur Beherzigung* (Oppeln, 1873), 14.

30. Max Joseph, "Haskarat Neschamot," 1452.

Yizkor: A Microcosm of Liturgical Interconnectivity, by Dr. Eric L. Friedland

1. The terms in German are *Seelenfeier* and *Totenfeier*. The French designation is, appropriately enough, *Office du Souvenir*.

2. The standard Ashkenazi equivalent is *El Malei Rachamim*. While essentially adhering to the Hamburg Temple *Totenfeier* for Yom Kippur, Adolph Huebsch (*Gebete für den öffentlichen Gottesdienst* [New York, 1875]) reverted for the last day of the Pilgrimage Festivals (except Shavuot) in his Bohemian-native synagogue in Manhattan (Ahawath Chesed Gemeinde, now Central Synagogue) to the more accustomed *El Malei Rachamim*, with verbal modifications, recited by the rabbi, not the cantor. As for the *Yizkor* part, it is a series of touching personalized invocations, which fall back on the ritual of the revolutionary Berlin *Reformgemeinde* (*Gebetbuch für jüdische Reformgemeinden* [Berlin, 1858]), to family and friends who are no more.

3. Cf. David de Sola Pool, *Prayers for the Day of Atonement* (New York, 1939).

4. Could it be that the drama of a nocturnal memorial service here was so as to fill the gap left by the dismissal of *Kol Nidre*, seen by many nineteenth-century reformers as little more than an *ex opere operato* legal procedure and one more way to raise gentile suspicions regarding the credibility of oaths made by Jews?

5. Just about every non-Orthodox memorial service would contain a long mood-setting preface in the vernacular, more or less a disquisition on the subject of immortality, a kind of theodicy or *tzidduk hadin*, and a general commemoration of dead relatives, friends, teachers, and leaders of the community. This would be either preceded or succeeded—*de rigueur*—by a choral or cantorial rendition of "O Lord, What Is Man" (*Adonai Mah Adam*), a composite of psalmodic verses, either in Hebrew or in the congregation's native tongue. This expansive and, as often as not, nostalgic opening provides, in a sense, a justification and rationale for the climactic personal *Yizkor* prayer(s) or any of the latter-day alternatives.

6. Doubtless because of the last two verses, which speak of an afterlife: "Into his hand I commend my spirit, when I sleep and when I awake, / And with my spirit, my body too, for Adonai is with me and I shall not fear."

7. His and Geiger's memorial services make up of two of the three alternative *Seelenfeier* that appear in the *Union Prayer Book* ("*Einheitsgebetbuch*") of German Liberal Judaism not long before the Nazi takeover (*Gebetbuch für das ganze Jahr* [Frankfurt am Main, 1929]).

8. It is less a doxology than a mosaic of Wisdom verses from the Bible concerning the destiny of humankind and an entreaty for the dead (*al yisrael v'al tzadikaya*) and peace for all (*Oseh Shalom* until *Alenu* only). This unconventional *Kaddish* may be found in Eric L. Friedland *"Were Our Mouths Filled with Song": Studies in Liberal Jewish Liturgy* (Cincinnati: Hebrew Union College Press, 1997), 182–83, 188. One can't help wondering how congregants at Kenesseth Israel accustomed to a virtually all-English prayer book were able

to recite this one-of-a-kind, newfangled Hebrew/Aramaic *Kaddish*. Perhaps the mourners just listened—reverently, one hopes—while their beloved Rabbi Krauskopf intoned it on their behalf.

9. Jakob J. Petuchowski, *Prayerbook Reform in Europe* (New York: World Union for Progressive Judaism, 1968), 331–32. To capture the flavor and *Schwung* of the original, here is the German as composed by the talented lay compilers Seckel Isaac Fränkel and M. J. Bresselau, for the earliest, 1819 edition:

> *Dein, o mein geliebter Vater! (o meine geliebte Mutter!) gedenk' ich in dieser frommen Stunde und der Liebe, Sorgfalt und Treue mit der du (ihr) mich geleitet, so lange du (ihr) auf Erden um mich gewesen. Du gingest (ihr ginget) von mir und liessest (liesset) mich allein zurück; aber der Lehren gedenk' ich die du (ihr) mir gabst (gabt) und mein Herz ist tief gerührt und schlägt deinem (eurem) unsterblichen Geiste, der droben weilt bei seinem himmlischen Vater, laut und warm entgegen. O! dass der Allgütige deine (eure) Seele aufgenommen in seinem väterlichen Schutze, im Bunde derer, die ewig leben und sich laben an dem Glanze der göttlichen Grösse und Herrlichkeit, in der du (ihr) mich umschweben mögest (möget), bis auch mein Geist zu dem deinen (euren) sich gesellt, und im Reiche des reinsten Lichtes denen begegnet, die auf Erden tugendhaft gewandelt und so theuer und lieb mir waren; und du, o himmlischer Vater, gedenke der frommen Spende, die ich zum Besten dieses Hauses, dem theuren Andenken des (der) Heimgegangenen widme, o dass dir wohlgefallen mögen meines Mundes willige Opfer. Amen!*

10. I think of the fearlessly Reform *Olat Tamid* (Baltimore, 1858) to the proto-Conservative *Avodat Yisrael* (Baltimore, 1864), by Benjamin Szold.

11. Cf. Nosson Scherman, ed., *The Complete ArtScroll Siddur* (Brooklyn: Mesorah, 1984), 810–12; Nissen Mangel, trans., *Siddur Tehillat Hashem* (Brooklyn: Kehot, 2002), 338.

12. On principle, Merzbacher showed remarkable fidelity to the Hebrew text when he translated it into English. This is the only departure in *Order of Prayer* I have come across.

13. Adler also wrote a special *Hashkavah*, titled *Av Harachamim*, in fine classical Hebrew—it takes the place of either *El Malei Rachamim* or *M'nuchah N'khonah*—which passed over to the 1927 and 1946 Conservative prayer books, but without displacing *El Malei Rachamim*. Adler's innovatory prayer is not to be confused with the martyrological *Av Harachamim* traditionally said in Ashkenazi synagogues most Sabbaths. Ben Zion Bokser adopted the novel British prayer for his right-of-center Conservative *Hamachzor* (New York: The Rabbinical Assembly of America and the United Synagogue of America, 1959). The Israeli *Masortiim* (*Va-Ani Tefillati* [Jerusalem: The Masorti Movement and the Rabbinical Assembly of Israel, 2009]) have taken it up, expanded upon it, and made it into a literarily fine prayer. None of the later Conservative rites have opted for this unique *Hashkavah*. Nor has the former chief rabbi Jonathan Sacks for *The Koren Siddur, The Authorised Daily Prayer Book*'s successor.

14. Since renamed the United Synagogue of Conservative Judaism.

15. The British Liberal *Gate of Repentance* (London: Union of Liberal and Progressive Synagogues, 1973) and *Machzor Ruach Chadashah* (London: Liberal Judaism, 2003) use the Adler/Conservative *Yizkor* through *ut'hi menuchatam kavod* as a preface to a single longer piece in English—for all one's departed kith and kin. For the succinct, moving English paraphrase see note 16.

16. The tender, endearing tone of Joel Rosenberg's translation in the Reconstructionist *Kol Haneshamah* High Holy Day volume, with its reconceptualization of the afterlife, is worthy of attention: "Let God remember the soul of ... who went to her place of eternal rest. Please let her soul be bound up with the living in the continuum of life, and may her rest be honorable. Grant her abundant joy in your presence, and sweet pleasures at your right hand for eternity" (*Kol Haneshamah: Prayerbook for the Days of Awe* [Elkins Park, PA: Reconstructionist Press, 1999], 1027).

17. The American Reform Movement's *Gates of Repentance* took over the Adler/Conservative *Yizkor*, pluralized. A second one is added for those who lost their lives in the Shoah, the opening line modified to "May God remember forever our brothers and sisters of the House of Israel who gave their lives for the Sanctification of the Divine Name (*shemasru et nafshoteihem al kiddush hashem*)." These *Yizkor* texts, generalized and in Hebrew as they are, depart from all the editions of the Reform *Union Prayer Book*, volume 2, beginning with the 1894 one, where prayers are spoken, individually and solely in English, to dead family members and companions.

18. The Conservative *Sabbath and Festival Prayer Book* (New York: Rabbinical Assembly, 1946) did, however, have in its one *El Malei Rachamim* the promissory *ba'avur she'anu nodrim litz'dakah* ("for which we pledge charity") but left it untranslated. Interestingly, the newest *Mahzor Lev Shalem* substitutes in its *Yizkor* prayer the Hebrew term *nodev* ("freely offer") for *noder* ("vow"), though the entire phrase is as rendered by Harlow. This mild change had already been introduced in 1998 edition of the Conservative *Siddur Sim Shalom*.

19. There's the occasional trenchant verse by a non-Jew, like the one by Christina Rossetti (*Machzor Ruach Chadashah*, 392) or Su Tung P'o (*Kol Haneshamah: Machzor l'Yamim Nora'im*, 1024).

20. There is a much more generous helping of psalms than ever: Psalms 8, 23, 63, 90, 91, and 121. The earliest I have been able to find of the widespread use of Psalm 23 today in a *Jewish* memorial service is in David Einhorn's *Olat Tamid* (Baltimore, 1858). Its use in a Jewish context derives from its ubiquitous appearance in the last rites of the church. The classical Christian exegesis of "And I shall dwell in the house of the Lord forever," namely, abide with God eternally in paradise, is, strictly speaking, at variance with the standard this-worldly Jewish interpretation from *Targum Jonathan ad locum* to *Metzudat David's gloss* on *v'shavti*, "my dwelling in the Temple will be for length of days, and I will no longer be banished or made to wander."

21. To be sure, the Hamburg, *Reformgemeinde*, and Geiger rites had a single prayer for all the departed, but in each case, the German *Yizkor* proxy was a touching fresh composition. Succeeding prayer books, e.g., Cäsar Seligmann's, provided *Yizkor* prayers in the vernacular that were much more individualized and specific, eloquent, and warm.

"Service for the Souls": The Origin of Modern Memorial Services, 1819 to 1938, by Dr. Annette M. Boeckler

1. On the roots of the traditional custom, see Solomon B. Freehof, *"Hazkarath Neshamoth," Hebrew Union College Annual* 36 (1965): 179–89 (reprinted in this volume, pp. 77–89).

2. E. Kley and C. S. Günsburg, *Die deutsche Synagoge* (Berlin: Mauersche Buchhandlung, 1817), iv–v, xiv–xv.

3. Isaiah 42:12.

4. *Der achtzehnte October: Ein heiliges Denkmahl in künftigen Zeiten für die Fürsten und Völker / Gesprochen im neuen Israelitischen Tempel zu Hamburg* von G. Salomon am 18. October 1825 (Hamburg: Joseph Ahrons, s.a., 1825 [small leaflet self-published by the Hamburg Temple]). Another sermon on this occasion is *Die neue Erde und der neue Himmel oder der Achtzehnte des Octobermonats ein dreifaches heiliges Denkmal der Zeit: Eine Predigt in neuen Israelitischen Tempel zu Hamburg am 18. October 1832 / gehalten und auf wiederholtes Verlangen zum Druck befördert von Gotthold Salomon* (Hamburg: Hartwig und Müller, s.a. 1832 [small leaflet self-published by the Hamburg Temple]).

5. The day, a Sunday, fell that year on the eighteenth of Tishrei, the fourth day of Sukkot.

6. The Prussian rulers were themselves Protestants. During the nineteenth century, Protestantism became more of a culture (*Kulturprotestantismus*) than a theologically based religion with its own "confessional" status. Catholicism already had its memorial day: on "All Souls' Day," people would visit the graves in the night between November 1 and 2 and place candles on them. The original medieval purpose was to say prayers for the souls of relatives. On *Totensonntag*, see, e.g., Karl-Heinz Bieritz, *Das Kirchenjahr: Feste, Gedenk- und Feiertage in Geschichte und Gegenwart* (Berlin: Union Verlag, 1988), 159f.; W. Jannasch, *"Totensonntag,"* in *Die Religion in Geschichte und Gegenwart* (1986), 6:956f.

7. *Seder Ha'avodah ... Ordnung der oeffentlichen Andacht für die Sabbath- und Festtage des ganzen Jahres: Nach dem Gebrauche des Neuen-Tempel-Vereins in Hamburg*, eds. Herausgegeben von S. J. Fraenkel und M. J. Bresselau (Hamburg, 5579 [1819]), 279–288.

8. An abridged translation can be found in Jakob J. Petuchowski, *Prayerbook Reform in Europe: The Liturgy of European Liberal and Reform Judaism* (New York: World Union for Progressive Judaism, 1968), 331.

9. An English translation of this text can be found in Petuchowski, *Prayerbook Reform in Europe*, 331f.

10. Mishnah Sanhedrin 10:1; Talmud, Berakhot 17a; and Mishnah Avot 2:16. The text with an English translation and a textual analysis can be found in Petuchowski, *Prayerbook Reform in Europe*, 325–27. This *Kaddish* with this introduction was also used in Hamburg to end all evening services on Shabbat or festivals. See ... *Ordnung der öffentlichen Andacht für die Sabbath—und Festtage des ganzen Jahres: Nach dem Gebrauche des Neuen-Tempel-Vereins in Hamburg* (Hamburg, 1819), 22–25.

11. *Seder Ha'avodah: Gebetbuch für die öffentliche und häusliche Andacht nach dem Gebrauch des Neuen Israelitischen Tempels in Hamburg* (Hamburg: B.S. Berendsohn, 1841), 306–16.

12. See, e.g., the meditations in Hamburg (1941), pp. 339–41, 364–67, and the insertion of the uplifting Sephardi hymn *El Nora Alilah* (p. 353).

13. שיר הכבוד מיט ווארטגעטרייער דייטשער איבערזעטצונג ... נעבזט הזכרת נשמות מיט איבערזעטצונג [*Shir Hakavod with literal German translation alongside the Memorial Service with translation*] (Hamburg: Jacob Joachim Levy, 1844; in Leo Baeck College Library Lewis Family Trust collection RB/8A.116).

14. *Israelitisches Gebets—und Andachtsbuch*, ed. Joseph Maier (Stuttgart, 1848), 29–31.

15. *Israelitische Gebetordnung*, Zweiter Band (Stuttgart, 1861), 554–55.

16. *Union Prayer Book* (New York, 1894), 297–98.

17. For example, Hamburg (1819), Philippson, Madgeburg (1864); Geiger (1870); Leipzig (1876); Vogelstein, Westphalen (1896); Seligmann, Frankfurt (1904).

18. Seligmann (1904), 305.

19. For example, Philippson (1864), Geiger (1870), Vogelstein (1896), Hamburg (1904), Seligmann (1904).

20. The six strophes of this *tokh'chah* can be found in I. Zangwill, *Selected Religious Poems of Solomon ibn Gabirol* (Philadelphia: Jewish Publication Society, 1923), 52–54.

21. Published in L. Lewandowski, *Todah W'simrah* (Berlin, 1876–82, Nr 227), 260–62.

22. See, e.g., the different ones in *Gesänge und Melodien zum Gebrauch der Jacobson Schule in Seesen* (Wolfenbüttel: E. Holle, s.a., post 1833, Nr 82), 18; and *Seder T'fillah Israelitische Gebetordnung für Synagoge und Schule*, ed. Joseph Maier (Stuttgart: J.B. Metzler, 1861), 554f. Rabbi Andrew Goldstein recently showed me a handwritten third melody that reproduced what he remembers from his childhood.

23. *Todah W'simrah*, Nr 228, 262–65.

24. For this custom and some of its reasons, see J. D. Eisenstein, Ozar Dinim u-Minhagim: *A Digest of Jewish Laws and Customs in Alphabetical Order* (New York, 1917; reprint, Tel Aviv, 1968), 96f. [Hebrew]. (I am grateful to Dr. Jeremy Schonfield for pointing my attention to this source.)

25. As, e.g., in a story about Abaye and Rav Pappa in Talmud, Yevamot 106a.
26. Berlin Fasanenstr (p. 302), Berlin Neue Synagoge (p. 302), *Einheitsgebetbuch* (p. 398).
27. Geiger, 1870 (p. 293); Joel (p. 318); Westfalen (p. 442); Stein, 1910 (p. 508); Danzig, 1905 (p. 361).
28. Hamburg, 1819; Hamburg, 1841 (p. 306).
29. *Einheitsgebetbuch* (p. 482).
30. Berlin Reform (p. 47); Seligmann, Frankfurt (p. 301); *Einheitsgebetbuch* (p. 528).
31. *T'fillot l'khol Hashanah: Gebetbuch für das ganze Jahr. Zweiter Teil: Neujahr und Versöhnungstag* (Ausgabe für Berlin, Frankfurt am Main: M. Lehrberger, 1931), 39–59.
32. *T'fillot L'khol Hashanah: Gebetbuch für das ganze Jahr. Zweiter Teil: Neujahr und Versöhnungstag* (Ausgabe für Berlin, Frankfurt am Main: M. Lehrberger, 1938), 345–51.

What Happens When We Die: Intimations of Immortality, by Rabbi Lawrence A. Englander, CM, DHL

1. Neil Gillman, *The Death of Death* (Woodstock, VT: Jewish Lights, 1997), especially 134ff.
2. George Wald, *International Journal of Quantum Chemistry*, symposium 11, 1984, 1.
3. This essay is dedicated to the memory of my aunt Rhoda Weltman, Rivka bat Yosef Tzvi u'Miriam. She had a passion for social justice and taught me a great deal about our participation in *tikkun olam*.
4. Talmud, Yevamot 97a.
5. Mishnah Sanhedrin 6:5.
6. Talmud, Ta'anit 22a.

Remembering through Forgetting: *Yizkor* as an Unshared Experience, by Rabbi Shoshana Boyd Gelfand

1. Jonah Lehrer, *Proust Was a Neuroscientist* (New York: Houghton Mifflin, 2007), 95.
2. Beth Kissileff, "Judaism: The World's Best Memory Palace," *Moment Magazine*, September/October 2012, 26.
3. Joshua Foer, *Moonwalking with Einstein*, as quoted in Kissileff, "Judaism," 26.
4. Joshua Foer, *Moonwalking with Einstein: The Art and Science of Remembering Everything* (London: Penguin Books, 2011), 82.
5. Lehrer, *Proust*, 94.
6. Jorge Luis Borges, *Funes the Memorious*, http://evans-experientialism. freewebspace.com/borges.htm.
7. Foer, *Moonwalking*, 29.

Hard to Plan the Day, by Rabbi Edwin Goldberg, DHL

1. Israel Shenker, "E. B. White: Notes and Comment by Author," *New York Times*, July 11, 1969.

Why Art Thou Cast Down? by Rabbi Andrew Goldstein, PhD

1. Jakob J. Petuchowski, *Prayerbook Reform in Europe* (New York: World Union for Progressive Judaism, 1968), 190, 193, 329ff.
2. Eric L. Friedland, *"Were Our Mouths Filled with Song": Studies in Liberal Jewish Liturgy* (Cincinnati: Hebrew Union College Press, 1997), 152.
3. Morris Jastrow and Max D. Klein, e.g., Ibid., 177n34.
4. Ibid., 171.
5. Ibid., 180n45. First published in 1819, with revised edition in 1833.
6. Published by Union of Liberal and Progressive Synagogues, London, 1973. The North American *Gates of Repentance* was based on this book and likewise omitted the hymn that had appeared in the edition of the *Union Prayer Book*.
7. I am grateful to Dr. Annette M. Boeckler for sharing with me a copy of his early music.
8. *Machzor Ruach Chadashah*, ed. Rabbi Dr. Andrew Goldstein and Rabbi Dr. Charles Middleburgh (London: Liberal Judaism, 2003).

Remembering Abraham Geiger,
by Rabbi Walter Homolka, PhD, DHL

1. Leo Baeck, *"Judentum,"* in *Religion in Geschichte und Gegenwart*, ed. Hermann Gunkel and Leopold Zscharnack (Tübingen: J.C.B. Mohr, 1929), 3:488.
2. Cited in Wilhelm Freund, *Zur Judenfrage in Deutschland vom Standpunkte des Rechts und der Gewissensfreiheit* (Berlin: Veit, 1843), 214–16.
3. Abraham Geiger, "Letter to Leopold Zunz, 22 April 1831," cited by Ludwig Geiger, *Abraham Geiger: Leben und Lebenswerk* (Berlin: Reimer, 1910), 17.
4. Abraham Geiger, "Das Judenthum unserer Zeit und die Bestrebungen in ihm," *Wissenschaftliche Zeitschrift für jüdische Theologie* 1, no. 1 (1835): 1–12.
5. Ludwig Geiger, *Abraham Geiger: Leben und Lebenswerk* (Berlin: Reimer, 1910), 296.
6. Abraham Geiger, "Die zwei verschiedenen Betrachtungsweisen. Der Schriftsteller und der Rabbiner," *Wissenschaftliche Zeitung für jüdische Theologie* 4, no. 3 (1839): 3–4.
7. Cited in Ludwig Geiger, "Abraham Geiger's Briefe an J. Dérenbourg [Joseph Dernburg] (1833–1842)," *Allgemeine Zeitung des Judenthums* 60, no. 18 (May 1, 1896): 214.
8. Max Dienemann, "Der Rabbiner," *Der Morgen* 9, no. 2 (1933): 95.
9. Ferdinand Rosenthal, *Was war, was ist und was soll der Rabbiner sein?* (1911), cited in Alexander Altmann, "The German Rabbi; 1910-1939," in *Leo Baeck Year Book*, v. 19 (1974), 31.

10. Abraham Geiger, "Tagebuch 1824–1832," in *Abraham Geigers Nachgelassene Schriften*, ed. Ludwig Geiger (Berlin: Gerschel, 1878), 5:3–42.
11. Abraham Geiger, "Abhandlung: Die Gründung einer jüdisch-theologischen Facultät, ein dringendes Bedürfnis unserer Zeit," *Wissenschaftliche Zeitung für jüdische Theologie* 1 (1836): 16.
12. Ludwig Philippson, "Aufforderung an alle Israeliten Deutschlands," *Allgemeine Zeitung des Judenthums* 88 (1837): 349–51.
13. Cited in Ludwig Geiger, *Abraham Geiger: Leben*, 220.
14. Demand for an independent Jewish theological faculty in a German university did not resonate, even after the founding of the Second German Reich in 1871, in large part because of the opposition of the Protestant Church. Cf. Christian Wiese, *Wissenschaft des Judentums und protestantische Theologie im wilhelminischen Deutschland: Ein Schrei ins Leere?* (Tübingen: Mohr Siebeck, 1999). See the English translation *Challenging Colonial Discourse: Jewish Studies and Protestant Theology in Wilhelmine Germany* (Leiden: Brill, 2005); and Benno Jacob, *Die Stellung des Rabbiners in dem Entwurf eines Gesetzes betreffend die Verfassung der jüdischen Religionsgemeinschaft in Preussen* (Hamburg: Lessmann, 1910), 15.
15. The Breslau and the Orthodox Hildesheimer seminary in Berlin in 1938; the famous liberal Hochschule in Berlin in 1942.

An Ongoing Conversation with Empty Chairs, by Rabbi Delphine Horvilleur

1. www.akadem.org/sommaire/colloques/livres-des-mondes-juifs-et-diasporas-en-dialogue-2012/recits-des-origines-14-02-2012-30252_4399.php.

"Empty-Handed before Adonai," by Rabbi Jonathan Magonet, PhD

1. A. Z. Idelsohn, *Jewish Liturgy and Its Development* (New York: Schocken Books, 1967), 230–31.
2. *Forms of Prayer for Jewish Worship*, vol. 3, *Prayers for the High Holydays*, 8th ed., ed. Assembly of Rabbis of the Reform Synagogues of Great Britain (London: Reform Synagogues of Great Britain, 1985), 606–25.

The Hippo of Recollection Stirring in the Muddy Waters of the Mind, by Rabbi Charles H. Middleburgh, PhD

Chapter title after Terry Pratchett, *Soul Music*.

1. Charles Middleburgh and Andrew Goldstein, eds., *Machzor Ruach Chadashah* (London: Liberal Judaism, 2003).
2. Israel I Mattuck, ed., *Liberal Jewish Prayer Book* (London: Liberal Jewish Synagogue, 1937).
3. John D. Rayner and Chaim Stern, eds., *Gate of Repentance* (London: Union of Liberal and Progressive Synagogues, 1973).

4. Christina Rossetti (1830–1894), "Remember me when I am gone away.... "
5. Chaim Nachman Bialik (1873–1934), "After I am dead.... "
6. Harold M. Schulweis (1925–), "The Yahrzeit candle is different.... "
7. Anon, "In many houses, all at once.... "
8. Gilda Radner (1946–1989), "I wanted a perfect ending.... "
9. Marjorie Pizer (1920–), "I had thought that your death.... "
10. *The Union Prayer Book for Jewish Worship*, rev. ed. (Cincinnati: Central Conference of American Rabbis, 1940; New York: Central Conference of American Rabbis, 1945).
11. *Gate of Repentance*, 374f.
12. *Machzor Ruach Chadashah*, 397f.
13. Ronald Aigen, ed., *Machzor Chadeish Yameinu: Renew Our Days; A Prayer Cycle for Days of Awe* (Quebec: Congregation Dorshei Emet, 2001).
14. Ibid., 554f.
15. *Machzor Ruach Chadashah*, 399.
16. Rabbi Sidney Brichto (1936–2009), former executive director of the Union of Liberal and Progressive Synagogues (in the United Kingdom and Ireland).
17. The textual inspiration for the sermon was the Rabbinic dictum "There are three partners in the making of a human being: the Holy One, ever to be praised, one's father, and one's mother" (Talmud, Kiddushin 30b).

Re-membering: *Yizkor* and the Dynamics of Death, by Rabbi Jay Henry Moses

1. Avivah Gottlieb Zornberg, *Genesis: The Beginning of Desire* (Philadelphia: Jewish Publication Society, 1995), 243–83.

Prayer for the Dead; Promise by the Living, by Rabbi Aaron D. Panken, PhD

1. Nahum N. Sarna, *Genesis, The JPS Torah Commentary* (Philadelphia: Jewish Publication Society, 1989), 56.
2. Leo Jung, "The Meaning of the *Kaddish*," in *Jewish Reflections on Death*, ed. Jack Riemer (New York: Schocken Books, 1974), 163.

A Soul-ar Eclipse, by Rabbi Sandy Eisenberg Sasso

1. Douglas Hofstadter, *I Am a Strange Loop* (New York: Basic Books, 2007), 259.
2. Theodore White, *The Mountain Road* (New York: William Sloan Associates, 1956), 340–41.
3. Hofstadter, *Strange Loop*, 258, 317.
4. Howard Schwartz, *Tree of Souls: The Mythology of Judaism* (New York: Oxford University Press, 2004), 203–4.

To Tear and to Sew, by Rabbi David Stern

1. Talmud, Mo'ed Katan 26a–b.
2. Quoted in Jack Stern, *The Right Not to Remain Silent* (Lincoln, NE: iUniverse, 2006), 317.
3. William Wordsworth, "Ode: Intimations of Immortality from Recollections of Early Childhood," in *English Romantic Writers*, ed. David Perkins (New York: Harcourt Brace Jovanovich, 1967), 282.

"For I Pledge *Tz'dakah* on Her Behalf," by Rabbi Margaret Moers Wenig, DD

1. *Gates of Repentance: The New Union Prayerbook for the Days of Awe* (New York: Central Conference of American Rabbis, 1978), "Memorial Service," 490.
2. Bruce D. Perry and Maia Szalavitz, *The Boy Who Was Raised as a Dog and Other Stories from a Child Psychiatrist's Notebook: What Traumatized Children Can Teach Us about Loss, Love and Healing* (New York: Basic Books, 2006), 19.
3. Ibid., 156.
4. Mark Doty, *Heaven's Coast: A Memoir* (New York: Harper Perennial, 1996), 287.
5. Perry and Szalavitz, *Boy Who Was Raised as a Dog*, 156.
6. Julian Barnes, *The Sense of an Ending* (New York: Knopf, 2011), 143.
7. Perry and Szalavitz, *Boy Who Was Raised as a Dog*, 156.
8. From the central prayer of *K'dushat Hayom* on Yom Kippur, *M'chal*, see Birnbaum Siddur, Philip Birnbaum, trans., *High Holiday Prayer Book* (New York: Hebrew Publishing Company, 1951), 507, 609–11, 691, 751, 863, 903, 947, 967, 1007.
9. Simcha Paul Raphael, *Jewish Views of the Afterlife* (New York: Jason Aronson, 1994), 353, quoting Martin Buber, *Tales of the Hasidim*, vol. 1.
10. *Mishneh Torah*, Laws of Repentance 2:11.
11. *Ba'avur* ... is also included in the *Yizkor* formula that is recited at the end of each of the three Pilgrimage Festivals. There, the pledge is understood to echo the festival offerings brought to the Temple.
12. With thanks to Helen Blumenthal, Daniel Fleshler, Rabbi Lawrence A. Hoffman D, Marion Marx, Elizabeth Lorris Ritter, Steven Rosenberg, Liba Rubenstein, Dr. Monica Saez, and Rabbi Elaine Zecher for reactions to an earlier draft.

Remembering Our Summers in the Autumns of Our Years, by Rabbi Daniel G. Zemel

1. Hans Meyerhoff, *Time in Literature* (Berkley: University of California Press, 1955), 109.

2. A. Bartlett Giamatti, "The Green Fields of the Mind," in *A Great and Glorious Game: Baseball Writings of A. Bartlett Giamatti*, ed. Kenneth S. Robson (Chapel Hill, NC: Algonquin Books, 1998), 7.

3. Ibid., 7–8.

4. Avishai Margalit, *The Ethics of Memory* (Cambridge, MA: Harvard University Press, 2002), 20.

5. Lawrence A. Hoffman, "*Zekher* and *Zikaron*: A Liturgical Theology of Memory," in *Memory in Jewish and Christian Traditions*, ed. Michael A. Signer (Notre Dame, IN: University of Notre Dame Press, 2001).

6. Giamatti, "Green Fields," 13.

Appendix A

1. *Book of Prayer According to the Custom of the Spanish and Portuguese Jews*, 2nd ed., ed. David de Sola Pool (New York: Union of Sephardic Congregations, 1983).

Appendix B

1. Eliezer Lazer ben Harav Meir Landshuth, *Amudei Ha'avodah* (Berlin, 1857–62; reprint, New York: Hermon Press, 1965).

2. Geographic references to the vast area in question are notoriously hard to pinpoint for modern readers. I am indebted to Yoram Bitton for identifying the modern-day equivalents of the geographic towns and villages, which the document provides in only their Yiddishized versions. I am similarly indebted to Dr. Carole Balin for her enormous guidance in finding my way through the secondary literature on the period.

〇∞〇

Glossary

The glossary presents names and Hebrew words used regularly throughout this volume and provides the way they are pronounced. Sometimes two pronunciations are common, in which case the first is the way the word is sounded in Hebrew, and the second is the way it is sometimes heard in common speech, under the influence of English or, sometimes, of Yiddish, the folk language of Jews in northern and eastern Europe (a combination, mostly, of Hebrew and German). Our goal is to provide the way that many Jews actually use these words, not just the technically correct version.

- The pronunciations are divided into syllables by dashes.
- The accented syllable is written in capital letters.
- "Kh" represents a guttural sound, similar to the German (as in "sprach").
- The most common vowel is "a" as in "father," which appears here as "ah."
- The short "e" (as in "get") is written as either "e" (when it is in the middle of a syllable) or "eh" (when it ends a syllable).
- Similarly, the short "i" (as in "tin") is written as either "i" (when it is in the middle of a syllable) or "ih" (when it ends a syllable).
- A long "o" (as in "Moses") is written as "oe" (as in the word "toe") or "oh" (as in the word "Oh!").

Adon Olam (pronounced ah-DOHN oh-LAHM): An early-morning prayer of unknown authorship, but dating from medieval times. We assume it may have been intended originally as a nighttime prayer, because it praises God for watching over our souls when we sleep. Nowadays it is used also as a concluding song, for which composers have provided a staggering variety of tunes.

Alenu (pronounced ah-LAY-noo): The first word and, therefore, the title of a well-known prayer, compiled in the second or third century as part of the New Year (Rosh Hashanah) service, but from about 1300 on, used also as a concluding prayer for every daily service. *Alenu* means "it is incumbent upon us ... " and introduces the prayer's theme: our duty to praise God.

Aliyah (pronounced ah-lee-YAH or, commonly, ah-LEE-yah; plural: *aliyot*, pronounced ah-lee-YOHT): Literally, "going up, ascending," and hence, the act of going up to the reader's lectern to recite blessings over the reading of Torah. In common parlance, one "receives an *aliyah*," that is, one is called up to the Torah to say the blessings.

Al kiddush hashem (pronounced AHL kee-DOOSH hah-SHEHM): Literally, "for the sanctification of God's name," but used technically as a euphemism for dying as a martyr.

Amidah (pronounced ah-mee-DAH or, commonly, ah-MEE-dah): One of three titles for the second of two central units in the worship service, the first being the *Sh'ma* and Its Blessings. It is composed of a series of blessings, many of which are petitionary, except on Sabbaths and holidays, when the petitions are removed out of deference to the holiness of the day. Also called *T'fillah* (pronounced t'-fee-LAH or, commonly, t'-FEE-lah) and *Sh'moneh Esreh* (pronounced sh'-moh-NEH ehs-RAY, or, commonly, sh'-MOH-neh EHS-ray). *Amidah* means "standing" and refers to the fact that the prayer is said standing up.

Arvit (pronounced ahr-VEET or, commonly, AHR-veet): From the Hebrew word *erev* (pronounced EH-rev), meaning "evening." One of two titles used for the evening worship service (also called *Ma'ariv*, pronounced mah-ah-REEV, or, commonly, MAH-ah-riv).

Ashkenazi (pronounced ahsh-k'-nah-ZEE or, commonly, ahsh-k'-NAH-zee): From the Hebrew word *Ashkenaz*, denoting the geographic area of northern and eastern Europe. Ashkenazi is the adjective, describing not just the inhabitants but also the liturgical rituals and customs practiced in Ashkenaz, as opposed to Sephardi (pronounced s'-fahr-DEE, or, commonly, s'-FAHR-dee), meaning rituals and customs derived from Sefarad, modern-day Spain and Portugal (see **Sephardi**).

Av Harachamim (pronounced AHV hah-rah-khah-MEEM or, commonly, AHV hah-RAH-khah-meem): Literally, "Father of mercy," a prayer composed in the wake of the Crusades to commemorate the death of Jewish martyrs in Germany; now part of the weekly Shabbat service (after reading Torah) and one of the main prayers comprising the memorial service (*Yizkor*).

Benediction (also called a "blessing"): One of two terms used for the Rabbis' favorite prose formula for composing prayers. The worship service is composed of many different literary genres, but most of it is benedictions. Long benedictions end with a summary line that begins *Barukh atah Adonai* ... (pronounced bah-RUKH ah-TAH ah-doh-NAH-ee), "Blessed are You, Adonai...." " Short blessings consist of the summary line alone.

Bet din (pronounced bayt DEEN): A law court, tribunal, or panel of judges.

Black Sabbath: The Sabbath before the ninth of Av.

Blessing: See **Benediction**.

B'rakhah (pronounced b'-rah-KHAH or, commonly, B'RUKH-uh; pl. *b'rakhot*, pronounced b'-rah-KHOT): See **Benediction**.

Chacham (pronounced khah-KHAHM): Literally, "wise," hence, a master of Talmudic study, a sage; but used technically in Sephardi tradition as the equivalent of "rabbi," the title given, therefore, to a Sephardi rabbi.

Chevra kaddisha (pronounced KHEHV-rah kah-DEE-shah): Literally, "The holy society," the Aramaic term used for the burial society charged with preparing the dead for interment.

Converso (pronounced kahn-VEHR-soh): A Jew forced to convert to Christianity during the period of the Spanish Inquisition.

Edot hamizrach (pronounced ay-DOHT hah-mihz-RAKH): Literally, "communities of the east," referring to the branch of Sephardim who were expelled from Spain in 1492 and settled in North Africa or the Mediterranean; and who were subsequently influenced by the sixteenth-century kabbalistic teachings of various teachers (most notably Isaac Luria, the Ari) in the Land of Israel.

El Malei Rachamim (pronounced AYL mah-LAY rah-khah-MEEM or, popularly, AYL mah-lay RAH-khah-meem): Literally, "God, full of compassion," a prayer associated with the Chmielnicki pogroms that devastated Jewish communities in Ukraine in 1648. Chmielnicki was the Cossack leader who initiated the destruction. The prayer was used to memorialize the victims and soon spread to become part of the funeral liturgy and the memorial service as well.

Gehinnom (pronounced gay-hee-NAHM or, popularly, g'-HIH-nuhm): Originally the biblical name for a valley south of Jerusalem. It was associated with a cult involving the burning of children, against which the prophets inveighed; and from that negative association, *Gehinnom* came to be used as a metaphoric term for hell, the place where evil people would receive punishment after death.

haftarah (pronounced hahf-tah-RAH or, commonly, hahf-TOH-rah): The section of Scripture taken from Prophets and read publicly as part of Shabbat and holiday worship services. From a word meaning "to conclude," because it is the "concluding reading," that is, it follows a reading of Torah (the Five Books of Moses).

Halakhah (pronounced hah-lah-KHAH or, commonly, hah-LAH-khah): The Hebrew word for Jewish law. Used adjectivally in the anglicized form, "halakhic" (pronounced hah-LAH-khic), meaning "legal." From the Hebrew root *h.l.kh*, meaning "to walk" or "to go," denoting the way one should walk or go through life.

Hashkavah (pronounced hash-kah-VAH): Literally, "laying down" or "requiem," hence, the name given to the Sephardi memorial prayer recited in the synagogue for the deceased.

Hazkarat hametim (pronounced hahz-kah-RAHT hah-may-TEEM; sing. *Hazkarat hamet*, pronounced hahz-kah-RAHT hah-MAYT): Literally, "remembering the dead," hence, an alternative term for the act of *hazkarat n'shamot*. See *Hazkarat n'shamot*.

Hazkarat n'shamot (pronounced hahz-kah-RAHT n'-shah-MOHT): Literally, "remembering of the souls," hence, the proper term for *Yizkor*, both the concept and the general act of remembering the deceased. By extension, also the *Yizkor* service in its entirety, that service's opening prayer (titled *Yizkor*) and *Av Harachamim*, the third of the *Yizkor* prayers, which itself began as a prayer for *hazkarat n'shamot* following the Crusades.

Kabbalah (pronounced kah-bah-LAH or, popularly, kah-BAH-lah): A general term for Jewish mysticism, but used properly for a specific set of mystical doctrines that began in western Europe in the eleventh and twelfth centuries, was recorded in the *Zohar* (pronounced ZOH-hahr) in the thirteenth century, and then was further elaborated, especially in the Land of Israel (in Safed), in the sixteenth century. From a Hebrew word meaning "to receive" or to "welcome," it means also "tradition," implying the receiving of tradition from one's past.

Kabbalat Shabbat (pronounced kah-bah-LAHT shah-BAHT): Literally, "welcoming Shabbat [the Sabbath]" and, therefore, a term for the introductory synagogue prayers that lead up to the arrival of the Sabbath at sundown on Friday night.

Kabbalist: A devotee of Kabbalah. See **Kabbalah.**

Kaddish (pronounced kah-DEESH or, popularly, KAH-dihsh): One of several prayers from a Hebrew word meaning "holy" and, therefore, the name given to a prayer that affirms God's holiness. It was composed in the first century but later found its way into the service in several forms, including the one known as the Mourner's *Kaddish* (see *Kaddish Yatom*) and used as a mourner's prayer. It also punctuates the service in various formats: a full *Kaddish* (containing an extra line, compared to the mourner's version) and a "half *Kaddish* (just half the size of the full version).

Kaddish D'rabbanan (pronounced kah-DEESH d'-rah-bah-NAHN): Literally, "the Rabbis' *Kaddish*," that is, the form of *Kaddish* recited after study. See *Kaddish.*

Kaddish Yatom (pronounced kah-DEESH yah-TOHM or, commonly, KAH-deech yah-TOHM): Literally, "orphan's *Kaddish*," that is, the form of *Kaddish* said by mourners. See *Kaddish.*

K'lipot (pronounced k'lee-POHT; sing. *klipah*, pronounced k'-lee-PAH): Literally, "shards," the name given in Kabbalah for the "shards of evil" that are said to have entered the universe as part of the process by which it was created.

K'matnat yad (pronounced k'-maht-naht YAHD or, popularly, k'-MAHT-naht YAHD): Literally, "each according to the gift of his hand," a citation from Deuteronomy 16:17, the reading from the second day of the three Pilgrimage Festivals, whence we get the custom of reciting *Yizkor* then, and giving charity in honor of the dead.

Machzor (pronounced mahkh-*ZOHR* or, commonly, MAHKH-zohr; pl. *machzorim*, pronounced mahkh-zoh-REEM): Literally, "cycle," as in "the annual cycle" of time; hence, the name given to the prayer book for holy days that occur once annually and that mark the passing of the year. Separate *machzorim* exist for Rosh Hashanah and Yom Kippur.

Matnat yad: See *K'matnat yad.*

Minchah (pronounced meen-KHAH or, commonly, MIN-khah): Literally, "afternoon." Originally, the name of a type of sacrifice; but the name now of the afternoon service, usually scheduled just before nightfall.

Minhag, minhagim (pronounced mihn-HAHG, mihn-hah-GEEM): Literally "custom, customs," referring to liturgical customs as opposed to hard and fast liturgical laws. Used to refer to a specific custom (the custom of saying *Yizkor*, visiting a grave, breaking a glass at weddings, and such), but also for the general manner in which a given community goes about doing things: for example, *minhag ashkenaz* ("the Ashkenazi manner of prayer"), as opposed to *minhag sepharad* ("the Sephardi manner of prayer").

Mitzvah (pronounced meetz-VAH or, commonly, MITZ-vah; pl. *mitzvot*, pronounced meetz-VOHT): A Hebrew word used commonly to mean "good deed," but in the more technical sense, a commandment from God; from the Hebrew root *tz.v.h*, meaning "command."

Musaf (pronounced moo-SAHF or, commonly, MOO-sahf): The Hebrew word meaning "extra" or "added" and, therefore, the title of the additional sacrifice that was offered in the Temple on Shabbat and holy days; now the name given to the additional service of worship appended to the morning service on those days.

Nachalah (pronounced nah-khah-LAH): Literally, "possession, inheritance, bequest, or legacy," but used technically by Sephardim as the term that is equivalent to the Ashkenazi *yahrzeit*, the anniversary of someone's death.

N'ilah (pronounced n'-ee-LAH or, commonly, n'-EE-lah): Literally, "locking," hence (1) the time at night when the gates to the sacrificial Temple of late antiquity were closed; and (2) additional worship services that developed then just for fast days, one of which, the final service for Yom Kippur, is still the norm today.

Pidyon (pronounced peed-YOHN): Literally, "redemption," both in the legal secular context of redeeming a pledge or bailment and in the religious ritual of *pidyon haben* (pronounced peed-YOHN hah-BEHN), "redemption of the first-born." Used here as a halakhic conception pertinent to the halakhic understanding of *Yizkor*.

Pidyon haben: See *Pidyon*.

Pidyon sh'vuyim (pronounced peed-YOHN sh'voo-YEEM): Literally, "redemption of captives," the Jewish obligation to redeem those who have been captured and held captive, as hostages or prisoners of war, for example. See *Pidyon*.

Pogrom (pronounced puh-GRUHM): A Yiddish word from the Russian for an attack, usually against a particular ethnic people, accompanied by large-scale theft, murder, and mayhem; used in a Jewish context to denote anti-Jewish attacks in Russia from 1881 to 1921; and then extended, nowadays, to mean anti-Jewish attacks in general.

Rosh Chodesh (pronounced rohsh KHOH-dehsh): Literally, "head of the moon or month," hence, the twenty-four-hour holy-day period introduced by the new moon, the first of the month.

Rosh Hashanah (pronounced rohsh hah-shah-NAH, or, commonly ROHSH hah-SHAH-nah): Literally, "head of the year," hence, the New Year.

Seelenfeier: Literally, "service for souls," hence, a name given to the memorial service.

Sephardi (pronounced s'-fahr-DEE or, commonly, s'-FAHR-dee): From the Hebrew word *Sefarad* (pronounced s'-fah-RAHD), meaning the geographic area of modern-day Spain and Portugal. Sephardi is the adjective, describing the liturgical rituals and customs that are derived from *Sefarad* prior to the expulsion of Jews from there at the end of the fifteenth century; as opposed to Ashkenazi (see **Ashkenazi**), meaning the liturgical rituals and customs common to northern and eastern Europe. Nowadays, Sephardi refers also to customs of Jews from North Africa and Arab lands whose ancestors came from Spain.

Shabbat p'kudato (pronounced shah-BAHT p'-koo-dah-TOH): Literally, the Sabbath on which one is "visited, chastised, called up, or ordered"; used technically by Sephardim as the week of mourning, the week that someone is "summoned" on high, so to speak. The equivalent to the Ashkenazi term *shivah*. See **Shivah.**

Shabbat Shachor (pronounced shah-BAHT shah-KHOHR): Literally, "the Black Sabbath"; see **Black Sabbath.**

Sheol (pronounced sh'-OHL): The biblical name for the netherworld to which one descends after death.

Shivah (pronounced shee-VAH but, commonly, SHIH-vah): Literally, "seven," hence, the usual Ashkenazi word for the seven days of mourning following the interment of a loved one. See also *Shabbat p'kudato.*

Sh'loshim (pronounced sh'-loh-SHEEM or, popularly, sh'-LOH-sheem): Literally, "thirty," hence, the name given to the first thirty days of mourning (the first seven being the days of shivah). See **Shivah.**

T'fillah (pronounced t'-fee-LAH or, commonly, t'-FEE-lah): A Hebrew word meaning "prayer," but used technically to denote a specific prayer, namely, the second of the two main units in the worship service; known also as the *Amidah* or the *Sh'moneh Esreh* (see *Amidah*). Also the title of the sixteenth blessing of the *Amidah*, a petition for God to accept our prayer.

Tikkun olam (pronounced tee-KOON oh-LAHM or, commonly, TEE-koon oh-LAHM): Literally, "repair of the world," a term taken today to denote social action, but originally a kabbalistic reference to the impact our actions have upon the world.

Totenfeier: Literally, "service for the dead," hence, a name given to the memorial service.

Totensonntag: Literally, "Sunday of the Dead," a Prussian holiday established in 1816 to remember those killed in the Napoleonic Wars.

T'shuvah (pronounced t'-shoo-VAH or, commonly t'-SHOO-vah): Literally "repentance"; also the title of the fifth blessing in the daily *Amidah*, a petition by worshipers that they successfully turn to God in heartfelt repentance.

Tz'dakah (pronounced tz'-dah-KAH but, commonly, ts'-DAH-kah): Literally, "[acts of] righteousness," hence, the normative rabbinic word for charity; here, the act of pledging charity on behalf of the dead as part of the *Yizkor* service.

Un'taneh Tokef (pronounced oo-n'-TAH-neh TOH-kehf): A *piyyut* (liturgical poem) for the High Holy Days emphasizing the awesome nature of these days when we stand before God for judgment; but originally, the climactic part of a longer poem for the *Amidah* called *k'dushta* (pronounced k'-doosh-TAH or, commonly, k'-DOOSH-tah). Although widely connected with a legend of Jewish martyrdom in medieval Germany, the poem more likely derives from a Byzantine poet, circa sixth century. It is known for its conclusion: "Penitence, prayer, and charity help the misfortune of the decree pass." See full treatment in Lawrence A. Hoffman, ed., *Who by Fire, Who by Water—Un'taneh Tokef* (Woodstock, VT: Jewish Lights, 2010).

Yahrzeit (pronounced YOHR- tzite): Yiddish for "time of year," but referring specifically, by extension, to the anniversary of the death of a mother, father, sibling, spouse, or child.

Yigdal Elohim Chai (pronounced yihg-DAHL eh-loh-HEEM CHA'i or, commonly, yihg-DAHL eh-LOH-heem CHA'i): A popular morning hymn that encapsulates the Thirteen Principles of Faith composed by prominent medieval philosopher Moses Maimonides (1135–1204). These Thirteen Principles were arranged poetically as *Yigdal* in the fourteenth century by Daniel ben Judah Dayyan (pronounced dah-YAHN) of Rome.

Yizkor (pronounced yihz-KOHR or, commonly, YIHZ-k'r): Literally, "May he remember," and hence, the first word (and title) of the main memorial prayer, titled "May God Remember" (*Yizkor Elohim,* pronounced yihz-KOHR eh-loh-HEEM).

Yom Hakippurim (pronounced YOHM hah-kee-poo-REEM): The formal rabbinic term for "Day of Atonement," nowadays, shortened in common speech to Yom Kippur. See **Yom Kippur.**

Yom Kippur (pronounced yohm kee-POOR or, commonly, yohm KIHp'r): Day of Atonement.

Zikhronot (pronounced zikh-roh-NOHT): Literally, "Remembrances," the name given to the second of three parts in the service of blowing the shofar on Rosh Hashanah, the part that emphasizes God's acts of remembering.

ๆ∕∩∩∩ᘺ

Bible Study / Midrash

Passing Life's Tests: Spiritual Reflections on the Trial of Abraham, the Binding of Isaac   *By Rabbi Bradley Shavit Artson, DHL*
Invites us to use this powerful tale as a tool for our own soul wrestling, to confront our existential sacrifices and enable us to face—and surmount—life's tests.
6 x 9, 176 pp, Quality PB, 978-1-58023-631-7 **$18.99**

The Messiah and the Jews: Three Thousand Years of Tradition, Belief and Hope   *By Rabbi Elaine Rose Glickman; Foreword by Rabbi Neil Gillman, PhD; Preface by Rabbi Judith Z. Abrams, PhD*
Explores and explains an astonishing range of primary and secondary sources, infusing them with new meaning for the modern reader.
6 x 9, 192 pp, Quality PB, 978-1-58023-690-4 **$16.99**

Speaking Torah: Spiritual Teachings from around the Maggid's Table—in Two Volumes   *By Arthur Green, with Ebn Leader, Ariel Evan Mayse and Or N. Rose*
The most powerful Hasidic teachings made accessible—from some of the world's preeminent authorities on Jewish thought and spirituality.
Volume 1—6 x 9, 512 pp, Hardcover, 978-1-58023-668-3 **$34.99**
Volume 2—6 x 9, 448 pp, Hardcover, 978-1-58023-694-2 **$34.99**

Masking and Unmasking Ourselves: Interpreting Biblical Texts on Clothing & Identity   *By Dr. Norman J. Cohen*
Presents ten Bible stories that involve clothing in an essential way, as a means of learning about the text, its characters and their interactions.
6 x 9, 240 pp, HC, 978-1-58023-461-0 **$24.99**

The Genesis of Leadership: What the Bible Teaches Us about Vision, Values and Leading Change   *By Rabbi Nathan Laufer; Foreword by Senator Joseph I. Lieberman*
6 x 9, 288 pp, Quality PB, 978-1-58023-352-1 **$18.99**

Hineini in Our Lives: Learning How to Respond to Others through 14 Biblical Texts and Personal Stories   *By Rabbi Norman J. Cohen, PhD*   6 x 9, 240 pp, Quality PB, 978-1-58023-274-6 **$16.99**

The Modern Men's Torah Commentary: New Insights from Jewish Men on the 54 Weekly Torah Portions   *Edited by Rabbi Jeffrey K. Salkin*
6 x 9, 368 pp, HC, 978-1-58023-395-8 **$24.99**

Moses and the Journey to Leadership: Timeless Lessons of Effective Management from the Bible and Today's Leaders   *By Rabbi Norman J. Cohen, PhD*
6 x 9, 240 pp, Quality PB, 978-1-58023-351-4 **$18.99**; HC, 978-1-58023-227-2 **$21.99**

The Other Talmud—*The Yerushalmi*: Unlocking the Secrets of The Talmud of Israel for Judaism Today   *By Rabbi Judith Z. Abrams, PhD*
6 x 9, 256 pp, HC, 978-1-58023-463-4 **$24.99**

Sage Tales: Wisdom and Wonder from the Rabbis of the Talmud
By Rabbi Burton L. Visotzky   6 x 9, 256 pp, HC, 978-1-58023-456-6 **$24.99**

The Torah Revolution: Fourteen Truths That Changed the World
By Rabbi Reuven Hammer, PhD   6 x 9, 240 pp, HC, 978-1-58023-457-3 **$24.99**

The Wisdom of Judaism: An Introduction to the Values of the Talmud
By Rabbi Dov Peretz Elkins   6 x 9, 192 pp, Quality PB, 978-1-58023-327-9 **$16.99**

Or phone, mail or e-mail to: **JEWISH LIGHTS** Publishing
An imprint of Turner Publishing Company
4507 Charlotte Avenue • Suite 100 • Nashville, Tennessee 37209
Tel: (615) 255-2665 • www.jewishlights.com
Prices subject to change.

Congregation Resources

Jewish Megatrends: Charting the Course of the American Jewish Future
By Rabbi Sidney Schwarz; Foreword by Ambassador Stuart E. Eizenstat
Visionary solutions for a community ripe for transformational change—from fourteen leading innovators of Jewish life.
6 x 9, 288 pp, HC, 978-1-58023-667-6 **$24.99**

Relational Judaism: Using the Power of Relationships to Transform the Jewish Community *By Dr. Ron Wolfson*
How to transform the model of twentieth-century Jewish institutions into twenty-first-century relational communities offering meaning and purpose, belonging and blessing.
6 x 9, 288 pp, HC, 978-1-58023-666-9 **$24.99**

Revolution of Jewish Spirit: How to Revive *Ruakh* in Your Spiritual Life, Transform Your Synagogue & Inspire Your Jewish Community
By Rabbi Baruch HaLevi, DMin, and Ellen Frankel, LCSW; Foreword by Dr. Ron Wolfson
A practical and engaging guide to reinvigorating Jewish life. Offers strategies for sustaining and expanding transformation, impassioned leadership, inspired programming and inviting sacred spaces.
6 x 9, 224 pp, Quality PB Original, 978-1-58023-625-6 **$19.99**

Building a Successful Volunteer Culture: Finding Meaning in Service in the Jewish Community *By Rabbi Charles Simon; Foreword by Shelley Lindauer; Preface by Dr. Ron Wolfson*
6 x 9, 192 pp, Quality PB, 978-1-58023-408-5 **$16.99**

The Case for Jewish Peoplehood: Can We Be One?
By Dr. Erica Brown and Dr. Misha Galperin; Foreword by Rabbi Joseph Telushkin
6 x 9, 224 pp, HC, 978-1-58023-401-6 **$21.99**

Empowered Judaism: What Independent Minyanim Can Teach Us about Building Vibrant Jewish Communities *By Rabbi Elie Kaunfer; Foreword by Prof. Jonathan D. Sarna*
6 x 9, 224 pp, Quality PB, 978-1-58023-412-2 **$18.99**

Finding a Spiritual Home: How a New Generation of Jews Can Transform the American Synagogue *By Rabbi Sidney Schwarz*
6 x 9, 352 pp, Quality PB, 978-1-58023-185-5 **$19.95**

Inspired Jewish Leadership: Practical Approaches to Building Strong Communities
By Dr. Erica Brown 6 x 9, 256 pp, HC, 978-1-58023-361-3 **$27.99**

Jewish Pastoral Care, 2nd Edition: A Practical Handbook from Traditional & Contemporary Sources *Edited by Rabbi Dayle A. Friedman, MSW, MAJCS, BCC*
6 x 9, 528 pp, Quality PB, 978-1-58023-427-6 **$35.00**

Jewish Spiritual Direction: An Innovative Guide from Traditional and Contemporary Sources
Edited by Rabbi Howard A. Addison, PhD, and Barbara Eve Breitman, MSW
6 x 9, 368 pp, HC, 978-1-58023-230-2 **$30.00**

A Practical Guide to Rabbinic Counseling
Edited by Rabbi Yisrael N. Levitz, PhD, and Rabbi Abraham J. Twerski, MD
6 x 9, 432 pp, HC, 978-1-58023-562-4 **$40.00**

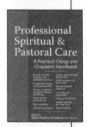

Professional Spiritual & Pastoral Care: A Practical Clergy and Chaplain's Handbook
Edited by Rabbi Stephen B. Roberts, MBA, MHL, BCJC
6 x 9, 480 pp, HC, 978-1-59473-312-3 **$50.00**

Reimagining Leadership in Jewish Organizations: Ten Practical Lessons to Help You Implement Change and Achieve Your Goals *By Dr. Misha Galperin*
6 x 9, 192 pp, Quality PB, 978-1-58023-492-4 **$16.99**

Rethinking Synagogues: A New Vocabulary for Congregational Life
By Rabbi Lawrence A. Hoffman, PhD 6 x 9, 240 pp, Quality PB, 978-1-58023-248-7 **$19.99**

Spiritual Community: The Power to Restore Hope, Commitment and Joy
By Rabbi David A. Teutsch, PhD
5½ x 8½, 144 pp, HC, 978-1-58023-270-8 **$19.99**

Spiritual Boredom: Rediscovering the Wonder of Judaism *By Dr. Erica Brown*
6 x 9, 208 pp, HC, 978-1-58023-405-4 **$21.99**

The Spirituality of Welcoming: How to Transform Your Congregation into a Sacred Community *By Dr. Ron Wolfson* 6 x 9, 224 pp, Quality PB, 978-1-58023-244-9 **$19.99**

Social Justice

Where Justice Dwells
A Hands-On Guide to Doing Social Justice in Your Jewish Community
By Rabbi Jill Jacobs; Foreword by Rabbi David Saperstein
Provides ways to envision and act on your own ideals of social justice.
7 x 9, 288 pp, Quality PB Original, 978-1-58023-453-5 **$24.99**

There Shall Be No Needy
Pursuing Social Justice through Jewish Law and Tradition
By Rabbi Jill Jacobs; Foreword by Rabbi Elliot N. Dorff, PhD; Preface by Simon Greer
Confronts the most pressing issues of twenty-first-century America from a deeply
Jewish perspective. 6 x 9, 288 pp, Quality PB, 978-1-58023-425-2 **$16.99**

There Shall Be No Needy Teacher's Guide 8½ x 11, 56 pp, PB, 978-1-58023-429-0 **$8.99**

Conscience
The Duty to Obey and the Duty to Disobey
By Rabbi Harold M. Schulweis
Examines the idea of conscience and the role conscience plays in our relationships
to government, law, ethics, religion, human nature, God—and to each other.
6 x 9, 160 pp, Quality PB, 978-1-58023-419-1 **$16.99**; HC, 978-1-58023-375-0 **$19.99**

Judaism and Justice
The Jewish Passion to Repair the World
By Rabbi Sidney Schwarz; Foreword by Ruth Messinger
Explores the relationship between Judaism, social justice and the Jewish identity
of American Jews. 6 x 9, 352 pp, Quality PB, 978-1-58023-353-8 **$19.99**

Spirituality / Women's Interest

New Jewish Feminism
Probing the Past, Forging the Future
Edited by Rabbi Elyse Goldstein; Foreword by Anita Diamant
Looks at the growth and accomplishments of Jewish feminism and what they
mean for Jewish women today and tomorrow.
6 x 9, 480 pp, HC, 978-1-58023-359-0 **$24.99**

The Divine Feminine in Biblical Wisdom Literature
Selections Annotated & Explained
Translation & Annotation by Rabbi Rami Shapiro
5½ x 8½, 240 pp, Quality PB, 978-1-59473-109-9 **$16.99**
(A book from SkyLight Paths, Jewish Lights' sister imprint)

The Quotable Jewish Woman
Wisdom, Inspiration & Humor from the Mind & Heart
Edited by Elaine Bernstein Partnow
6 x 9, 496 pp, Quality PB, 978-1-58023-236-4 **$19.99**

The Women's Haftarah Commentary
New Insights from Women Rabbis on the 54 Weekly Haftarah Portions,
the 5 Megillot & Special Shabbatot
Edited by Rabbi Elyse Goldstein
Illuminates the historical significance of female portrayals in the Haftarah and the
Five Megillot. 6 x 9, 560 pp, Quality PB, 978-1-58023-371-2 **$19.99**

The Women's Torah Commentary
New Insights from Women Rabbis on the 54 Weekly Torah Portions
Edited by Rabbi Elyse Goldstein
Over fifty women rabbis offer inspiring insights on the Torah, in a week-by-week format.
6 x 9, 496 pp, Quality PB, 978-1-58023-370-5 **$19.99**; HC, 978-1-58023-076-6 **$34.95**

See Passover for *The Women's Passover Companion: Women's Reflections on
the Festival of Freedom* and *The Women's Seder Sourcebook: Rituals &
Readings for Use at the Passover Seder.*

Holidays / Holy Days

Prayers of Awe Series

An exciting new series that examines the High Holy Day liturgy to enrich the praying experience of everyone—whether experienced worshipers or guests who encounter Jewish prayer for the very first time.

We Have Sinned—Sin and Confession in Judaism: *Ashamnu and Al Chet*
Edited by Rabbi Lawrence A. Hoffman, PhD
A varied and fascinating look at sin, confession and pardon in Judaism, as suggested by the centrality of *Ashamnu* and *Al Chet*, two prayers that people know so well, though understand so little. 6 x 9, 304 pp, HC, 978-1-58023-612-6 **$24.99**

Who by Fire, Who by Water—Un'taneh Tokef
Edited by Rabbi Lawrence A. Hoffman, PhD
Quality PB, 978-1-58023-672-0 **$19.99**; 6 x 9, 272 pp, HC, 978-1-58023-424-5 **$24.99**

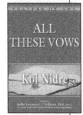

All These Vows—Kol Nidre
Edited by Rabbi Lawrence A. Hoffman, PhD 6 x 9, 288 pp, HC, 978-1-58023-430-6 **$24.99**

Rosh Hashanah Readings: Inspiration, Information and Contemplation
Yom Kippur Readings: Inspiration, Information and Contemplation
Edited by Rabbi Dov Peretz Elkins; Section Introductions from Arthur Green's These Are the Words
Rosh Hashanah: 6 x 9, 400 pp, Quality PB, 978-1-58023-437-5 **$19.99**
Yom Kippur: 6 x 9, 368 pp, Quality PB, 978-1-58023-438-2 **$19.99**; HC, 978-1-58023-271-5 **$24.99**

Reclaiming Judaism as a Spiritual Practice: Holy Days and Shabbat
By Rabbi Goldie Milgram 7 x 9, 272 pp, Quality PB, 978-1-58023-205-0 **$19.99**

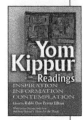

The Sabbath Soul: Mystical Reflections on the Transformative Power of Holy Time
Selection, Translation and Commentary by Eitan Fishbane, PhD
6 x 9, 208 pp,

Shabbat, 2nd Edition: The Family Guide to Preparing for and Celebrating the Sabbath
By Dr. Ron Wolfson 7 x 9, 320 pp, Illus., Quality PB, 978-1-58023-164-0 **$19.99**

Hanukkah, 2nd Edition: The Family Guide to Spiritual Celebration
By Dr. Ron Wolfson 7 x 9, 240 pp, Illus., Quality PB, 978-1-58023-122-0 **$18.95**

Passover

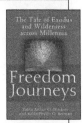

My People's Passover Haggadah
Traditional Texts, Modern Commentaries
Edited by Rabbi Lawrence A. Hoffman, PhD, and David Arnow, PhD
A diverse and exciting collection of commentaries on the traditional Passover Haggadah—in two volumes!
Vol. 1: 7 x 10, 304 pp, HC, 978-1-58023-354-5 **$24.99**
Vol. 2: 7 x 10, 320 pp, HC, 978-1-58023-346-0 **$24.99**

Freedom Journeys: The Tale of Exodus and Wilderness across Millennia
By Rabbi Arthur O. Waskow and Rabbi Phyllis O. Berman
Explores how the story of Exodus echoes in our own time, calling us to relearn and rethink the Passover story through social-justice, ecological, feminist and interfaith perspectives. 6 x 9, 288 pp, HC, 978-1-58023-445-0 **$24.99**

Leading the Passover Journey: The Seder's Meaning Revealed,
the Haggadah's Story Retold *By Rabbi Nathan Laufer*
Uncovers the hidden meaning of the Seder's rituals and customs.
6 x 9, 224 pp, Quality PB, 978-1-58023-399-6 **$18.99**

Creating Lively Passover Seders, 2nd Edition: A Sourcebook of Engaging Tales,
Texts & Activities *By David Arnow, PhD* 7 x 9, 464 pp, Quality PB, 978-1-58023-444-3 **$24.99**

Passover, 2nd Edition: The Family Guide to Spiritual Celebration
By Dr. Ron Wolfson with Joel Lurie Grishaver 7 x 9, 416 pp, Quality PB, 978-1-58023-174-9 **$19.95**

The Women's Passover Companion: Women's Reflections on the Festival of Freedom
Edited by Rabbi Sharon Cohen Anisfeld, Tara Mohr and Catherine Spector; Foreword by Paula E. Hyman
6 x 9, 352 pp, Quality PB, 978-1-58023-231-9 **$19.99**; HC, 978-1-58023-128-2 **$24.95**

The Women's Seder Sourcebook: Rituals & Readings for Use at the Passover Seder
Edited by Rabbi Sharon Cohen Anisfeld, Tara Mohr and Catherine Spector
6 x 9, 384 pp, Quality PB, 978-1-58023-232-6 **$19.99**

Theology / Philosophy / The Way Into... Series

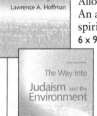

The Way Into... series offers an accessible and highly usable "guided tour" of the Jewish faith, people, history and beliefs—in total, an introduction to Judaism that will enable you to understand and interact with the sacred texts of the Jewish tradition. Each volume is written by a leading contemporary scholar and teacher, and explores one key aspect of Judaism. The Way Into... series enables all readers to achieve a real sense of Jewish cultural literacy through guided study.

The Way Into Encountering God in Judaism
By Rabbi Neil Gillman, PhD
For everyone who wants to understand how Jews have encountered God throughout history and today.
6 x 9, 240 pp, Quality PB, 978-1-58023-199-2 **$18.99**; HC, 978-1-58023-025-4 **$21.95**
Also Available: **The Jewish Approach to God:** A Brief Introduction for Christians
By Rabbi Neil Gillman, PhD
5½ x 8½, 192 pp, Quality PB, 978-1-58023-190-9 **$16.95**

The Way Into Jewish Mystical Tradition
By Rabbi Lawrence Kushner
Allows readers to interact directly with the sacred mystical texts of the Jewish tradition. An accessible introduction to the concepts of Jewish mysticism, their religious and spiritual significance, and how they relate to life today.
6 x 9, 224 pp, Quality PB, 978-1-58023-200-5 **$18.99**

The Way Into Jewish Prayer
By Rabbi Lawrence A. Hoffman, PhD
Opens the door to 3,000 years of Jewish prayer, making anyone feel at home in the Jewish way of communicating with God.
6 x 9, 208 pp, Quality PB, 978-1-58023-201-2 **$18.99**

The Way Into Jewish Prayer Teacher's Guide
By Rabbi Jennifer Ossakow Goldsmith
8½ x 11, 42 pp, PB, 978-1-58023-345-3 **$8.99**
Download a free copy at www.jewishlights.com.

The Way Into Judaism and the Environment
By Jeremy Benstein, PhD
Explores the ways in which Judaism contributes to contemporary social-environmental issues, the extent to which Judaism is part of the problem and how it can be part of the solution.
6 x 9, 288 pp, Quality PB, 978-1-58023-368-2 **$18.99**; HC, 978-1-58023-268-5 **$24.99**

The Way Into *Tikkun Olam* (Repairing the World)
By Rabbi Elliot N. Dorff, PhD
An accessible introduction to the Jewish concept of the individual's responsibility to care for others and repair the world.
6 x 9, 304 pp, Quality PB, 978-1-58023-328-6 **$18.99**

The Way Into Torah
By Rabbi Norman J. Cohen, PhD
Helps guide you in the exploration of the origins and development of Torah, explains why it should be studied and how to do it.
6 x 9, 176 pp, Quality PB, 978-1-58023-198-5 **$16.99**

The Way Into the Varieties of Jewishness
By Sylvia Barack Fishman, PhD
Explores the religious and historical understanding of what it has meant to be Jewish from ancient times to the present controversy over "Who is a Jew?"
6 x 9, 288 pp, Quality PB, 978-1-58023-367-5 **$18.99**; HC, 978-1-58023-030-8 **$24.99**

Theology / Philosophy

From Defender to Critic: The Search for a New Jewish Self
By Dr. David Hartman
A daring self-examination of Hartman's goals, which were not to strip halakha of its authority but to create a space for questioning and critique that allows for the traditionally religious Jew to act out a moral life in tune with modern experience.
6 x 9, 336 pp, HC, 978-1-58023-515-0 **$35.00**

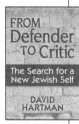

The God Who Hates Lies: Confronting & Rethinking Jewish Tradition
A deeply personal look at the struggle between commitment to Jewish religious tradition and personal morality.
By Dr. David Hartman with Charlie Buckholtz 6 x 9, 208 pp, HC, 978-1-58023-455-9 **$24.99**

Our Religious Brains: What Cognitive Science Reveals about Belief, Morality, Community and Our Relationship with God
By Rabbi Ralph D. Mecklenburger; Foreword by Dr. Howard Kelfer; Preface by Dr. Neil Gillman
This is a groundbreaking, accessible look at the implications of cognitive science for religion and theology, intended for laypeople. 6 x 9, 224 pp, HC, 978-1-58023-508-2 **$24.99**

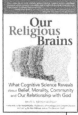

The Other Talmud—The Yerushalmi: Unlocking the Secrets of The Talmud of Israel for Judaism Today *By Rabbi Judith Z. Abrams, PhD*
A fascinating—and stimulating—look at "the other Talmud" and the possibilities for Jewish life reflected there. 6 x 9, 256 pp, HC, 978-1-58023-463-4 **$24.99**

The Way of Man: According to Hasidic Teaching
By Martin Buber; New Translation and Introduction by Rabbi Bernard H. Mehlman and Dr. Gabriel E. Padawer; Foreword by Paul Mendes-Flohr
An accessible and engaging new translation of Buber's classic work—*available as an e-book only.* E-book, 978-1-58023-601-0 Digital List Price **$14.99**

The Death of Death: Resurrection and Immortality in Jewish Thought
By Rabbi Neil Gillman, PhD 6 x 9, 336 pp, Quality PB, 978-1-58023-081-0 **$18.95**

Doing Jewish Theology: God, Torah & Israel in Modern Judaism *By Rabbi Neil Gillman, PhD*
6 x 9, 304 pp, Quality PB, 978-1-58023-439-9 **$18.99**; HC, 978-1-58023-322-4 **$24.99**

A Heart of Many Rooms: Celebrating the Many Voices within Judaism
By Dr. David Hartman 6 x 9, 352 pp, Quality PB, 978-1-58023-156-5 **$19.95**

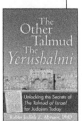

Jewish Theology in Our Time: A New Generation Explores the Foundations and Future of Jewish Belief *Edited by Rabbi Elliot J. Cosgrove, PhD; Foreword by Rabbi David J. Wolpe; Preface by Rabbi Carole B. Balin, PhD* 6 x 9, 240 pp, Quality PB, 978-1-58023-630-1, **$19.99**; HC, 978-1-58023-413-9 **$24.99**

Maimonides—Essential Teachings on Jewish Faith & Ethics: The Book of Knowledge & the Thirteen Principles of Faith—Annotated & Explained
Translation and Annotation by Rabbi Marc D. Angel, PhD
5½ x 8½, 224 pp, Quality PB Original, 978-1-59473-311-6 **$18.99***

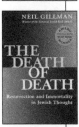

Maimonides, Spinoza and Us: Toward an Intellectually Vibrant Judaism
By Rabbi Marc D. Angel, PhD 6 x 9, 224 pp, HC, 978-1-58023-411-5 **$24.99**

Your Word Is Fire: The Hasidic Masters on Contemplative Prayer
Edited and translated by Rabbi Arthur Green, PhD, and Barry W. Holtz
6 x 9, 160 pp, Quality PB, 978-1-879045-25-5 **$16.99**

I Am Jewish
Personal Reflections Inspired by the Last Words of Daniel Pearl
Almost 150 Jews—both famous and not—from all walks of life, from all around the world, write about many aspects of their Judaism.
Edited by Judea and Ruth Pearl 6 x 9, 304 pp, Deluxe PB w/ flaps, 978-1-58023-259-3 **$19.99**
Download a free copy of the *I Am Jewish Teacher's Guide* at www.jewishlights.com.

Hannah Senesh: Her Life and Diary, The First Complete Edition
By Hannah Senesh; Foreword by Marge Piercy; Preface by Eitan Senesh; Afterword by Roberta Grossman
6 x 9, 368 pp, b/w photos, Quality PB, 978-1-58023-342-2 **$19.99**

*A book from SkyLight Paths, Jewish Lights' sister imprint

Spirituality

Amazing Chesed: Living a Grace-Filled Judaism
By Rabbi Rami Shapiro
Drawing from ancient and contemporary, traditional and non-traditional Jewish wisdom, reclaims the idea of grace in Judaism.
6 x 9, 176 pp, Quality PB, 978-1-58023-624-9 **$16.99**

Jewish with Feeling: A Guide to Meaningful Jewish Practice
By Rabbi Zalman Schachter-Shalomi with Joel Segel
Takes off from basic questions like "Why be Jewish?" and whether the word God still speaks to us today and lays out a vision for a whole-person Judaism.
5½ x 8½, 288 pp, Quality PB, 978-1-58023-691-1 **$19.99**

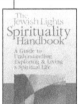

The Jewish Lights Spirituality Handbook: A Guide to Understanding, Exploring & Living a Spiritual Life *Edited by Stuart M. Matlins*
What exactly is "Jewish" about spirituality? How do I make it a part of my life? Fifty of today's foremost spiritual leaders share their ideas and experience with us.
6 x 9, 456 pp, Quality PB, 978-1-58023-093-3 **$19.99**

Aleph-Bet Yoga: Embodying the Hebrew Letters for Physical and Spiritual Well-Being
By Steven A. Rapp; Foreword by Tamar Frankiel, PhD, and Judy Greenfeld; Preface by Hart Lazer
7 x 10, 128 pp, b/w photos, Quality PB, Lay-flat binding, 978-1-58023-162-6 **$16.95**

A Book of Life: Embracing Judaism as a Spiritual Practice
By Rabbi Michael Strassfeld 6 x 9, 544 pp, Quality PB, 978-1-58023-247-0 **$19.99**

Bringing the Psalms to Life: How to Understand and Use the Book of Psalms
By Rabbi Daniel F. Polish, PhD 6 x 9, 208 pp, Quality PB, 978-1-58023-157-2 **$16.95**

Does the Soul Survive? A Jewish Journey to Belief in Afterlife, Past Lives & Living with Purpose *By Rabbi Elie Kaplan Spitz; Foreword by Brian L. Weiss, MD*
6 x 9, 288 pp, Quality PB, 978-1-58023-165-7 **$18.99**

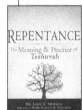

Entering the Temple of Dreams: Jewish Prayers, Movements and Meditations for the End of the Day *By Tamar Frankiel, PhD, and Judy Greenfeld*
7 x 10, 192 pp, illus., Quality PB, 978-1-58023-079-7 **$16.95**

First Steps to a New Jewish Spirit: Reb Zalman's Guide to Recapturing the Intimacy & Ecstasy in Your Relationship with God *By Rabbi Zalman M. Schachter-Shalomi with Donald Gropman* 6 x 9, 144 pp, Quality PB, 978-1-58023-182-4 **$16.95**

Foundations of Sephardic Spirituality: The Inner Life of Jews of the Ottoman Empire
By Rabbi Marc D. Angel, PhD 6 x 9, 224 pp, Quality PB, 978-1-58023-341-5 **$18.99**

God & the Big Bang: Discovering Harmony between Science & Spirituality
By Dr. Daniel C. Matt 6 x 9, 216 pp, Quality PB, 978-1-879045-89-7 **$18.99**

God in Our Relationships: Spirituality between People from the Teachings of Martin Buber *By Rabbi Dennis S. Ross* 5½ x 8½, 160 pp, Quality PB, 978-1-58023-147-3 **$16.95**

Judaism, Physics and God: Searching for Sacred Metaphors in a Post-Einstein World
By Rabbi David W. Nelson 6 x 9, 352 pp, Quality PB, inc. reader's discussion guide,
978-1-58023-306-4 **$18.99**; HC, 352 pp, 978-1-58023-252-4 **$24.99**

Meaning & Mitzvah: Daily Practices for Reclaiming Judaism through Prayer, God, Torah, Hebrew, Mitzvot and Peoplehood *By Rabbi Goldie Milgram*
7 x 9, 336 pp, Quality PB, 978-1-58023-256-2 **$19.99**

Repentance: The Meaning and Practice of Teshuvah
By Dr. Louis E. Newman; Foreword by Rabbi Harold M. Schulweis; Preface by Rabbi Karyn D. Kedar
6 x 9, 256 pp, HC, 978-1-58023-426-9 **$24.99** Quality PB, 978-1-58023-718-5 **$18.99**

The Sabbath Soul: Mystical Reflections on the Transformative Power of Holy Time
Selection, Translation and Commentary by Eitan Fishbane, PhD
6 x 9, 208 pp, Quality PB, 978-1-58023-459-7 **$18.99**

***Tanya*, the Masterpiece of Hasidic Wisdom:** Selections Annotated & Explained
Translation & Annotation by Rabbi Rami Shapiro; Foreword by Rabbi Zalman M. Schachter-Shalomi
5½ x 8½, 240 pp, Quality PB, 978-1-59473-275-1 **$16.99**

These Are the Words, 2nd Edition: A Vocabulary of Jewish Spiritual Life
By Rabbi Arthur Green, PhD 6 x 9, 320 pp, Quality PB, 978-1-58023-494-8 **$19.99**

Spirituality / Prayer

Davening: A Guide to Meaningful Jewish Prayer
By Rabbi Zalman Schachter-Shalomi with Joel Segel; Foreword by Rabbi Lawrence Kushner
A fresh approach to prayer for all who wish to appreciate the power of prayer's poetry, song and ritual, and to join the age-old conversation that Jews have had with God. 6 x 9, 240 pp, Quality PB, 978-1-58023-627-0 **$18.99**

Jewish Men Pray: Words of Yearning, Praise, Petition, Gratitude and Wonder from Traditional and Contemporary Sources
Edited by Rabbi Kerry M. Olitzky and Stuart M. Matlins; Foreword by Rabbi Bradley Shavit Artson, DHL
A celebration of Jewish men's voices in prayer—to strengthen, heal, comfort, and inspire—from the ancient world up to our own day.
5 x 7¼, 400 pp, HC, 978-1-58023-628-7 **$19.99**

Making Prayer Real: Leading Jewish Spiritual Voices on Why Prayer Is Difficult and What to Do about It *By Rabbi Mike Comins* 6 x 9, 320 pp, Quality PB, 978-1-58023-417-7 **$18.99**

Witnesses to the One: The Spiritual History of the *Sh'ma*
By Rabbi Joseph B. Meszler; Foreword by Rabbi Elyse Goldstein
6 x 9, 176 pp, Quality PB, 978-1-58023-400-9 **$16.99**; HC, 978-1-58023-309-5 **$19.99**

My People's Prayer Book Series: Traditional Prayers, Modern Commentaries *Edited by Rabbi Lawrence A. Hoffman, PhD*
Provides diverse and exciting commentary to the traditional liturgy. Will help you find new wisdom in Jewish prayer, and bring liturgy into your life. Each book includes Hebrew text, modern translations and commentaries from all perspectives of the Jewish world.
Vol. 1—The *Sh'ma* and Its Blessings
  7 x 10, 168 pp, HC, 978-1-879045-79-8 **$29.99**
Vol. 2—The *Amidah* 7 x 10, 240 pp, HC, 978-1-879045-80-4 **$24.95**
Vol. 3—*P'sukei D'zimrah* (Morning Psalms)
  7 x 10, 240 pp, HC, 978-1-879045-81-1 **$29.99**
Vol. 4—*Seder K'riat Hatorah* (The Torah Service)
  7 x 10, 264 pp, HC, 978-1-879045-82-8 **$29.99**
Vol. 5—*Birkhot Hashachar* (Morning Blessings)
  7 x 10, 240 pp, HC, 978-1-879045-83-5 **$24.95**
Vol. 6—*Tachanun* and Concluding Prayers
  7 x 10, 240 pp, HC, 978-1-879045-84-2 **$24.95**
Vol. 7—Shabbat at Home 7 x 10, 240 pp, HC, 978-1-879045-85-9 **$24.95**
Vol. 8—*Kabbalat Shabbat* (Welcoming Shabbat in the Synagogue)
  7 x 10, 240 pp, HC, 978-1-58023-121-3 **$24.99**
Vol. 9—Welcoming the Night: *Minchah* and *Ma'ariv* (Afternoon and Evening Prayer) 7 x 10, 272 pp, HC, 978-1-58023-262-3 **$24.99**
Vol. 10—Shabbat Morning: *Shacharit* and *Musaf* (Morning and Additional Services) 7 x 10, 240 pp, HC, 978-1-58023-240-1 **$29.99**

Spirituality / Lawrence Kushner

I'm God; You're Not: Observations on Organized Religion & Other Disguises of the Ego
6 x 9, 256 pp, Quality PB, 978-1-58023-513-6 **$18.99**; HC, 978-1-58023-441-2 **$21.99**

The Book of Letters: A Mystical Hebrew Alphabet
Popular HC Edition, 6 x 9, 80 pp, 2-color text, 978-1-879045-00-2 **$24.95**
Collector's Limited Edition, 9 x 12, 80 pp, gold-foil-embossed pages, w/ limited-edition silkscreened print, 978-1-879045-04-0 **$349.00**

The Book of Miracles: A Young Person's Guide to Jewish Spiritual Awareness
6 x 9, 96 pp, 2-color illus., HC, 978-1-879045-78-1 **$16.95** *For ages 9–13*

God Was in This Place & I, i Did Not Know: Finding Self, Spirituality and Ultimate Meaning 6 x 9, 192 pp, Quality PB, 978-1-879045-33-0 **$16.95**

Honey from the Rock: An Introduction to Jewish Mysticism
6 x 9, 176 pp, Quality PB, 978-1-58023-073-5 **$16.95**

Invisible Lines of Connection: Sacred Stories of the Ordinary
5½ x 8½, 160 pp, Quality PB, 978-1-879045-98-9 **$16.99**

The Way Into Jewish Mystical Tradition
6 x 9, 224 pp, Quality PB, 978-1-58023-200-5 **$18.99**; HC, 978-1-58023-029-2 **$21.95**

About Jewish Lights

People of all faiths and backgrounds yearn for books that attract, engage, educate, and spiritually inspire.

Our principal goal is to stimulate thought and help all people learn about who the Jewish People are, where they come from, and what the future can be made to hold. While people of our diverse Jewish heritage are the primary audience, our books speak to people in the Christian world as well and will broaden their understanding of Judaism and the roots of their own faith.

We bring to you authors who are at the forefront of spiritual thought and experience. While each has something different to say, they all say it in a voice that you can hear.

Our books are designed to welcome you and then to engage, stimulate, and inspire. We judge our success not only by whether or not our books are beautiful and commercially successful, but by whether or not they make a difference in your life.

For your information and convenience, at the back of this book we have provided a list of other Jewish Lights books you might find interesting and useful. They cover all the categories of your life:

Bar/Bat Mitzvah	Life Cycle
Bible Study / Midrash	Meditation
Children's Books	Men's Interest
Congregation Resources	Parenting
Current Events / History	Prayer / Ritual / Sacred Practice
Ecology / Environment	Social Justice
Fiction: Mystery, Science Fiction	Spirituality
Grief / Healing	Theology / Philosophy
Holidays / Holy Days	Travel
Inspiration	Twelve Steps
Kabbalah / Mysticism / Enneagram	Women's Interest

Stuart M. Matlins, Publisher

Or phone, mail or e-mail to: **JEWISH LIGHTS Publishing**
An imprint of Turner Publishing Company
4507 Charlotte Avenue • Suite 100 • Nashville, Tennessee 37209
Tel: (615) 255-2665 • www.jewishlights.com
Prices subject to change.

For more information about each book, visit our website at www.jewishlights.com

Printed in the USA
CPSIA information can be obtained
at www.ICGtesting.com
JSHW022211140824
68134JS00018B/980